THE JOHN HARVARD LIBRARY

Bernard Bailyn

Editor-in-Chief

ENGLISH TRAITS

By

Ralph Waldo Emerson

Edited by Howard Mumford Jones

THE BELKNAP PRESS OF
HARVARD UNIVERSITY PRESS
Cambridge, Massachusetts
1 9 6 6

Distributed in Great Britain by Oxford University Press, London

Library of Congress Catalog Card Number 66-23464

Printed in the United States of America

Preface

In this edition of *English Traits* I have tried to supply dates and occasional brief biographical tags for the scores of persons Emerson refers to in his text. In order to save space this information is given on the first appearance of a name in the book and is not repeated in subsequent notes. I have also tried to locate all of Emerson's quotations and allusions as to source. Some I have not been able to find; readers of this edition may be more fortunate. In most cases I of course consulted, where I could, editions or books Emerson used or might have used; but in the case of more common standard writers I have referred to editions likely to be accessible to modern readers. Thus, though Emerson read Plato in a translation by Thomas Taylor that came out at the beginning of the nineteenth century, it seemed to me more sensible to use the Jowett translation, which is widely available.

I am indebted to so many colleagues at Harvard University and out of it, it would take up a great deal of space to thank them individually, but I trust this general statement of gratitude for the aid that is the finer spirit of scholarship will do. I must, however, pay tribute to my research assistant, Edith Gray, for the endless hours she spent turning over a multitude of books in search of a single fact or a quoted line.

Howard Mumford Jones

Cambridge, Massachusetts
April 1, 1966

Contents

ENGLISH TRAITS

CONTENTS

Introduction

Historians of American culture have made rich use of interpretations of life in the United States by visiting foreigners, for example, Mrs. Trollope, Michel Chevalier, Alexis de Tocqueville, Lord Bryce, and Paul Bourget. They have paid less attention, and literary historians have paid virtually no attention at all, to a distinguished library of books by American writers about other countries. Works like *Venetian Life* by William Dean Howells, which preserves the charm of a whole vanished way of life, *Life in Mexico* by Madame Calderon de la Barca, who, as Frances Erskine Inglis, once taught school in Boston, Baltimore, and Staten Island, *Japan Day by Day* by Edward Sylvester Morse, *Two Years in the French West Indies* by Lafcadio Hearn, a marvelous exercise in death, luxuriance, and decay, *Castilian Days* by John Hay, and *Chinese Characteristics* by the missionary Arthur Henderson Smith not only decreased American parochialism, but by shaping American opinion may have subtly influenced foreign policy. In this library *English Traits* by Ralph Waldo Emerson must rank high. Despite faults of construction, despite Emerson's lack of contact with certain important sides of British industrial life, no better book by an American about Victorian England (or rather Great Britain at mid-century) has ever been written. Its excellence arises from a number of causes. Emerson was an Anglophile from a characteristically Anglophilic portion of the United States and therefore a sympathetic observer; he wrote the book at the height of his powers; and, as the annotation required to explain it amply testifies, he toiled terribly in writing it. A work that draws casually upon sources as diverse as Iamblichus, Hansard's *Parliamentary Debates,* the *Heimskringla,* Montesquieu, Tacitus, Sharon Turner's *History of the Anglo-Saxons,* the *Mémoires* of Philippe de Commines, Fuller's *Worthies,* and the London *Times* is no mere journalistic job.

Emerson had visited Europe in 1833. He went again in 1847–48 when, barring a brief excursion to revolutionary Paris, he spent his time in England and Scotland. The two visits differed radically in character and purpose. Emerson briefly sets forth the record of the earlier one in the first chapter of *English Traits,* a record that can be supplemented from his letters and journals.

In 1833 he was a sorely stricken and bewildered young man. He had suffered a series of domestic and professional trials and calamities. His wife, the beautiful Ellen Tucker, had died of consumption in February 1831, the seventeenth month of their marriage; it is significant of the lasting memory of this loss that in 1839 he named his daughter by his second wife, Lidian Jackson Emerson, Ellen. He knew that his two beloved brothers, Edward and Charles, were threatened by this characteristic plague of New England, and in fact each of them died not long after his return from abroad. Then there was his other brother, Bulkeley, whose mind, it is gently said, "remained undeveloped" and who had somehow to be taken care of. There was his widowed mother. There was the problem of his own health, far from normal: he had been forced to spend the winter of 1826–27 in Georgia and Florida to fend off consumption. He was, moreover, uncertain what he was good for in the world. He had tried school-teaching in a series of casual engagements and, though he was conscientious and was liked by his pupils, he thought himself a failure as a pedagogue. After some equally casual work at the Harvard Divinity School, he had, as the phrase went, been "approbated to preach" by the Middlesex Association of Ministers in 1826; once past the usual wanderings of the neophyte preacher, he had been called, in March 1829, to be the junior colleague of the Reverend Henry Ware of the Second (Unitarian) Church in Boston, a solid and relatively liberal-minded society. But Mr. Ware also suffered from bad health, resigned, leaving Emerson in charge, and devoted himself during his few remaining years to the professorship of pulpit eloquence and pastoral care at the Divinity School. Emerson came to have increasing doubts about religious formularies, and in September 1832 he relinquished his parish, his resignation being accepted (with good will on both sides) on October 28. In September his brother Charles had noted that "Waldo is very feeble," and in November, "Waldo is sick again — and very much dispirited."

What to do? He could not altogether accept the indulgent Christian theology of Unitarianism, if, indeed, it was Christian, which many doubted. He had thoughts of giving up religion altogether: "I have sometimes thought that in order to be a good minister it was necessary to leave the ministry. The profession is antiquated." But how to live? What to believe? He went abroad in February 1833 partly to improve his health (he did), partly to forget Ellen (he did not), and partly to think things through, to consult, if he could, some of the leaders of literature in the Old World. He tells us in chapter one that, like other young men of his generation, he had been much indebted to Scotch genius, especially evident in the *Edinburgh Review,* and that he wanted to see the faces of three or four great writers — Landor, Coleridge, Wordsworth, and Carlyle, not yet famous, not yet known. He wanted to talk with them, motivated not by the gossip-collecting ability that made Nathaniel Parker Willis the ancestor of our social columnists but by the need to form a philosophic outlook of his own. In the Jardin des Plantes in Paris he even seriously thought of turning scientist; and science is a primary concern in his writing. There is no evidence that the great Europeans received him other than kindly, each in his own manner, and of course his visit to Carlyle was to be an epochal event. He came home well on his way to a new philosophy, expressed in *Nature* (1836), "The American Scholar" (1837), and the "Divinity School Address" (1838), that scandalous performance that shocked Andrews Norton. In maturer form he expressed it in lectures and books; and the two series of his *Essays* (1841 and 1844) were to be republished in Great Britain with introductions by Carlyle. His first visit was private and self-centered. He had not yet acquired the experience, the social and political shrewdness, that went into the making of *English Traits* (1856).

The second venture was quite another matter. He was fourteen years older and much more experienced. He had in fact become a public character, famous and a little feared at home and abroad — in Great Britain, for example, the alarm and indignation of religious conservatives were forcibly expressed, and some of them even tried to get his lectures canceled. He had become a professional publicist, a representative American intellectual. Alexander Ireland, the young Scotsman who had learned to admire him and who had left Edinburgh for Manchester where he had risen to the managership of the *Examiner*, an influential liberal organ, had invited Emerson to come. Ireland and his associates had arranged a whole program of appearances in the north of England and the south of Scotland for Emerson, principally at the Mechanics' Institutes (or Institutions), which, however, had ceased to appeal to working men and had become lyceum centers for the middle class. In preparation for Emerson Ireland and his friends launched a remarkable publicity campaign,* and the

---

* Carefully analyzed by Townsend Scudder III in "Emerson's British Lecture Tour, 1847–1848," *American Literature*, 7 (1935): 15–36; 166–180. See also

visitor lectured before public men, intellectuals, statesmen, editors, the clergy. If there had been doubts about an engagement in London, these were removed when Emerson was asked to lecture there in the spring of 1848, and if the series had not been remunerative, it had drawn distinguished audiences. No longer did an introspective young man from America have to present letters of introduction to famous men; on the contrary, he was everywhere feted, dined, and made much of, asked to speak, asked to travel, asked to spend weekends here and there, given memberships in clubs, taken to Parliament, taken to the office of that mighty power the London *Times*. He had so many invitations that he complained about it in letters home. I see "the best of the people," he wrote Lidian in December 1847; and the lists of social engagements he sent her and Margaret Fuller in the spring of 1848 show a certain shy pride. Unfortunately for his book, all this meant that he had little or no contact with British agriculturists, who were having their troubles, or with the industrial proletariat. Their hideous existence was being revealed in parliamentary blue books and in novels like Mrs. Gaskell's *Mary Barton* (1848), set in the slums of Manchester, the very city where Emerson began his tour. A young man named Marx, who came to London in 1849 and spent the rest of his life writing and reading in the British Museum, was alert to this misery as Emerson was not.* Emerson wrote Elizabeth Hoar from Manchester in December 1847 about "the great manufacturers who exercise a paternal patronage & providence over their district. Such are the Brights at Rochdale, whom

---

"A Chronological List of Emerson's Lectures on His British Lecture Tour of 1847–1848," *PMLA*, 51 (1936): 243–248. I prefer these sober factual accounts to the somewhat lush expansion of this material in Scudder's *The Lonely Wayfaring Man: Emerson and Some Englishmen*, New York, 1936.

* It is interesting to contrast chap. viii, pt. III, vol. I of *Das Kapital* with Emerson's statements about British industry. It is of course in no way surprising that the visiting lecturer had not heard of *The Communist Manifesto* of 1848.

I visited, and the Schwanns at Huddersfield, — best of their sort. And England will stand many a day & year yet, and tis all idle the talk of revolution & decay, for they have the energy now which made all these things." Emerson saw English poverty only at rare intervals during his lecturing, and the sight did not basically influence his book.

His journey had been expensive so that, when he returned, Emerson had to set about lecturing once more. He had already read some lectures on things English; now with these fresh experiences in hand, he expanded and enriched what may be called the British gambit in his list of topics. On December 27, 1848, he lectured at Tremont Temple in Boston on "England," a lecture he repeated many times — in New York, in Brooklyn, in Cleveland, in Cincinnati, in Pittsburgh, even in Montreal and Galena, Illinois. There were other lectures, for example, one on "London" and one on "The Anglo-American," which, though he seems to have once thought about making a chapter out of it, did not go into the book. He had read widely in British history and English literature, and now, book devourer that he was, he read even more. He was doubtful about his ability to do justice to the theme. At one time he hoped that Arthur Hugh Clough would come to live at Concord and help him with critical commentary on his writing, but Clough did not come. Yet the subject would not down, it continued to tease him and he worked at it. In December 1852 he wrote William Emerson from Cincinnati that "my English notes have now assumed the size of a pretty book, which I am eager to complete." (His last work in prose had been *Representative Men* in 1850.) But not until October 1855 did he send Moses D. Phillips of Phillips, Sampson and Company, a publishing firm that was to disintegrate during the panic of 1857, "the first of sixteen or seventeen chapters." Like any other author he grew tired of his task. On June 2, 1856, he wrote William he was toiling at the "weary, refractory concluding chapters," and he was even then uncertain how to end the volume. But by the middle of June the manuscript was done, and on August 6, 1856, it was advertised as officially published.

English Traits is made up of nineteen chapters, seventeen of which are the real body of the work, and two of which (the first and last) I find it difficult to justify. Emerson's speech at Manchester (altered from the original version) would have been better printed as an appendix, in which case the sense of anticlimax created by its coming after the admirable summary ("Results") in chapter eighteen would not have occurred. As for the opening chapter, though we know Emerson was puzzled how to begin, one would think that his businesslike account of the ocean voyage would have done very well. If the chapter is there to lead the reader to expect some illuminating comparison between Britain in 1833 and Britain in 1848, no such comparison is made. The vignettes of Landor, Coleridge, Wordsworth, and Carlyle have a certain value, but they are too reportorial, too suggestive of an "interview," and verge perilously close to the slick manner of Willis in a book like *Hurry-Graphs* that came out in 1851. Could it be that the Sage of Concord was trying to be "popular"?

The seventeen chapters that make up the essential *English Traits* fall into three unequal categories. Chapters II, XVI, and XVII are personalized accounts: Emerson's experience of transatlantic travel, Emerson's exploration of Stonehenge, Emerson's general letter of thanks to the scores of persons who had befriended him during his visit. These chapters, though not irrelevant like the first and last ones, might have appeared in any travel book about England. In the second group are chapters XII and XV, which examine with particularity two characteristic institutions, Oxford University as an ancient creation, and the London *Times* as the characteristic creation of modern interest and energy. The remaining chapters (III through XI, XIII, XIV, and XVIII) are generalizations about phases of British life laconically expressed in their titles and backed up by specific examples. One is glad that Emerson went to Stonehenge just as one is happy to note the author's good manners in chapter XVII, and of course Stonehenge is further justified as a study in the antiquity of man on the island, but the brilliance of the book lies mainly in the great generalizing chapters.

The Britain Emerson studied was Britain near the top of her greatness. Behind her lay the glories of the Napoleonic wars, and it is interesting to note how many of Emerson's illustrations are drawn from the statesmen, soldiers, and sailors of that heroic time, nor should it be forgotten that when Emerson was in England the Duke of Wellington, Tennyson's "great duke," was still living. Despite the economic stringencies of the hungry forties, despite popular unrest (Emerson in the main only glances at Chartism), despite the population problem — emigrants pouring out, he says, at the rate of a thousand a day and Irishmen and others pouring in — despite the military incompetence revealed in the Crimean War (which of course did not begin until four years after his visit), and despite the gloomy irascibilities of his friend Carlyle, Emerson was convinced that Great Britain was the most powerful nation in the world. When revolution swept over the Continent in 1848, Britain remained tranquil. Despite the absurdities and inconsistencies of its political and social systems, it was the refuge of liberals and the hope of liberalism. It had somehow reconciled feudal traditions and popular liberties. It was the money center of the globe. It was the workshop of mankind. It headed a gigantic empire on which it seemed to be slowly imposing popular institutions, as the mid-century understood popular institutions. Its offspring, whether independent like the United

States or still in a pupillary state like Australia and Canada, extended the range of the English language, of English thought, and of Anglo-Saxon energy. What were the elements of British success? This is the problem Emerson set himself to solve.

Emerson was a leading American transcendentalist, and it might be expected he would measure British society in such transcendental terms as Time, Eternity, the Ideal, and the Over-Soul. He did nothing of the kind. Emerson was an idealist, but he was also a hardheaded Yankee, and he was never more the Yankee than when writing *English Traits,* the tone of which is so radically different from that, say, of *Nature* that if, a thousand years from now, both books were dug up and the name of the author had disappeared, a cautious scholar of the thirty-first century would scarcely dare assign them to the same pen. Emerson was never less the rhapsode than in this great study. His analysis is not metaphysical but flexible and pragmatic. Environment, race, inheritance, tradition, behavior, commerce and industry, the structure of this amazing society, its religion, its education, its literature — he studies all these phases of its life. In the back of his mind, I think, was also the theme of the chapter he never included, that on "The Anglo-American." From Britain's present superiority, what could be predicted of the United States? If Tocqueville analyzed democracy in America as a lesson to the French, Emerson analyzed a limited monarchy, product of centuries of tradition, as a lesson to the United States. If he did not make the lesson explicit, it was because he found the problem of analysis so absorbing he could not work out the problem of comparison.

Emerson is not only a sociologist (he read widely in the literature of that young subject); he is also a historian. A child of the nineteenth century, he tends to seek the genetic explanation, to go back in time to origins, to trace development and disuse, insisting that the power of Britain can be understood best in a temporal context. This assumption is nowhere more evident than in the chapters on religion, aristocracy, and race. Inevitably, being Emerson, he felt that "no people at the present day can be explained by their national religion," and yet there it was, the Anglican church, as much a part of England as the Tower of London. Moreover, the island had written important chapters in the history of Christianity. Even though in England (at least the social England he was studying) religion was now mainly "part of good-breeding," a function of a bourgeois mercantile culture, the architecture of the churches "still glows with faith in immortality." He devotes himself to the Established Church because both literally and in our sense of the word the church was part of the establishment, and one could no more ignore it than one could ignore the factory system. But he was not satisfied with a merely negative report; and if the final paragraph of the chapter begins by ushering the church out of the door, it ends by opening wide the window for the return of religion, since "if religion be the doing of all good, and for its sake the suffering of all evil . . . that divine secret has existed from the days of Alfred to those of Romilly, of Clarkson, and of Florence Nightingale, and in thousands who have no fame." Emerson could not forget that Britain had abolished slavery and America had not.

The chapter on aristocracy has a somewhat weaker polarity. Emerson traces the origins of the nobility to warlords who were no better than thieves, takes a thoroughly American view of aristocratic idleness, privilege, and decay, and concludes by observing that there are about seventy thousand people in London who make up what is called high society and who cannot shut their eyes to the truth that the visiting Englishman goes about the world in the character of an untitled nobleman because he has economic power, "drawing more than all the advantages which the strongest of his kings could command." Aristocracy is an outmoded social form. Power belongs to those who work, who know how to wield it, who invent, who accumulate capital. English history, wisely read, "is the vindication of the brain of that people." Nevertheless he notes that excellence and integrity are not denied the nobleman merely because he was born or was made noble; he admires the personal force evident in characters as diverse as Lord Eldon, Lord Shaftesbury, the Duke of Wellington. "You cannot," he writes, "wield great agencies without lending yourself to them, and when it happens that the spirit of the earl meets his rank and duties, we have the best examples of behavior." It is a mistake to think the upper classes have only birth, "they have the sense of superiority, the absence of all the ambitious effort which disgusts in the aspiring classes, a pure tone of thought and feeling, and the power to command, among their other luxuries, the presence of the most accomplished men in their festive meetings." It is not cynicism to say that Emerson had been so commanded; his social engagements had given him wonderful opportunities to observe.

The chapter on race is puzzling. Emerson's terminology is confused and inconsistent. Sometimes by "race" he means mankind in general, sometimes one or more of the three or five or eleven "fixed" races his authorities told him about, sometimes a particular racial strain (Caucasian, Celt, Saxon), sometimes an amalgam of various racial stocks that is tagged by the name of one among them. Moreover, he fails to differentiate the Scotch and the English; in many passages all the inhabitants of the island at any time are "English," and only in a few does he note the Celtic origins of Scotland. Sometimes Celt and Saxon are lumped together as progenitors; sometimes it is important to keep them apart. Nor, though he uses all the terms, does he discriminate carefully

among Teutons, Germans, Scandinavians, Norsemen, Northmen, Danes, Saxons, and Normans. He annexes the *Heim-*
skringla and other early sagas to the prehistory of his theme,
which is, among other matters, that the Teutonic strain is
marked by honesty, energy, and "truth"; yet the treachery
latent in the episodes he selects from the sagas does not seem
to differ from his contemptuous dismissal of the army of
William the Conqueror as "twenty thousand thieves,"
"greedy and ferocious dragoons," who "burned, harried,
violated, tortured and killed," because the Scandinavian in-
vaders of Normandy left France for England worse men than
when they came to Normandy. It is difficult to see how the
contribution of "comity, social talent and fine manners"
emerges from any of these racial strains. In truth Emerson
had no great faith in the racial theorists he read, and I think
he unconsciously transferred his bewilderment to his manuscript.

These infelicities should not, however, obscure his central
point, which is that we are dealing not with the Mediterranean world but with the world of the North, a world
that contains an island called Britain anchored like a ship
off the coast of Europe. On this island various racial strains
were amalgamated by force of environment, circumstance,
and time to produce a people called the English, whose survival value has been and is extraordinarily high. In England
(and here one must regret his failure to explore the mines,
the mills, and the slums) manliness is taken for granted,
vigorous health is common, people are fair and comely, and
the "race" displays "more constitutional energy than any
other people." The amalgam is a race that has practical sense,
a supreme eye for facts, self-respect, an instinct for fair play,
and a Teutonic love for "truth." The very felons, he says,
have their pride in each other's staunchness, the charm of
Nelson's story lies in his assurance of being supported to the

uttermost by those whom he supports to the uttermost. The chapter concludes with a sentence so syntactically tangled one must read it two or three times — a quite uncharacteristic defect — which expresses for Emerson the admirable outcome of the racial history he has been thus cloudily tracing: "Whilst they are some ages ahead of the rest of the world in the art of living; whilst in some directions they do not represent the modern spirit but constitute it; — this vanguard of civility and power they coldly hold, marching in phalanx, lockstep, foot after foot, file after file of heroes, ten thousand deep." *

Since Emerson consciously adopted the genetic point of view, historical considerations are not absent from the other generalizing chapters, but the rest of these deal more directly with contemporary life in Great Britain than do the three just examined, it being understood that chapter V ("Ability") is a kind of pendant to chapter IV. The Englishman Emerson pictures is a superior John Bull, chiefly living in London but establishing great industrial works in other parts of the island or going abroad as a bagman or commercial traveler or as a colonizer or colonial administrator. The analysis of British character emphasizes individualism and self-respect, and above all Emerson admires the empirical adaptability of the British nation, a surprising tribute from an idealist. He also pays humorous tribute to the British talent for eccentricity. The society he analyzes is chiefly male. Surprising also is the lengthy chapter on wealth, in which Emerson, whose cutting sarcasms directed against Boston mercantile values are well known, seems virtually to adopt the so-called Protestant ethic,

---

* As the extraordinary survival value of the English seems to be central in Emerson's estimate, in view of the number of passages of like kind in the book, I am at a loss to understand why, in his otherwise admirable *Emerson on Race and History: An Examination of English Traits* (New York, 1961), Philip L. Nicoloff thinks that Emerson was demonstrating the coming decadence of Great Britain. Is this not to read history backward?

or if not that, the Carlylean doctrine that tools are to him
that can use them.

True, England is responsible "for the despotism of expense." True also that antidotes to materialism are "frightfully inadequate" and that England is "no divinity, or wise
and instructed soul." But there England stands, striding the
world like a colossus. How else explain the power and greatness of a kingdom in which respect for wealth is paralleled
by respect for the truth of fact? Emerson cannot but admire
the solvency of the empire, the universal belief in economy,
or wise management, the power of invention to create more
wealth, the creation of which in the last ninety years "is a
main fact in modern history." How can one despise so rich
a nation that any Englishman "is a king in a plain coat"?
The chapter ends, of course, on a note of moral warning,
including some sarcasms on death as a reduction in family
expenses, but on balance, as the summarizing chapter ("Result") plainly shows, though the American system is more
democratic, the Americans do not produce abler or more
inventive men. "The English have given importance to individuals, a principal end and fruit of every society. Every
man is allowed and encouraged to be what he is, and is
guarded in the indulgence of his whim . . . By this general
activity and by this sacredness of individuals, they have in
seven hundred years evolved the principle of freedom. It is
the land of patriots, martyrs, sages and bards, and if the
ocean out of which it emerged should wash it away, it will
be remembered as an island famous for immortal laws, for
the announcements of original right which makes the stone
tables of liberty." Approbation can scarcely go further. Even
Oxford, which he thought might, like the church, be principally an influence for conformity, has its place: "England
is the land of mixture and surprise, and when you have settled it that the universities are moribund, out comes a poetic

influence from the heart of Oxford, to mould the opinions
of cities, to build their houses as simply as birds their nests,
to give veracity to art and charm mankind, as an appeal to
moral order always must." I take this to be a tribute to
Ruskin, who, curiously enough, is not discussed in the chapter on literature.

Chapter XIV ("Literature") is the only part of the book
that seems to announce a drift toward decline. After the age
of Shakespeare, the age of Milton, "who was the stair or high
table-land to let down the English genius from the summits"
to the dullness of Hallam, the low realism of Dickens, the
empiricism of Macaulay, a literature wherein "no hope, no
sublime augury cheers the student, no secure striding from
experiment onward to a foreseen law." We who regard the
Victorian period as a great age in British letters are a little
taken aback by a condemnation so wholesale that it scarcely
frees Carlyle and Wordsworth from the charge of meanness,
"the limitary tone of English thought," and makes the great
exceptions to the mediocrity of intellect "John Hunter, a
man of ideas," perhaps "Robert Brown, the botanist," and
"Richard Owen, who has imported into Britain the German
homologists." Students of the history of ideas may be a little
bewildered by this list and the omissions from it; for example,
Faraday, of whose work Emerson apparently knew little or
nothing.* I think the harshness of these judgments can be
explained by a variety of causes. In the first place a great age
seldom appears great to those who live in it. In the second
place the transcendentalist, not the Yankee, writes the chapter; and the transcendentalist is committed to the proposition
that British genius at its highest is always Platonic, even in
the case of Francis Bacon. Though the chapter begins by

---

* Faraday's name appears once in the text (the chapter called "Personal")
as somebody Emerson had met, and does not appear in the correspondence
until 1857.

apparently accepting the notion that "a strong common sense
. . . marks the English mind for a thousand years," the
writer is impatient with empiricism and fashion. A discussion
that devotes a paragraph to "Wilkinson, the editor of Swedenborg," and fails to discuss Hazlitt, Lamb, De Quincey, Shelley, and Keats and says little or nothing about Byron,
Thackeray, Dickens, and Scott (and that little unsympathetic)
is scarcely an example of adequate analysis. Emerson's judgment that the Elizabethans were at the top of British genius
is conventional; and it is a curious paradox that the leading
literary light of New England was at his weakest in surveying
contemporary British literature. One's sense of incongruity
is increased when one turns to the shrewd account of the
London *Times* in the following chapter.

Such, then, is *English Traits,* one of the most remarkable
studies of a foreign nation ever published by an American
author, a tough-minded analysis of a complex modern industrial society, the most potent then in the world, by a
writer least likely to have produced a book of this kind. It is,
however, a silent rebuke to the school of criticism that dismisses Emerson as a thin idealist. Like most American books
of the period, the study, it is true, is not wholly unified, but
what may be called the centrifugal parts are minor and the
centripetal forces dominate and drive home the theme. For
the most part the analysis is forward-going and orderly —
the land, the biological inheritance, some examination of
their social patterns and their peculiar traits as a people, the
traditional education of the governing class, their religion,
their literature and that most striking of British inventions,
the London *Times,* then the most powerful newspaper in the
world. If two or three chapters are mere makeweight affairs,
Emerson's powerful summary, laconic and just, within the
limits of his study, leads the reader back to his central theme,

the demonstration that "England is the best of actual nations." There are inequities and inequalities in the British system, British foreign policy is sometimes contradictory and even tyrannous, and the British acquisition of random real estate around the globe is no lovelier than that by other powers. Yet the British expiate the wrongs they have done by conferring benefits, as in the case of India; and, after all, let Americans remember that freedom "is double-edged and dangerous to any but the wise and good." If there is a "cramp limitation" on the British mind, the right measure of the country is the men it has bred; better, he says, one Alfred, one Shakespeare, one Milton, one Sidney, one Raleigh, one Wellington than a million foolish democrats. And what reserves of power in that island population! "What variety of power and talent; what facility and plenteousness of knighthood, lordship, ladyship, royalty, loyalty . . . ! What dignity resting on what reality and stoutness! What courage in war, what sinew in labor, what cunning workmen, what inventors and engineers, what seamen and pilots, what clerks and scholars!"

The best life of Emerson is that by Ralph Leslie Rusk, New York, 1949. Rusk also edited in six volumes *The Letters of Ralph Waldo Emerson,* New York, 1939. Edward Waldo Emerson and Waldo Emerson Forbes edited Emerson's *Journals* in ten volumes, Boston, 1909–1914, but this edition is inadequate and is being superseded by an edition now (1966) being published by Harvard University Press under various editors. The only book-length study of *English Traits* is that mentioned in a note above, Philip L. Nicoloff, *Emerson on Race and History: An Examination of English Traits,* New York, 1961, which has great value by setting the book in the context of Emerson's mature thinking. And as I have also indicated in a note, Townsend Scudder, *The Lonely Wayfaring Man: Emerson and Some Englishmen,* New York, 1936, is devoted to his second English visit. The bibliography in Scudder is a valuable guide to further biographical study of this period of Emerson's life. See also William J. Sowder, *Emerson's Impact on the British Isles and Canada: A Study in Literary History,* Charlottesville, The University Press of Virginia, 1966.

A NOTE ON THE TEXT

English Traits was originally published by Phillips, Sampson and Company of Boston in 1856 as a 12mo. of 312 pages; and from the plates of this edition a number of subsequent printings were made. In 1876 James R. Osgood and Company, ancestors of Houghton, Mifflin and Company, brought out a "new and revised" edition in an 18mo. of 236 pages, the basis of all subsequent reprintings. Examination shows few important textual changes: Emerson corrected a few typographical errors and indicated in the revised edition the dates of some of his statistical information, and he, or some one for him, altered the punctuation here and there. But the substance of the work remained essentially unchanged. This text was reset for the Centenary edition of Emerson's *Complete Works* in 1901, to which the editor, Edward Waldo Emerson, added a good deal of annotation. I have, however, preferred the printing of the so-called "new and revised edition" as this was gathered into the Riverside edition of Emerson in 1883 because it retains Emerson's original footnotes. I am indebted to the annotations of the Centenary edition for some of my own notes.

ENGLISH TRAITS

First Visit To England

I have been twice in England. In 1833, on my return from a short tour in Sicily, Italy and France, I crossed from Boulogne and landed in London at the Tower stairs. It was a dark Sunday morning; there were few people in the streets, and I remember the pleasure of that first walk on English ground, with my companion, an American artist,[1] from the Tower up through Cheapside and the Strand to a house in Russell Square, whither we had been recommended to good chambers. For the first time for many months we were forced to check the saucy habit of travellers' criticism, as we could no longer speak aloud in the streets without being understood. The shop-signs spoke our language; our country names were on the door-plates, and the public and private buildings wore a more native and wonted front.

Like most young men at that time, I was much indebted to the men of Edinburgh and of the Edinburgh Review, — to Jeffrey, Mackintosh, Hallam, and to Scott, Playfair and De Quincey;[2] and my narrow and desultory reading had inspired the wish to see the faces of three or four writers, — Coleridge, Wordsworth, Landor, De Quincey, and the latest and strongest contributor to the critical journals, Carlyle;[3] and I suppose if I had sifted the reasons that led me to Europe, when I was ill and was advised to travel, it was mainly the attraction of these persons. If Goethe had been still living I might have wandered into Germany also. Besides those I have named (for Scott was dead), there was not in Britain the man living whom I cared to behold, unless it were the Duke of Wellington,[4] whom I afterwards saw at Westminster Abbey at the funeral of Wilberforce.[5] The young scholar fancies it happiness enough to live with people who can give an inside to the world; without reflecting that they are prisoners, too, of their own thought, and cannot apply themselves to yours. The conditions of literary success are almost destructive of the best social power, as they do not leave that frolic liberty which only can encounter a companion on the best terms. It is probable you left some obscure comrade at a tavern, or in the farms, with right mother-wit and equality to life, when you crossed sea and land to play bo-peep with celebrated scribes. I have, however, found writers superior to their books, and I cling to my first belief that a strong head will dispose fast enough of these impediments and give one the satisfaction of reality, the sense of having been met, and a larger horizon.

On looking over the diary of my journey in 1833,[6] I find nothing to publish in my memoranda of visits to places. But I have copied the few notes I made of visits to persons, as they respect parties quite too good and too transparent to the whole world to make it needful to affect any prudery of suppression about a few hints of those bright personalities.

At Florence, chief among artists I found Horatio Greenough,[7] the American sculptor. His face was so handsome and his person so well formed that he might be pardoned, if, as was alleged, the face of his Medora and the figure of a colossal Achilles in clay, were idealizations of his own. Greenough was a superior man, ardent and eloquent, and all his opinions had elevation and magnanimity. He believed that the Greeks had wrought in schools or fraternities, — the genius of the master imparting his design to his friends and inflaming them with it, and when his strength was spent, a new hand with equal heat continued the work; and so by relays, until it was finished in every part with equal fire. This was necessary in so refractory a material as stone; and he thought art would never prosper until we left our shy jealous ways and worked in society as they. All his thoughts breathed the same generosity. He was an accurate and a deep man. He was a votary of the Greeks, and impatient of Gothic art. His paper on Architecture,[8] published in 1843, announced in advance the leading thoughts of Mr. Ruskin on the *morality* in architecture,[9] notwithstanding the antagonism in their views of the history of art. I have a private letter from him,[10] — later, but respecting the same period, — in which he roughly sketches his own theory. "Here is my theory of structure: A scientific arrangement of spaces and forms to functions and to site; an emphasis of features proportioned to their *gradated* importance in function; color and ornament to be decided and arranged and varied by strictly organic laws, having a distinct reason for each decision; the entire and immediate banishment of all make-shift and make-believe."

Greenough brought me, through a common friend, an invitation from Mr. Landor,[11] who lived at San Domenica di Fiesole. On the 15th May I dined with Mr. Landor. I found him noble and courteous, living in a cloud of pictures at his Villa Gherardesca, a fine house commanding a beautiful landscape.[12] I had inferred from his books, or magnified from some anecdotes, an impression of Achillean wrath,[13] — an untamable petulance. I do not know whether the imputation were just or not, but certainly on this May day his courtesy veiled that haughty mind and he was the most patient and gentle of hosts. He praised the beautiful cyclamen which grows all about Florence; he admired Washington; talked of Wordsworth, Byron, Massinger, Beaumont and Fletcher.[14] To be sure, he is decided in his opinions, likes to surprise, and is well content to impress, if possible, his English whim upon the immutable past. No great man ever had a great son, if Philip and Alexander be not an exception; and Philip he calls the greater man.[15] In art, he loves the Greeks, and in sculpture, them only. He prefers the Venus to everything else, and, after that, the head of Alexander, in the gallery here.[16] He prefers John of Bologna to Michael Angelo; in painting, Raffaelle, and shares the growing taste for Perugino and the early masters.[17] The Greek histories he thought the only good; and after them, Voltaire's.[18] I could not make him praise Mackintosh, nor my more recent friends; Montaigne very cordially, — and Charron also,[19] which seemed undiscriminating. He thought Degerando[20] indebted to "Lucas on Happiness" and "Lucas on Holiness"![21] He pestered me with Southey; but who is Southey?[22]

He invited me to breakfast on Friday. On Friday I did not fail to go, and this time with Greenough. He entertained us at once with reciting half a dozen hexameter lines of Julius Cæsar's! — from Donatus, he said.[23] He glorified Lord Chesterfield[24] more than was necessary, and undervalued Burke, and undervalued Socrates; designated as three of the greatest of men, Washington, Phocion and Timoleon,[25] — much as our pomologists, in their lists, select the three or the six best pears "for a small orchard;" — and did not even omit to remark the similar termination of their names. "A great man," he said, "should make great sacrifices and kill his hundred oxen without knowing whether they would be consumed by gods and heroes, or whether the flies would eat them." I had visited Professor Amici,[26] who had shown me his microscopes, magnifying (it was said) two thousand diameters; and I spoke of the uses to which they were applied. Landor despised entomology, yet, in the same breath, said, "the sublime was in a grain of dust." I suppose I teased him about recent writers, but he professed never to have heard of

Herschel, *not even by name.*[27] One room was full of pictures, which he likes to show, especially one piece, standing before which he said "he would give fifty guineas to the man that would swear it was a Domenichino." [28] I was more curious to see his library, but Mr. H——,[29] one of the guests, told me that Mr. Landor gives away his books and has never more than a dozen at a time in his house.

Mr. Landor carries to its height the love of freak which the English delight to indulge, as if to signalize their commanding freedom. He has a wonderful brain, despotic, violent and inexhaustible, meant for a soldier, by what chance converted to letters; in which there is not a style nor a tint not known to him, yet with an English appetite for action and heroes. The thing done avails, and not what is said about it. An original sentence, a step forward, is worth more than all the censures. Landor is strangely undervalued in England; usually ignored and sometimes savagely attacked in the Reviews. The criticism may be right or wrong, and is quickly forgotten; but year after year the scholar must still go back to Landor for a multitude of elegant sentences; for wisdom, wit, and indignation that are unforgetable.

From London, on the 5th August, I went to Highgate,[30] and wrote a note to Mr. Coleridge, requesting leave to pay my respects to him. It was near noon. Mr. Coleridge sent a verbal message that he was in bed, but if I would call after one o'clock he would see me. I returned at one, and he appeared, a short, thick old man, with bright blue eyes and fine clear complexion, leaning on his cane. He took snuff freely, which presently soiled his cravat and neat black suit. He asked whether I knew Allston,[31] and spoke warmly of his merits and doings when he knew him in Rome; what a master of the Titianesque he was, &c., &c. He spoke of Dr. Channing.[32] It was an unspeakable misfortune that he should have turned out a Unitarian after all. On this, he burst into a declamation on the folly and ignorance of Unitarianism, — its high unreasonableness; and taking up Bishop Waterland's book,[33] which lay on the table, he read with vehemence two or three pages written by himself in the fly-leaves, — passages, too, which, I believe, are printed in the "Aids to Reflection."[34] When he stopped to take breath, I interposed that "whilst I highly valued all his explanations, I was bound to tell him that I was born and bred a Unitarian." "Yes," he said, "I supposed so;" and continued as before. It was a wonder that after so many ages of unquestioning acquiescence in the doctrine of St. Paul, — the doctrine of the Trinity, which was also according to Philo Judæus[35] the doctrine of the Jews before Christ, — this handful of Priestleians[36] should take on themselves to deny it, &c., &c. He was very sorry that Dr. Channing, a man to whom he looked up, — no, to say that he looked *up* to him would be to speak falsely, but a man whom he looked *at* with so much interest, — should embrace such views. When he saw Dr. Channing he had hinted to him that he was afraid he loved Christianity for what was lovely and excellent, — he loved the good in it, and not the true; — "And I tell you, sir, that I have known ten persons who loved the good, for one person who loved the true; but it is a far greater virtue to love the true for itself alone, than to love the good for itself alone." He (Coleridge) knew all about Unitarianism perfectly well, because he had once been a Unitarian and knew what quackery it was. He had been called "the rising star of Unitarianism." He went on defining, or rather refining: "The Trinitarian doctrine was realism; the idea of God was not essential, but super-essential;" talked of *trinism* and *tetrakism*[37] and much more, of which I only caught this, "that the will was that by which a person is a person; because, if one should push me in the street, and so I should force the man next me into the kennel, I should at once exclaim, I did not do it, sir, meaning it was not my will." And this also, that "if you should insist on your faith here in England, and I on mine, mine would be the hotter side of the fagot."

I took advantage of a pause to say that he had many readers of all religious opinions in America and I proceeded to inquire if the "extract" from the Independent's pamphlet, in the third volume of the Friend, were a veritable quotation. He replied that it was really taken from a pamphlet in his possession entitled "A Protest of one of the Independents," or something to that effect.[38] I told him how excellent I thought it and how much I wished to see the entire work. "Yes," he said, "the man was a chaos of truths, but lacked the knowledge that God was a God of order. Yet the passage would no doubt strike you more in the quotation than in the original, for I have filtered it."

When I rose to go, he said, "I do not know whether you care about poetry, but I will repeat some verses I lately made on my baptismal anniversary," and he recited with strong emphasis, standing, ten or twelve lines beginning, —

"Born unto God in Christ ——" [39]

He inquired where I had been travelling; and on learning that I had been in Malta and Sicily, he compared one island with the other, repeating what he had said to the Bishop of London when he returned from that country, that Sicily was an excellent school of political economy;[40] for, in any town there, it only needed to ask what the government enacted, and reverse that, to know what ought to be done; it was the most felicitously opposite legislation to anything good and wise. There were only three things which the government had brought into that garden of delights, namely, itch, pox and famine. Whereas in Malta, the force of law and mind was seen, in making that barren rock of semi-Saracen inhabitants[41] the seat of population and plenty. Going out, he showed me in the next apartment a picture of Allston's, and told me that Montague,[42] a picture-dealer, once came to see him, and glancing towards this, said "Well, you have got a picture!" thinking it the work of an old master; afterwards, Montague, still talking with his back to the canvas, put up his hand and touched it, and exclaimed, "By Heaven! this picture is not ten years old:" — so delicate and skilful was that man's touch.

I was in his company for about an hour, but find it impossible to recall the largest part of his discourse, which was often like so many printed paragraphs in his book, — perhaps the same, — so readily did he fall into certain commonplaces. As I might have foreseen, the visit was rather a spectacle than a conversation, of no use beyond the satisfaction of my curiosity. He was old and preoccupied, and could not bend to a new companion and think with him.

From Edinburgh I went to the Highlands. On my return I came from Glasgow to Dumfries,[43] and being intent on delivering a letter which I had brought from Rome, inquired for Craigenputtock.[44] It was a farm in Nithsdale, in the parish of Dunscore, sixteen miles distant. No public coach passed near it, so I took a private carriage from the inn. I found the house amid desolate heathery hills, where the lonely scholar nourished his mighty heart. Carlyle was a man from his youth, an author who did not need to hide from his readers, and as absolute a man of the world, unknown and exiled on that hill-farm, as if holding on his own terms what is best in London. He was tall and gaunt, with a cliff-like brow, self-possessed and holding his extraordinary powers of conversation in easy command; clinging to his northern accent with evident relish; full of lively anecdote and with a streaming humor which floated every thing he looked upon. His talk playfully exalting the familiar objects, put the companion at once into an acquaintance with his Lars and Lemurs,[45] and it was very pleasant to learn what was predestined to be a pretty mythology. Few were the objects and lonely the man; "not a person to speak to within sixteen miles except the minister of Dunscore;" so that books inevitably made his topics.

He had names of his own for all the matters familiar to his discourse. Blackwood's was the "sand magazine;" Fraser's nearer approach to possibility of life was the "mud magazine;" a piece of road near by, that marked some failed enterprise, was the "grave of the last sixpence." [46] When too much praise of any genius annoyed him he professed hugely to admire the talent shown by his pig. He had spent much time and contrivance in confining the poor beast to one enclosure in his pen, but pig, by great strokes of judgment, had found out how to let a board down, and had foiled him. For all that he still thought man the most plastic little fellow in the planet, and he liked Nero's death, *"Qualis artifex pereo!"* [47] better than most history. He worships a man that will manifest any truth to him. At one time he had inquired and read a good deal about America. Landor's principle was mere rebellion; and *that* he feared was the American principle. The best thing he knew of that country was that in it a man can have meat for his labor. He had read in Stewart's book[48] that when he inquired in a New York hotel for the Boots, he had been shown across the street and had found Mungo[49] in his own house dining on roast turkey.

We talked of books. Plato he does not read, and he disparaged Socrates; and, when pressed, persisted in making Mirabeau a hero.[50] Gibbon he called the "splendid bridge from the old world to the new." His own reading had been multifarious. Tristram Shandy[51] was one of his first books after Robinson Crusoe, and Robertson's America[52] an early favorite. Rousseau's Confessions had discovered to him that he was not a dunce; and it was now ten years since he had learned German, by the advice of a man who told him he would find in that language what he wanted.[53]

He took despairing or satirical views of literature at this moment; recounted the incredible sums paid in one year by the great booksellers for puffing. Hence it comes that no newspaper is trusted now, no books are bought, and the booksellers are on the eve of bankruptcy.

He still returned to English pauperism, the crowded country, the selfish abdication by public men of all that public persons should perform. Government should direct poor men what to do. Poor Irish folk come wandering over these moors. My dame[54] makes it a rule to give to every son of Adam bread to eat, and supplies his wants to the next house. But here are thousands of acres which might give them all meat, and nobody to bid these poor Irish go to the moor and till it. They burned the stacks and so found a way to force the rich people to attend to them.[55]

We went out to walk over long hills, and looked at Criffel, then without his cap, and down into Wordsworth's country.[56] There we sat down and talked of the immortality of the soul. It was not Carlyle's fault that we talked on that topic, for he had the natural disinclination of every nimble spirit to bruise itself against walls, and did not like to place himself where no step can be taken. But he was honest and true, and cognizant of the subtile links that bind ages together, and saw how every event affects all the future. "Christ died on the tree; that built Dunscore kirk yonder; that brought you and me together. Time has only a relative existence."

He was already turning his eyes towards London with a scholar's appreciation. London is the heart of the world he said, wonderful only from the mass of human beings. He liked the huge machine. Each keeps its own round. The baker's boy brings muffins to the window at a fixed hour every day, and that is all the Londoner knows or wishes to know on the subject. But it turned out good men. He named certain individuals, especially one man of letters, his friend, the best mind he knew, whom London had well served.[57]

On the 28th August I went to Rydal Mount, to pay my respects to Mr. Wordsworth.[58] His daughters called in their father, a plain, elderly, white-haired man, not prepossessing, and disfigured by green goggles. He sat down, and talked with great simplicity. He had just returned from a journey. His health was good, but he had broken a tooth by a fall, when walking with two lawyers, and had said that he was glad it did not happen forty years ago; whereupon they had praised his philosophy.

He had much to say of America, the more that it gave occasion for his favorite topic, — that society is being enlightened by a superficial tuition, out of all proportion to its being restrained by moral culture. Schools do no good. Tuition is not education. He thinks more of the education of circumstances than of tuition. 'Tis not question whether there are offences of which the law takes cognizance, but whether there are offences of which the law does not take cognizance. Sin is what he fears, — and how society is to escape without gravest mischiefs from this source? He has even said, what seemed a paradox, that they needed a civil war in America, to teach the necessity of knitting the social ties stronger. "There may be," he said, "in America some vulgarity in manner, but that's not important. That comes of the pioneer state of things. But I fear they are too much given to the making of money; and secondly, to politics; that they make political distinction the end and not the means. And I fear they lack a class of men of leisure, — in short, of gentlemen, — to give a tone of honor to the community. I am told that things are boasted

of in the second class of society there, which, in England, —
God knows, are done in England every day, but would never
be spoken of. In America I wish to know not how many
churches or schools, but what newspapers? My friend Colonel
Hamilton,[59] at the foot of the hill, who was a year in America, assures me that the newspapers are atrocious, and accuse
members of Congress of stealing spoons!" He was against
taking off the tax on newspapers in England,[60] — which the
reformers represent as a tax upon knowledge, — for this reason, that they would be inundated with base prints. He said
he talked on political aspects, for he wished to impress on
me and all good Americans to cultivate the moral, the conservative, &c., &c., and never to call into action the physical
strength of the people, as had just now been done in England in the Reform Bill, — a thing prophesied by Delolme.[61]
He alluded once or twice to his conversation with Dr. Channing, who had recently visited him, (laying his hand on a
particular chair in which the Doctor had sat.) [62]

The conversation turned on books. Lucretius he esteems a
far higher poet than Virgil; not in his system, which is nothing, but in his power of illustration. Faith is necessary to
explain anything and to reconcile the foreknowledge of God
with human evil. Of Cousin (whose lectures we had all been
reading in Boston), he knew only the name.[63]

I inquired if he had read Carlyle's critical articles and
translations. He said he thought him sometimes insane. He
proceeded to abuse Goethe's Wilhelm Meister heartily.[64] It
was full of all manner of fornication. It was like the crossing
of flies in the air. He had never gone farther than the first
part; so disgusted was he that he threw the book across the
room. I deprecated this wrath, and said what I could for the
better parts of the book, and he courteously promised to look
at it again. Carlyle he said wrote most obscurely. He was
clever and deep, but he defied the sympathies of every body.

Even Mr. Coleridge wrote more clearly, though he had always wished Coleridge would write more to be understood. He led me out into his garden, and showed me the gravel walk in which thousands of his lines were composed. His eyes are much inflamed. This is no loss except for reading, because he never writes prose, and of poetry he carries even hundreds of lines in his head before writing them. He had just returned from a visit to Staffa, and within three days had made three sonnets on Fingal's Cave, and was composing a fourth when he was called in to see me.[65] He said "If you are interested in my verses perhaps you will like to hear these lines." I gladly assented, and he recollected himself for a few moments and then stood forth and repeated, one after the other, the three entire sonnets with great animation. I fancied the second and third more beautiful than his poems are wont to be. The third is addressed to the flowers, which, he said, especially the ox-eye daisy, are very abundant on the top of the rock. The second alludes to the name of the cave, which is "Cave of Music;" the first to the circumstance of its being visited by the promiscuous company of the steamboat.

This recitation was so unlooked for and surprising, — he, the old Wordsworth, standing apart, and reciting to me in a garden-walk, like a schoolboy declaiming, — that I at first was near to laugh; but recollecting myself, that I had come thus far to see a poet and he was chanting poems to me, I saw that he was right and I was wrong, and gladly gave myself up to hear. I told him how much the few printed extracts had quickened the desire to possess his unpublished poems. He replied he never was in haste to publish; partly because he corrected a good deal, and every alteration is ungraciously received after printing; but what he had written would be printed, whether he lived or died. I said "Tintern Abbey" [66] appeared to be the favorite poem with the public, but more contemplative readers preferred the first books of the "Excursion," and the Sonnets.[67] He said "Yes, they are better." He preferred such of his poems as touched the affections, to any others; for whatever is didactic, — what theories of society, and so on, — might perish quickly; but whatever combined a truth with an affection was κτῆμα 'ες 'αεί,[68] good to-day and good forever. He cited the sonnet "On the feelings of a high-minded Spaniard," [69] which he preferred to any other (I so understood him), and the "Two Voices;" [70] and quoted, with evident pleasure, the verses addressed "To the Skylark." [71] In this connection he said of the Newtonian theory that it might yet be superseded and forgotten; and Dalton's atomic theory.

When I prepared to depart he said he wished to show me what a common person in England could do, and he led me into the enclosure of his clerk, a young man to whom he had given this slip of ground, which was laid out, or its natural capabilities shown, with much taste. He then said he would show me a better way towards the inn; and he walked a good part of a mile, talking and ever and anon stopping short to impress the word or the verse, and finally parted from me with great kindness and returned across the fields.

Wordsworth honored himself by his simple adherence to truth, and was very willing not to shine; but he surprised by the hard limits of his thought. To judge from a single conversation, he made the impression of a narrow and very English mind; of one who paid for his rare elevation by general tameness and conformity. Off his own beat, his opinions were of no value. It is not very rare to find persons loving sympathy and ease, who expiate their departure from the common in one direction, by their conformity in every other.

CHAPTER II

Voyage to England

The occasion of my second visit to England was an invitation from some Mechanics' Institutes in Lancashire and Yorkshire, which separately are organized much in the same way as our New England Lyceums,[1] but in 1847 had been linked into a "Union," which embraced twenty or thirty towns and cities and presently extended into the middle counties and northward into Scotland.[2] I was invited, on liberal terms, to read a series of lectures in them all. The request was urged with every kind suggestion and every assurance of aid and comfort, by friendliest parties in Manchester,[3] who, in the sequel, amply redeemed their word. The remuneration was equivalent to the fees at that time paid in this country for the like services. At all events it was sufficient to cover any travelling expenses, and the proposal offered an excellent opportunity of seeing the interior of England and Scotland, by means of a home and a committee of intelligent friends awaiting me in every town.

I did not go very willingly. I am not a good traveller, nor have I found that long journeys yield a fair share of reasonable hours. But the invitation was repeated and pressed at a moment of more leisure and when I was a little spent by some unusual studies. I wanted a change and a tonic, and England was proposed to me. Besides, there were at least the dread attraction and salutary influences of the sea. So I took my berth in the packet-ship Washington Irving and sailed from Boston on Tuesday, 5th October, 1847.

On Friday at noon we had only made one hundred and thirty-four miles. A nimble Indian would have swum as far; but the captain affirmed that the ship would show us in time all her paces, and we crept along through the floating drift of boards, logs and chips, which the rivers of Maine and New Brunswick pour into the sea after a freshet.

At last, on Sunday night, after doing one day's work in four, the storm came, the winds blew, and we flew before a north-wester which strained every rope and sail. The good ship darts through the water all day, all night, like a fish; quivering with speed, gliding through liquid leagues, sliding from horizon to horizon. She has passed Cape Sable;[4] she has reached the Banks;[5] the land-birds are left; gulls, haglets,[6] ducks, petrels, swim, dive and hover around; no fishermen; she has passed the Banks, left five sail behind her far on the edge of the west at sundown, which were far east of us at morn, — though they say at sea a stern chase is a long race, — and still we fly for our lives. The shortest sea-line from Boston to Liverpool is 2,850 miles. This a steamer keeps, and saves 150 miles. A sailing ship can never go in a shorter line than 3,000, and usually it is much longer. Our good master keeps his kites up to the last moment, studding-sails alow and aloft, and by incessant straight steering, never loses a rod of way.[7] Watchfulness is the law of the ship, — watch on watch, for advantage and for life. Since the ship was built, it seems, the master never slept but in his day-clothes whilst on board. "There are many advantages," says Saadi,[8] "in sea-voyaging, but security is not one of them." Yet in hurrying over these abysses, whatever dangers we are running into, we are certainly running out of the risks of hundreds of miles every day, which have their own chances of squall, collision, sea-stroke, piracy, cold and thunder. Hour for hour, the risk on a steamboat is greater;[9] but the speed is safety, or twelve days of danger instead of twenty-four.

Our ship was registered 750 tons, and weighed perhaps, with all her freight, 1,500 tons.[10] The mainmast, from the deck to the top-button,[11] measured 115 feet; the length of the deck from stem to stern, 155. It is impossible not to personify a ship; every body does, in every thing they say: — she behaves well; she minds her rudder; she swims like a duck; she runs her nose into the water; she looks into a port. Then that wonderful *esprit du corps* by which we adopt into our self-love every thing we touch, makes us all champions of her sailing qualities.

The conscious ship hears all the praise. In one week she had made 1,467 miles, and now, at night, seems to hear the steamer behind her, which left Boston to-day at two; has mended her speed and is flying before the gray south wind eleven and a half knots the hour. The sea-fire[12] shines in her wake and far around wherever a wave breaks. I read the hour, 9h. 45', on my watch by this light. Near the equator you can read small print by it; and the mate describes the phosphoric insects, when taken up in a pail, as shaped like a Carolina potato.[13]

I find the sea-life an acquired taste, like that for tomatoes and olives. The confinement, cold, motion, noise and odor are not to be dispensed with. The floor of your room is sloped at an angle of twenty or thirty degrees, and I waked every morning with the belief that some one was tipping up my berth. Nobody likes to be treated ignominiously, upset, shoved against the side of the house, rolled over, suffocated with bilge, mephitis and stewing oil.[14] We get used to these annoyances at last, but the dread of the sea remains longer. The sea is masculine, the type of active strength. Look, what egg-shells are drifting all over it, each one, like ours, filled with men in ecstasies of terror, alternating with cockney con-

ceit, as the sea is rough or smooth. Is this sad-colored circle an
eternal cemetery? In our graveyards we scoop a pit, but this
aggressive water opens mile-wide pits and chasms and makes
a mouthful of a fleet. To the geologist the sea is the only
firmament; the land is in perpetual flux and change, now
blown up like a tumor, now sunk in a chasm, and the registered observations of a few hundred years find it in a perpetual tilt, rising and falling. The sea keeps its old level; and
't is no wonder that the history of our race is so recent, if
the roar of the ocean is silencing our traditions. A rising of
the sea, such as has been observed, say an inch in a century,
from east to west on the land, will bury all the towns, monuments, bones, and knowledge of mankind, steadily and in-
sensibly. If it is capable of these great and secular mischiefs,
it is quite as ready at private and local damage; and of this
no landsman seems so fearful as the seaman. Such discomfort
and such danger as the narratives of the captain and mate
disclose are bad enough as the costly fee we pay for entrance
to Europe; but the wonder is always new that any sane man
can be a sailor. And here on the second day of our voyage,
stepped out a little boy in his shirt-sleeves, who had hid himself whilst the ship was in port, in the bread-closet, having no
money and wishing to go to England. The sailors have dressed
him in Guernsey frock,[15] with a knife in his belt, and he is
climbing nimbly about after them; — "likes the work first-
rate, and if the captain will take him, means now to come
back again in the ship." The mate avers that this is the history of all sailors; nine out of ten are runaway boys; and adds
that all of them are sick of the sea, but stay in it out of pride.
Jack has a life of risks, incessant abuse and the worst pay. It
is a little better with the mate and not very much better with
the captain. A hundred dollars a month is reckoned high pay.
If sailors were contented, if they had not resolved again and
again not to go to sea any more, I should respect them.

Of course the inconveniences and terrors of the sea are not of any account to those whose minds are preoccupied. The water-laws,[16] arctic frost, the mountain, the mine, only shatter cockneyism; every noble activity makes room for itself. A great mind is a good sailor, as a great heart is. And the sea is not slow in disclosing inestimable secrets to a good naturalist.

'T is a good rule in every journey to provide some piece of liberal study to rescue the hours which bad weather, bad company and taverns steal from the best economist.[17] Classics which at home are drowsily read, have a strange charm in a country inn, or in the transom of a merchant brig.[18] I remember that some of the happiest and most valuable hours I have owed to books, passed, many years ago, on shipboard. The worst impediment I have found at sea is the want of light in the cabin.

We found on board the usual cabin library; Basil Hall, Dumas, Dickens, Bulwer, Balzac and Sand were our sea-gods.[19] Among the passengers there was some variety of talent and profession; we exchanged our experiences and all learned something. The busiest talk with leisure and convenience at sea, and sometimes a memorable fact turns up, which you have long had a vacant niche for, and seize with the joy of a collector. But, under the best conditions, a voyage is one of the severest tests to try a man. A college examination is nothing to it. Sea-days are long — these lack-lustre, joyless days which whistled over us; but they were few — only fifteen, as the captain counted, sixteen according to me. Reckoned from the time when we left soundings, our speed was such that the captain drew the line of his course in red ink on his chart, for the encouragement or envy of future navigators.

It has been said that the King of England would consult his dignity by giving audience to foreign ambassadors in the cabin of a man-of-war. And I think the white path of an

Atlantic ship the right avenue to the palace front of this sea-faring people, who for hundreds of years claimed the strict sovereignty of the sea, and exacted toll and the striking sail from the ships of all other peoples. When their privilege was disputed by the Dutch[20] and other junior marines, on the plea that you could never anchor on the same wave, or hold property in what was always flowing, the English did not stick to claim the channel, or bottom of all the main: "As if," said they, "we contended for the drops of the sea, and not for its situation, or the bed of those waters. The sea is bounded by his majesty's empire."

As we neared the land, its genius was felt. This was inevitably the British side. In every man's thought arises now a new system, English sentiments, English loves and fears, English history and social modes. Yesterday every passenger had measured the speed of the ship by watching the bubbles over the ship's bulwarks. To-day, instead of bubbles, we measure by Kinsale, Cork, Waterford and Ardmore.[21] There lay the green shore of Ireland, like some coast of plenty. We could see towns, towers, churches, harvests; but the curse of eight hundred years we could not discern.[22]

CHAPTER III

Land

Alfieri[1] thought Italy and England the only countries worth living in; the former because there Nature vindicates her rights and triumphs over the evils inflicted by the governments; the latter because art conquers nature and transforms a rude, ungenial land into a paradise of comfort and plenty. England is a garden. Under an ash-colored sky, the fields have been combed and rolled till they appear to have been finished with a pencil instead of a plough. The solidity of the structures that compose the towns speaks the industry of ages. Nothing is left as it was made. Rivers, hills, valleys, the sea itself, feel the hand of a master. The long habitation of a powerful and ingenious race has turned every rood of land to its best use, has found all the capabilities, the arable soil, the quarriable rock, the highways, the byways, the fords, the navigable waters; and the new arts of intercourse meet you every where; so that England is a huge phalanstery,[2] where all that man wants is provided within the precinct. Cushioned and comforted in every manner, the traveller rides as on a cannon-ball, high and low, over rivers and towns, through mountains in tunnels of three or four miles, at near twice the speed of our trains; and reads quietly the "Times" newspaper, which, by its immense correspondence and reporting seems to have machinized the rest of the world for his occasion.

The problem of the traveller landing at Liverpool is, Why England is England? What are the elements of that power which the English hold over other nations? If there be one test of national genius universally accepted, it is success; and if there be one successful country in the universe for the last millennium, that country is England.

A wise traveller will naturally choose to visit the best of actual nations; and an American has more reasons than another to draw him to Britain. In all that is done or begun by the Americans towards right thinking or practice, we are met by a civilization already settled and overpowering. The culture of the day, the thoughts and aims of men, are English thoughts and aims. A nation considerable for a thousand years since Egbert,[3] it has, in the last centuries, obtained the ascendant, and stamped the knowledge, activity and power of mankind with its impress. Those who resist it do not feel it or obey it less. The Russian in his snows is aiming to be English. The Turk and Chinese also are making awkward efforts to be English. The practical common-sense of modern society, the utilitarian direction which labor, laws, opinion, religion take, is the natural genius of the British mind. The influence of France is a constituent of modern civility, but not enough opposed to the English for the most wholesome effect. The American is only the continuation of the English genius into new conditions, more or less propitious.

See what books fill our libraries. Every book we read, every biography, play, romance, in whatever form, is still English history and manners. So that a sensible Englishman once said to me, "As long as you do not grant us copyright, we shall have the teaching of you." [4]

But we have the same difficulty in making a social or moral estimate of England, that the sheriff finds in drawing a jury to try some cause which has agitated the whole community and on which every body finds himself an interested party.

Officers, jurors, judges have all taken sides. England has
inoculated all nations with her civilization, intelligence and
tastes; and to resist the tyranny and prepossession of the
British element, a serious man must aid himself by comparing with it the civilizations of the farthest east and west, the
old Greek, the Oriental, and, much more, the ideal standard;
if only by means of the very impatience which English forms
are sure to awaken in independent minds.

Besides, if we will visit London, the present time is the
best time, as some signs portend that it has reached its highest point. It is observed that the English interest us a little
less within a few years; and hence the impression that the
British power has culminated, is in solstice, or already declining.

As soon as you enter England, which, with Wales, is no
larger than the State of Georgia,[5] this little land stretches by
an illusion to the dimensions of an empire. The innumerable
details, the crowded succession of towns, cities, cathedrals,
castles and great and decorated estates, the number and
power of the trades and guilds, the military strength and
splendor, the multitudes of rich and of remarkable people,
the servants and equipages, — all these catching the eye and
never allowing it to pause, hide all boundaries by the impression of magnificence and endless wealth.

I reply to all the urgencies that refer me to this and that
object indispensably to be seen, — Yes, to see England well
needs a hundred years; for what they told me was the merit of
Sir John Soane's Museum,[6] in London, — that it was well
packed and well saved, — is the merit of England; — it is
stuffed full, in all corners and crevices, with towns, towers,
churches, villas, palaces, hospitals and charity-houses. In the
history of art it is a long way from a cromlech to York minster;[7] yet all the intermediate steps may still be traced in this
all-preserving island.

The territory has a singular perfection. The climate is warmer by many degrees than it is entitled to by latitude. Neither hot nor cold, there is no hour in the whole year when one cannot work. Here is no winter, but such days as we have in Massachusetts in November, a temperature which makes no exhausting demand on human strength, but allows the attainment of the largest stature. Charles the Second said "It invited men abroad more days in the year and more hours in the day than another country." Then England has all the materials of a working country except wood. The constant rain, — a rain with every tide, in some parts of the island, — keeps its multitude of rivers full and brings agricultural production up to the highest point. It has plenty of water, of stone, of potter's clay, of coal, of salt and of iron. The land naturally abounds with game; immense heaths and downs are paved with quails, grouse and woodcock, and the shores are animated by water-birds. The rivers and the surrounding sea spawn with fish; there are salmon for the rich and sprats and herrings for the poor. In the northern lochs, the herring are in innumerable shoals; at one season, the country people say, the lakes contain one part water and two parts fish.

The only drawback on this industrial conveniency is the darkness of its sky. The night and day are too nearly of a color. It strains the eyes to read and to write. Add the coal smoke. In the manufacturing towns, the fine soot or *blacks* darken the day, give white sheep the color of black sheep, discolor the human saliva, contaminate the air, poison many plants and corrode the monuments and buildings.

The London fog aggravates the distempers of the sky, and sometimes justifies the epigram on the climate by an English wit, "in a fine day, looking up a chimney; in a foul day, looking down one." [8] A gentleman in Liverpool told me that he found he could do without a fire in his parlor about one day in the year. It is however pretended that the enormous con-

sumption of coal in the island is also felt in modifying the
general climate.

Factitious climate, factitious position. England resembles
a ship in its shape, and if it were one, its best admiral could
not have worked it or anchored it in a more judicious or
effective position. Sir John Herschel said "London is the
centre of the terrene globe." [9] The shopkeeping nation, to
use a shop word, has a *good stand*. The old Venetians pleased
themselves with the flattery that Venice was in 45°, midway
between the poles and the line; as if that were an imperial
centrality. Long of old, the Greeks fancied Delphi the navel
of the earth, in their favorite mode of fabling the earth to be
an animal.[10] The Jews believed Jerusalem to be the centre.
I have seen a kratometric chart[11] designed to show that the
city of Philadelphia was in the same thermic belt,[12] and by
inference in the same belt of empire, as the cities of Athens,
Rome and London. It was drawn by a patriotic Philadel-
phian, and was examined with pleasure, under his showing,
by the inhabitants of Chestnut Street. But when carried to
Charleston, to New Orleans and to Boston, it somehow failed
to convince the ingenious scholars of all those capitals.

But England is anchored at the side of Europe, and right
in the heart of the modern world. The sea, which, according
to Virgil's famous line,[13] divided the poor Britons utterly
from the world, proved to be the ring of marriage[14] with all
nations. It is not down in the books, — it is written only in
the geologic strata, — that fortunate day when a wave of the
German Ocean[15] burst the old isthmus which joined Kent
and Cornwall[16] to France, and gave to this fragment of
Europe its impregnable sea-wall, cutting off an island of eight
hundred miles in length, with an irregular breadth reaching
to three hundred miles; a territory large enough for independence, enriched with every seed of national power, so
near that it can see the harvests of the continent, and so far

that who would cross the strait must be an expert mariner, ready for tempests. As America, Europe and Asia lie, these Britons have precisely the best commercial position in the whole planet, and are sure of a market for all the goods they can manufacture. And to make these advantages avail, the river Thames must dig its spacious outlet to the sea from the heart of the kingdom, giving road and landing to innumerable ships, and all the conveniency to trade that a people so skilful and sufficient in economizing waterfront by docks, warehouses and lighters required. When James the First declared his purpose of punishing London by removing his Court, the Lord Mayor replied that "in removing his royal presence from his lieges, they hoped he would leave them the Thames." [17]

In the variety of surface, Britain is a miniature of Europe, having plain, forest, marsh, river, seashore; mines in Cornwall; caves in Matlock[18] and Derbyshire; delicious landscape in Dovedale,[19] delicious sea-view at Tor Bay,[20] Highlands in Scotland, Snowdon in Wales,[21] and in Westmoreland and Cumberland a pocket Switzerland,[22] in which the lakes and mountains are on a sufficient scale to fill the eye and touch the imagination. It is a nation conveniently small. Fontenelle[23] thought that nature had sometimes a little affectation; and there is such an artificial completeness in this nation of artificers as if there were a design from the beginning to elaborate a bigger Birmingham.[24] Nature held counsel with herself and said, 'My Romans are gone. To build my new empire, I will choose a rude race, all masculine, with brutish strength. I will not grudge a competition of the roughest males. Let buffalo gore buffalo, and the pasture to the strongest! For I have work that requires the best will and sinew. Sharp and temperate northern breezes shall blow, to keep that will alive and alert. The sea shall disjoin the people from others, and knit them to a fierce nationality. It shall

give them markets on every side. Long time I will keep them
on their feet, by poverty, border-wars, seafaring, sea-risks and
the stimulus of gain. An island, — but not so large, the people not so many as to glut the great markets and depress one
another, but proportioned to the size of Europe and the continents.'

With its fruits, and wares, and money, must its civil influence radiate. It is a singular coincidence to this geographic
centrality, the spiritual centrality which Emanuel Swedenborg ascribes to the people. "For the English nation, the best
of them are in the centre of all Christians, because they have
interior intellectual light. This appears conspicuously in the
spiritual world. This light they derive from the liberty of
speaking and writing, and thereby of thinking." [25]

CHAPTER IV

Race

An ingenious anatomist has written a book[1] to prove that races are imperishable, but nations are pliant political constructions, easily changed or destroyed. But this writer did not found his assumed races on any necessary law, disclosing their ideal or metaphysical necessity; nor did he on the other hand count with precision the existing races and settle the true bounds; a point of nicety, and the popular test of the theory. The individuals at the extremes of divergence in one race of men are as unlike as the wolf to the lapdog. Yet each variety shades down imperceptibly into the next, and you cannot draw the line where a race begins or ends. Hence every writer makes a different count. Blumenbach reckons five races; Humboldt three; and Mr. Pickering, who lately in our Exploring Expedition thinks he saw all the kinds of men that can be on the planet, makes eleven.[2]

The British Empire is reckoned to contain (in 1848) 222,-000,000 souls, — perhaps a fifth of the population of the globe; and to comprise a territory of 5,000,000 square miles. So far have British people predominated. Perhaps forty of these millions are of British stock. Add the United States of America, which reckon (in the same year), exclusive of slaves, 20,000,000 of people, on a territory of 3,000,000 square miles, and in which the foreign element, however considerable, is rapidly assimilated, and you have a population of English descent and language of 60,000,000, and governing a population of 245,000,000 souls.

The British census proper reckons twenty-seven and a half millions in the home countries. What makes this census important is the quality of the units that compose it. They are free forcible men, in a country where life is safe and has reached the greatest value. They give the bias to the current age; and that, not by chance or by mass, but by their character and by the number of individuals among them of personal ability. It has been denied that the English have genius. Be it as it may, men of vast intellect have been born on their soil, and they have made or applied the principal inventions. They have sound bodies and supreme endurance in war and in labor. The spawning force of the race has sufficed to the colonization of great parts of the world; yet it remains to be seen whether they can make good the exodus of millions from Great Britain, amounting in 1852 to more than a thousand a day. They have assimilating force, since they are imitated by their foreign subjects; and they are still aggressive and propagandist, enlarging the dominion of their arts and liberty. Their laws are hospitable, and slavery does not exist under them. What oppression exists is incidental and temporary; their success is not sudden or fortunate, but they have maintained constancy and self-equality for many ages.

Is this power due to their race, or to some other cause? Men hear gladly of the power of blood or race. Every body likes to know that his advantages cannot be attributed to air, soil, sea, or to local wealth, as mines and quarries, nor to laws and traditions, nor to fortune; but to superior brain, as it makes the praise more personal to him.

We anticipate in the doctrine of race something like that law of physiology that whatever bone, muscle, or essential organ is found in one healthy individual, the same part or organ may be found in or near the same place in its congener;

and we look to find in the son every mental and moral property that existed in the ancestor. In race, it is not the broad shoulders, or litheness, or stature that give advantage, but a symmetry that reaches as far as to the wit. Then the miracle and renown begin. Then first we care to examine the pedigree, and copy heedfully the training, — what food they ate, what nursing, school, and exercises they had, which resulted in this mother-wit, delicacy of thought and robust wisdom. How came such men as King Alfred, and Roger Bacon, William of Wykeham, Walter Raleigh, Philip Sidney, Isaac Newton, William Shakspeare, George Chapman, Francis Bacon, George Herbert, Henry Vane, to exist here? [3] What made these delicate natures? was it the air? was it the sea? was it the parentage? For it is certain that these men are samples of their contemporaries. The hearing ear is always found close to the speaking tongue, and no genius can long or often utter any thing which is not invited and gladly entertained by men around him.

It is race, is it not? that puts the hundred millions of India under the dominion of a remote island in the north of Europe. Race avails much, if that be true which is alleged, that all Celts are Catholics and all Saxons are Protestants; that Celts love unity of power, and Saxons the representative principle. Race is a controlling influence in the Jew, who, for two millenniums, under every climate, has preserved the same character and employments. Race in the negro is of appalling importance. The French in Canada, cut off from all intercourse with the parent people, have held their national traits. I chanced to read Tacitus "On the Manners of the Germans," [4] not long since, in Missouri and the heart of Illinois,[5] and I found abundant points of resemblance between the Germans of the Hercynian forest, and our *Hoosiers, Suckers* and *Badgers* of the American woods.[6]

But whilst race works immortally to keep its own, it is

resisted by other forces. Civilization is a re-agent, and eats away the old traits. The Arabs of to-day are the Arabs of Pharaoh; but the Briton of to-day is a very different person from Cassibelaunus or Ossian.[7] Each religious sect has its physiognomy. The Methodists have acquired a face; the Quakers, a face; the nuns, a face. An Englishman will pick out a dissenter by his manners. Trades and professions carve their own lines on face and form. Certain circumstances of English life are not less effective; as personal liberty; plenty of food; good ale and mutton; open market, or good wages for every kind of labor; high bribes to talent and skill; the island life, or the million opportunities and outlets for expanding and misplaced talent; readiness of combination among themselves for politics or for business; strikes; and sense of superiority founded on habit of victory in labor and in war: and the appetite for superiority grows by feeding.

It is easy to add to the counteracting forces to race. Credence is a main element. 'T is said that the views of nature held by any people determine all their institutions. Whatever influences add to mental or moral faculty, take men out of nationality as out of other conditions, and make the national life a culpable compromise.

These limitations of the formidable doctrine of race suggest others which threaten to undermine it, as not sufficiently based. The fixity or inconvertibleness of races as we see them is a weak argument for the eternity of these frail boundaries, since all our historical period is a point to the duration in which nature has wrought. Any the least and solitariest fact in our natural history, such as the melioration of fruits and of animal stocks, has the worth of a *power* in the opportunity of geologic periods. Moreover, though we flatter the self-love of men and nations by the legend of pure races, all our experience is of the gradation and resolution of races, and strange resemblances meet us everywhere. It need not puzzle us that

Malay and Papuan, Celt and Roman, Saxon and Tartar
should mix, when we see the rudiments of tiger and baboon
in our human form, and know that the barriers of races are
not so firm but that some spray sprinkles us from the ante-
diluvian seas.

The low organizations are simplest; a mere mouth, a jelly,
or a straight worm. As the scale mounts, the organizations
become complex. We are piqued with pure descent, but
nature loves inoculation. A child blends in his face the faces
of both parents and some feature from every ancestor whose
face hangs on the wall. The best nations are those most
widely related; and navigation, as effecting a world-wide
mixture, is the most potent advancer of nations.

The English composite character betrays a mixed origin.
Every thing English is a fusion of distant and antagonistic
elements. The language is mixed; the names of men are of
different nations, — three languages,[8] three or four nations;
— the currents of thought are counter: contemplation and
practical skill; active intellect and dead conservatism; world-
wide enterprise and devoted use and wont; aggressive freedom and hospitable law with bitter class-legislation; a people
scattered by their wars and affairs over the face of the whole
earth, and homesick to a man; a country of extremes, —
dukes and chartists,[9] Bishops of Durham[10] and naked heathen colliers; — nothing can be praised in it without damn-
ing exceptions, and nothing denounced without salvos of
cordial praise.

Neither do this people appear to be of one stem, but col-
lectively a better race than any from which they are derived.
Nor is it easy to trace it home to its original seats. Who can
call by right names what races are in Britain? Who can trace
them historically? Who can discriminate them anatomically,
or metaphysically?

In the impossibility of arriving at satisfaction on the his-

torical question of race, and — come of whatever disputable
ancestry — the indisputable Englishman before me, himself
very well marked, and nowhere else to be found, — I fancied
I could leave quite aside the choice of a tribe as his lineal
progenitors. Defoe said in his wrath, "the Englishman was
the mud of all races." [11] I incline to the belief that, as water,
lime, and sand make mortar, so certain temperaments marry
well, and, by well-managed contrarieties, develop as drastic
a character as the English. On the whole it is not so much a
history of one or of certain tribes of Saxons, Jutes, or Frisians,
coming from one place and genetically identical, as it is an
anthology of temperaments out of them all. Certain temperaments suit the sky and soil of England, say eight or ten or
twenty varieties, as, out of a hundred pear-trees, eight or ten
suit the soil of an orchard and thrive,[12] — whilst all the un-
adapted temperaments die out.

The English derive their pedigree from such a range of
nationalities that there needs sea-room and land-room to
unfold the varieties of talent and character. Perhaps the
ocean serves as a galvanic battery, to distribute acids at one
pole and alkalies at the other. So England tends to accumulate her liberals in America, and her conservatives at London.
The Scandinavians in her race still hear in every age the
murmurs of their mother, the ocean; the Briton in the blood
hugs the homestead still.

Again, as if to intensate the influences that are not of race,
what we think of when we talk of English traits really nar-
rows itself to a small district. It excludes Ireland and Scotland and Wales, and reduces itself at last to London, that is,
to those who come and go thither. The portraits that hang
on the walls in the Academy Exhibition at London,[13] the
figures in Punch's drawings of the public men or of the
club-houses, the prints in the shop-windows, are distinctive
English, and not American, no, nor Scotch, nor Irish: but 't is

a very restricted nationality. As you go north into the manu-facturing and agricultural districts, and to the population that never travels; as you go into Yorkshire,[14] as you enter Scotland, the world's Englishman is no longer found. In Scotland there is a rapid loss of all grandeur of mien and manners; a provincial eagerness and acuteness appear; the poverty of the country makes itself remarked, and a coarse-ness of manners; and, among the intellectual, is the insanity of dialectics. In Ireland are the same climate and soil as in England, but less food, no right relation to the land, political dependence, small tenantry and an inferior or misplaced race.

These queries concerning ancestry and blood may be well allowed, for there is no prosperity that seems more to depend on the kind of man than British prosperity. Only a hardy and wise people could have made this small territory great. We say, in a regatta or yacht-race, that if the boats are anywhere nearly matched, it is the man that wins. Put the best sailing-master into either boat, and he will win.

Yet it is fine for us to speculate in face of unbroken tradi-tions, though vague and losing themselves in fable. The traditions have got footing, and refuse to be disturbed. The kitchen-clock is more convenient than sidereal time.[15] We must use the popular category, as we do the Linnæan classi-fication,[16] for convenience, and not as exact and final. Other-wise we are presently confounded when the best-settled traits of one race are claimed by some new ethnologist as precisely characteristic of the rival tribe.

I found plenty of well-marked English types, the ruddy complexion fair and plump, robust men, with faces cut like a die, and a strong island speech and accent; a Norman type, with the complacency that belongs to that constitution. Others who might be Americans, for any thing that appeared in their complexion or form; and their speech was much less marked and their thought much less bound. We will call them Saxons. Then the Roman has implanted his dark complexion in the trinity or quaternity of bloods.

1. The sources from which tradition derives their stock are mainly three. And first they are of the oldest blood of the world, — the Celtic. Some peoples are deciduous or transitory. Where are the Greeks? Where the Etrurians? Where the Romans? But the Celts or Sidonides[17] are an old family, of whose beginning there is no memory, and their end is likely to be still more remote in the future; for they have endurance and productiveness. They planted Britain, and gave to the seas and mountains names which are poems and imitate the pure voices of nature. They are favorably remembered in the oldest records of Europe. They had no violent feudal tenure,[18] but the husbandman owned the land. They had an alphabet, astronomy, priestly culture and a sublime creed. They have a hidden and precarious genius. They made the best popular literature of the Middle Ages in the songs of Merlin and the tender and delicious mythology of Arthur.[19]

2. The English come mainly from the Germans, whom the Romans found hard to conquer in two hundred and ten years, — say impossible to conquer, when one remembers the long sequel; — a people about whom in the old empire the rumor ran there was never any that meddled with them that repented it not.

3. Charlemagne, halting one day in a town of Narbonnese Gaul, looked out of a window and saw a fleet of Northmen cruising in the Mediterranean. They even entered the port of the town where he was, causing no small alarm and sudden manning and arming of his galleys. As they put out to sea again, the emperor gazed long after them, his eyes bathed in tears. "I am tormented with sorrow," he said, "when I foresee the evils they will bring on my posterity." [20] There was

reason for these Xerxes' tears.[21] The men who have built a ship and invented the rig, cordage, sail, compass and pump; the working in and out of port, have acquired much more than a ship. Now arm them and every shore is at their mercy. For if they have not numerical superiority where they anchor, they have only to sail a mile or two to find it. Bonaparte's art of war, namely of concentrating force on the point of attack, must always be theirs who have the choice of the battle-ground. Of course they come into the fight from a higher ground of power than the land-nations; and can engage them on shore with a victorious advantage in the retreat. As soon as the shores are sufficiently peopled to make piracy a losing business, the same skill and courage are ready for the service of trade.

The "Heimskringla,"[22] or Sagas of the Kings of Norway, collected by Snorro Sturleson, is the Iliad and Odyssey of English history. Its portraits, like Homer's, are strongly individualized. The Sagas describe a monarchical republic like Sparta. The government disappears before the importance of citizens. In Norway, no Persian masses fight and perish to aggrandize a king, but the actors are bonders[23] or landholders, every one of whom is named and personally and patronymically described, as the king's friend and companion. A sparse population gives this high worth to every man. Individuals are often noticed as very handsome persons, which trait only brings the story nearer to the English race. Then the solid material interest predominates, so dear to English understanding, wherein the association is logical, between merit and land. The heroes of the Sagas are not the knights of South Europe. No vaporing of France and Spain has corrupted them. They are substantial farmers whom the rough times have forced to defend their properties. They have weapons which they use in a determined manner, by no means for chivalry, but for their acres. They are people considerably advanced in rural arts, living amphibiously on a rough coast, and drawing half their food from the sea and half from the land. They have herds of cows, and malt, wheat, bacon, butter, and cheese. A king among these farmers has a varying power, sometimes not exceeding the authority of a sheriff. They fish in the fiord and hunt the deer. A king was maintained, much as in some of our country districts a winter-schoolmaster is quartered, a week here, a week there, and a fortnight on the next farm, — on all the farms in rotation. This the king calls going into guest-quarters; and it was the only way in which, in a poor country, a poor king with many retainers could be kept alive when he leaves his own farm to collect his dues through the kingdom.

These Norsemen are excellent persons in the main, with good sense, steadiness, wise speech and prompt action. But they have a singular turn for homicide; their chief end of man is to murder or to be murdered; oars, scythes, harpoons, crowbars, peatknives[24] and hayforks are tools valued by them all the more for their charming aptitude for assassinations. A pair of kings, after dinner, will divert themselves by thrusting each his sword through the other's body, as did Yngve and Alf.[25] Another pair ride out on a morning for a frolic, and finding no weapon near, will take the bits out of their horses' mouths and crush each other's heads with them, as did Alric and Eric.[26] The sight of a tent-cord or a cloak-string puts them on hanging somebody, a wife, or a husband, or, best of all, a king. If a farmer has so much as a hayfork, he sticks it into a King Dag. King Ingiald finds it vastly amusing to burn up half a dozen kings in a hall, after getting them drunk. Never was poor gentleman so surfeited with life, so furious to be rid of it, as the Northman. If he cannot pick any other quarrel, he will get himself comfortably gored by a bull's horns, like Egil, or slain by a land-slide, like the agricultural King Onund. Odin died in his bed, in Sweden; but it was a proverb of ill condition to die the death of old age. King Hake of Sweden cuts and slashes in battle, as long as he can stand, then orders his war-ship, loaded with his dead men and their weapons, to be taken out to sea, the tiller shipped and the sails spread; being left alone he sets fire to some tar-wood and lies down contented on deck. The wind blew off the land, the ship flew, burning in clear flame, out between the islets into the ocean, and there was the right end of King Hake.

The early Sagas are sanguinary and piratical; the later are of a noble strain. History rarely yields us better passages than the conversation between King Sigurd the Crusader and King Eystein, his brother, on their respective merits, — one the soldier, and the other a lover of the arts of peace.[27]

But the reader of the Norman[28] history must steel himself by holding fast the remote compensations which result from animal vigor. As the old fossil world shows that the first steps of reducing the chaos were confided to saurians and other huge and horrible animals, so the foundations of the new civility were to be laid by the most savage men.

The Normans came out of France into England worse men than they went into it one hundred and sixty years before. They had lost their own language and learned the Romance or barbarous Latin of the Gauls, and had acquired, with the language, all the vices it had names for. The conquest has obtained in the chronicles the name of the "memory of sorrow." Twenty thousand thieves[29] landed at Hastings. These founders of the House of Lords were greedy and ferocious dragoons, sons of greedy and ferocious pirates. They were all alike, they took everything they could carry, they burned, harried, violated, tortured and killed, until every thing English was brought to the verge of ruin. Such however is the illusion of antiquity and wealth, that decent and dignified men now existing boast their descent from these filthy thieves, who showed a far juster conviction of their own merits, by assuming for their types the swine, goat, jackal, leopard, wolf and snake, which they severally resembled.

England yielded to the Danes and Northmen in the tenth and eleventh centuries, and was the receptacle into which all the mettle of that strenuous population was poured. The continued draught of the best men in Norway, Sweden and Denmark to these piratical expeditions exhausted those countries, like a tree which bears much fruit when young, and these have been second-rate powers ever since. The power of the race migrated and left Norway void. King Olaf said "When King Harold, my father, went westward to England, the chosen men in Norway followed him; but Norway was so emptied then, that such men have not since been to find in the country, nor especially such a leader as King Harold was for wisdom and bravery." [30]

It was a tardy recoil of these invasions, when, in 1801, the British government sent Nelson to bombard the Danish forts in the Sound, and, in 1807, Lord Cathcart, at Copenhagen, took the entire Danish fleet, as it lay in the basins, and all the equipments from the Arsenal, and carried them to England.[31] Konghelle, the town where the kings of Norway, Sweden and Denmark were wont to meet,[32] is now rented to a private English gentleman for a hunting ground.

It took many generations to trim and comb and perfume the first boat-load of Norse pirates into royal highnesses and most noble Knights of the Garter;[33] but every sparkle of ornament dates back to the Norse boat.[34] There will be time enough to mellow this strength into civility and religion. It is a medical fact that the children of the blind see; the children of felons have a healthy conscience. Many a mean, dastardly boy is, at the age of puberty, transformed into a serious and generous youth.

The mildness of the following ages has not quite effaced these traits of Odin; as the rudiment of a structure matured in the tiger is said to be still found unabsorbed in the Caucasian man.[35] The nation has a tough, acrid, animal nature, which centuries of churching and civilizing have not been able to sweeten. Alfieri said "the crimes of Italy were the proof of the superiority of the stock;"[36] and one may say of England that this watch moves on a splinter of adamant. The English uncultured are a brutal nation. The crimes recorded in their calendars leave nothing to be desired in the way of cold malignity. Dear to the English heart is a fair stand-up fight. The brutality of the manners in the lower class appears in the boxing, bear-baiting, cock-fighting, love of executions, and in the readiness for a set-to in the streets, delightful to the English of all classes. The costermongers of London streets hold cowardice in loathing: — "we must work our fists well; we are all handy with our fists." The public schools are charged with being bear-gardens of brutal strength, and are liked by the people for that cause. The fagging is a trait of the same quality. Medwin, in the Life of Shelley,[37] relates that at a military school they rolled up a young man in a snowball, and left him so in his room while the other cadets went to church; — and crippled him for life. They have retained impressment, deck-flogging, army-flogging and school-flogging. Such is the ferocity of the army discipline that a soldier, sentenced to flogging, sometimes prays that his sentence may be commuted to death. Flogging, banished from the armies of Western Europe, remains here by the sanction of the Duke of Wellington. The right of the husband to sell the wife has been retained down to our times. The Jews have been the favorite victims of royal and popular

persecution. Henry III. mortgaged all the Jews in the kingdom to his brother the Earl of Cornwall, as security for
money which he borrowed.[38] The torture of criminals, and
the rack for extorting evidence, were slowly disused. Of the
criminal statutes, Sir Samuel Romilly said "I have examined
the codes of all nations, and ours is the worst, and worthy
of the Anthropophagi." [39] In the last session (1848), the House
of Commons was listening to the details of flogging and torture practised in the jails.[40]

As soon as this land, thus geographically posted, got a
hardy people into it, they could not help becoming the sailors
and factors of the globe. From childhood, they dabbled in
water, they swam like fishes, their playthings were boats. In
the case of the ship-money,[41] the judges delivered it for law,
that "England being an island, the very midland shires
therein are all to be accounted maritime;" and Fuller[42] adds,
"the genius even of landlocked counties driving the natives
with a maritime dexterity." As early as the conquest it is
remarked, in explanation of the wealth of England, that its
merchants trade to all countries.

The English at the present day have great vigor of body
and endurance. Other countrymen look slight and under-
sized beside them, and invalids. They are bigger men than
the Americans. I suppose a hundred English taken at random
out of the street would weigh a fourth more than so many
Americans. Yet, I am told, the skeleton is not larger. They
are round, ruddy, and handsome; at least the whole bust is
well formed, and there is a tendency to stout and powerful
frames. I remarked the stoutness on my first landing at
Liverpool; porter, drayman, coachman, guard, — what substantial, respectable, grandfatherly figures, with costume and
manners to suit. The American has arrived at the old man-
sion-house and finds himself among uncles, aunts and grand-
sires. The pictures on the chimney-tiles of his nursery were

pictures of these people. Here they are in the identical costumes and air which so took him.

It is the fault of their forms that they grow stocky, and
the women have that disadvantage, — few tall, slender figures of flowing shape, but stunted and thickset persons. The
French say that the Englishwomen have two left hands. But
in all ages they are a handsome race. The bronze monuments
of crusaders lying cross-legged in the Temple Church at London, and those in Worcester and in Salisbury Cathedrals,[43]
which are seven hundred years old, are of the same type as
the best youthful heads of men now in England; — please
by beauty of the same character, an expression blending
good nature, valor and refinement, and mainly by that un-
corrupt youth in the face of manhood, which is daily seen
in the streets of London.

Both branches of the Scandinavian race are distinguished
for beauty. The anecdote of the handsome captives which
Saint Gregory found at Rome, A. D. 600, is matched by the
testimony of the Norman chroniclers, five centuries later,
who wondered at the beauty and long flowing hair of the
young English captives.[44] Meantime the "Heimskringla" has
frequent occasion to speak of the personal beauty of its
heroes. When it is considered what humanity, what resources
of mental and moral power the traits of the blonde race
betoken, its accession to empire marks a new and finer epoch,
wherein the old mineral force shall be subjugated at last by
humanity and shall plough in its furrow henceforward. It is
not a final race, once a crab always crab, — but a race with
a future.

On the English face are combined decision and nerve with
the fair complexion, blue eyes and open and florid aspect.
Hence the love of truth, hence the sensibility, the fine perception and poetic construction. The fair Saxon man, with

open front and honest meaning, domestic, affectionate, is not
the wood out of which cannibal, or inquisitor, or assassin is
made, but he is moulded for law, lawful trade, civility, marriage, the nurture of children, for colleges, churches, charities and colonies.

They are rather manly than warlike. When the war is
over, the mask falls from the affectionate and domestic tastes,
which make them women in kindness. This union of qualities is fabled in their national legend of "Beauty and the
Beast," [45] or, long before, in the Greek legend of Hermaphro-
dite.[46] The two sexes are co-present in the English mind.
I apply to Britannia, queen of seas and colonies, the words
in which her latest novelist[47] portrays his heroine; "She is
as mild as she is game, and as game as she is mild." The
English delight in the antagonism which combines in one
person the extremes of courage and tenderness. Nelson, dying
at Trafalgar, sends his love to Lord Collingwood, and like
an innocent schoolboy that goes to bed, says "Kiss me,
Hardy," and turns to sleep.[48] Lord Collingwood, his comrade,
was of a nature the most affectionate and domestic. Admiral
Rodney's figure approached to delicacy and effeminacy, and
he declared himself very sensible to fear, which he sur-
mounted only by considerations of honor and public duty.[49]
Clarendon says the Duke of Buckingham was so modest and
gentle, that some courtiers attempted to put affronts on him,
until they found that this modesty and effeminacy was only
a mask for the most terrible determination.[50] And Sir Edward Parry said of Sir John Franklin, that "if he found
Wellington Sound open, he explored it; for he was a man
who never turned his back on a danger, yet of that tenderness that he would not brush away a mosquito." [51] Even
for their highwaymen the same virtue is claimed, and Robin
Hood comes described to us as *mitissimus prædonum;* the

gentlest thief. But they know where their war-dogs lie. Crom-
well, Blake, Marlborough, Chatham, Nelson and Wellington
are not to be trifled with,[52] and the brutal strength which
lies at the bottom of society, the animal ferocity of the quays
and cockpits, the bullies of the costermongers of Shoreditch,
Seven Dials and Spitalfields, they know how to wake up.[53]

They have a vigorous health and last well into middle
and old age. The old men are as red as roses, and still handsome. A clear skin, a peach-bloom complexion and good
teeth are found all over the island. They use a plentiful and
nutritious diet. The operative cannot subsist on watercresses.
Beef, mutton, wheat-bread and malt-liquors are universal
among the first-class laborers. Good feeding is a chief point
of national pride among the vulgar, and in their caricatures
they represent the Frenchman as a poor, starved body. It is
curious that Tacitus found the English beer already in use
among the Germans: "They make from barley or wheat a
drink corrupted into some resemblance to wine." [54] Lord
Chief Justice Fortescue, in Henry VI.'s time, says "The inhabitants of England drink no water, unless at certain times
on a religious score and by way of penance." The extremes
of poverty and ascetic penance, it would seem, never reach
cold water in England. Wood the antiquary, in describing
the poverty and maceration of Father Lacey, an English
Jesuit, does not deny him beer. He says "His bed was under
a thatching, and the way to it up a ladder; his fare was coarse;
his drink, of a penny a gawn, or gallon." [55]

They have more constitutional energy than any other people. They think, with Henri Quatre,[56] that manly exercises
are the foundation of that elevation of mind which gives one
nature ascendant over another; or with the Arabs, that the
days spent in the chase are not counted in the length of life.
They box, run, shoot, ride, row, and sail from pole to pole.

They eat and drink, and live jolly in the open air, putting a
bar of solid sleep between day and day. They walk and ride
as fast as they can, their head bent forward, as if urged on
some pressing affair. The French say that Englishmen in the
street always walk straight before them like mad dogs. Men
and women walk with infatuation. As soon as he can handle
a gun, hunting is the fine art of every Englishman of condition. They are the most voracious people of prey that ever
existed. Every season turns out the aristocracy into the country to shoot and fish. The more vigorous run out of the island
to America, to Asia, to Africa and Australia, to hunt with
fury by gun, by trap, by harpoon, by lasso, with dog, with
horse, with elephant or with dromedary, all the game that
is in nature. These men have written the game-books of all
countries, as Hawker, Scrope, Murray, Herbert, Maxwell,
Cumming and a host of travellers.[57] The people at home
are addicted to boxing, running, leaping and rowing matches.

I suppose the dogs and horses must be thanked for the fact
that the men have muscles almost as tough and supple as
their own. If in every efficient man there is first a fine animal,
in the English race it is of the best breed, a wealthy, juicy,
broad-chested creature, steeped in ale and good cheer and a
little overloaded by his flesh. Men of animal nature rely, like
animals, on their instincts. The Englishman associates well
with dogs and horses. His attachment to the horse arises from
the courage and address required to manage it. The horse
finds out who is afraid of it, and does not disguise its opinion.
Their young boiling clerks and lusty collegians like the company of horses better than the company of professors. I
suppose the horses are better company for them. The horse
has more uses than Buffon noted.[58] If you go into the streets,
every driver in 'bus or dray is a bully, and if I wanted a good
troop of soldiers, I should recruit among the stables. Add a

certain degree of refinement to the vivacity of these riders, and you obtain the precise quality which makes the men and women of polite society formidable.

They come honestly by their horsemanship, with *Hengst* and *Horsa* for their Saxon founders.[59] The other branch of their race had been Tartar nomads. The horse was all their wealth. The children were fed on mares' milk. The pastures of Tartary were still remembered by the tenacious practice of the Norsemen to eat horseflesh at religious feasts. In the Danish invasions the marauders seized upon horses where they landed, and were at once converted into a body of expert cavalry.

At one time this skill seems to have declined. Two centuries ago the English horse never performed any eminent service beyond the seas; and the reason assigned was that the genius of the English hath always more inclined them to foot-service, as pure and proper manhood, without any mixture; whilst in a victory on horseback, the credit ought to be divided betwixt the man and his horse. But in two hundred years a change has taken place. Now, they boast that they understand horses better than any other people in the world, and that their horses are become their second selves.

"William the Conqueror being," says Camden, "better affected to beasts than to men, imposed heavy fines and punishments on those that should meddle with his game." The Saxon Chronicle says "he loved the tall deer as if he were their father." [60] And rich Englishmen have followed his example, according to their ability, ever since, in encroaching on the tillage and commons with their game-preserves. It is a proverb in England that it is safer to shoot a man than a hare. The severity of the game-laws certainly indicates an extravagant sympathy of the nation with horses and hunters. The gentlemen are always on horseback, and have brought horses to an ideal perfection; the English racer is a factitious breed. A score or two of mounted gentlemen may frequently be seen running like centaurs down a hill nearly as steep as the roof of a house. Every inn-room is lined with pictures of races; telegraphs communicate, every hour, tidings of the heats from Newmarket and Ascot; and the House of Commons adjourns over the "Derby Day."

CHAPTER V

Ability

The Saxon and the Northman are both Scandinavians. History does not allow us to fix the limits of the application of these names with any accuracy, but from the residence of a portion of these people in France, and from some effect of that powerful soil on their blood and manners, the Norman has come popularly to represent in England the aristocratic, and the Saxon the democratic principle. And though, I doubt not, the nobles are of both tribes, and the workers of both, yet we are forced to use the names a little mythically, one to represent the worker and the other the enjoyer.

The island was a prize for the best race. Each of the dominant races tried its fortune in turn. The Phœnician, the Celt and the Goth had already got in.[1] The Roman came, but in the very day when his fortune culminated.[2] He looked in the eyes of a new people that was to supplant his own. He disembarked his legions, erected his campus and towers, — presently he heard bad news from Italy, and worse and worse, every year; at last, he made a handsome compliment[3] of roads and walls, and departed. But the Saxon seriously settled in the land, builded, tilted, fished and traded, with German truth and adhesiveness. The Dane came and divided with him.[4] Last of all the Norman or French-Dane arrived,[5] and formally conquered, harried and ruled the kingdom. A century later it came out that the Saxon had the most bottom[6] and longevity, had managed to make the victor speak the language and accept the law and usage of the victim;[7] forced the baron to dictate Saxon terms to Norman kings;[8] and, step by step, got all the essential securities of civil liberty invented and confirmed. The genius of the race and the genius of the place conspired to this effect. The island is lucrative to free labor, but not worth possession on other terms. The race was so intellectual that a feudal or military tenure could not last longer than the war.[9] The power of the Saxon-Danes, so thoroughly beaten in the war that the name of English and villein[10] were synonymous, yet so vivacious as to extort charters from the kings, stood on the strong personality of these people. Sense and economy must rule in a world which is made of sense and economy, and the banker, with his seven *per cent.*,[11] drives the earl out of his castle. A nobility of soldiers cannot keep down a commonalty of shrewd scientific persons. What signifies a pedigree of a hundred links, against a cotton-spinner with steam in his mill; or against a company of broad-shouldered Liverpool merchants, for whom Stephenson and Brunel [12] are contriving locomotives and a tubular bridge?

These Saxons are the hands of mankind. They have the taste for toil, a distaste for pleasure or repose, and the telescopic appreciation of distant gain. They are the wealth-makers, — and by dint of mental faculty which has its own conditions. The Saxon works after liking, or only for himself; and to set him at work and to begin to draw his monstrous values out of barren Britain, all dishonor, fret and barrier must be removed, and then his energies begin to play.

The Scandinavian fancied himself surrounded by Trolls, — a kind of goblin men with vast power of work and skilful production, — divine stevedores, carpenters, reapers, smiths and masons, swift to reward every kindness done them, with gifts of gold and silver. In all English history this dream comes to pass. Certain Trolls or working brains, under the names of Alfred, Bede, Caxton, Bracton, Camden, Drake, Selden, Dugdale, Newton, Gibbon, Brindley, Watt, Wedgwood, dwell in the troll-mounts of Britain and turn the sweat of their face to power and renown.[13]

If the race is good, so is the place. Nobody landed on this spellbound island with impunity. The enchantments of barren shingle and rough weather transformed every adventurer into a laborer. Each vagabond that arrived bent his neck to the yoke of gain, or found the air too tense for him. The strong survived, the weaker went to the ground. Even the pleasure-hunters and sots of England are of a tougher texture. A hard temperament had been formed by Saxon and Saxon-Dane, and such of these French or Normans as could reach it were naturalized in every sense.

All the admirable expedients or means hit upon in England must be looked at as growths or irresistible offshoots of the expanding mind of the race. A man of that brain thinks and acts thus; and his neighbor, being afflicted with the same kind of brain, though he is rich and called a baron or a duke, thinks the same thing, and is ready to allow the justice of the thought and act in his retainer or tenant, though sorely against his baronial or ducal will.

The island was renowned in antiquity for its breed of mastiffs, so fierce that when their teeth were set you must cut their heads off to part them. The man was like his dog. The people have that nervous bilious temperament which is known by medical men to resist every means employed to make its possessor subservient to the will of others. The English game is main force to main force, the planting of foot to foot, fair play and open field, — a rough tug without trick or dodging, till one or both come to pieces. King Ethelwald spoke the language of his race when he planted himself at Wimborne and said he "would do one of two things, or there live, or there lie." [14] They hate craft and subtlety. They neither poison, nor waylay, nor assassinate; and when they have pounded each other to a poultice, they will shake hands and be friends for the remainder of their lives.

You shall trace these Gothic touches at school, [15] at country fairs, at the hustings and in parliament. No artifice, no breach of truth and plain dealing, — not so much as secret ballot, [15a] is suffered in the island. In parliament, the tactics of the opposition is to resist every step of the government by a pitiless attack: and in a bargain, no prospect of advantage is so dear to the merchant as the thought of being tricked is mortifying.

Sir Kenelm Digby, a courtier of Charles and James, who won the sea-fight of Scanderoon, was a model Englishman in his day. "His person was handsome and gigantic, he had so graceful elocution and noble address, that, had he been dropt out of the clouds in any part of the world, he would have made himself respected: he was skilled in six tongues, and master of arts and arms." [16] Sir Kenelm wrote a book, "Of Bodies and of Souls," in which he propounds, that "syllogisms do breed or rather are all the variety of man's life. They are the steps by which we walk in all our businesses. Man, as he is man, doth nothing else but weave such chains. Whatsoever he doth, swarving from this work, he doth as deficient from the nature of man: and, if he do aught beyond this, by breaking out into divers sorts of exterior actions, he findeth, nevertheless, in this linked sequel of simple discourses, the art, the cause, the rule, the bounds and the model of it." [17]

There spoke the genius of the English people. There is a necessity on them to be logical. They would hardly greet the good that did not logically fall, — as if it excluded their own merit, or shook their understandings. They are jealous of minds that have much facility of association, from an instinctive fear that the seeing many relations to their thought might impair this serial continuity and lucrative concentration. They are impatient of genius, or of minds addicted to contemplation, and cannot conceal their contempt for sallies of thought, however lawful, whose steps they cannot count by their wonted rule. Neither do they reckon better a syllogism that ends in syllogism. For they have a supreme eye to facts, and theirs is a logic that brings salt to soup, hammer to nail, oar to boat; the logic of cooks, carpenters and chemists, following the sequence of nature, and one on which words make no impression. Their mind is not dazzled by its own means, but locked and bolted to results. They love men who, like Samuel Johnson, a doctor in the schools, would jump out of his syllogism the instant his major proposition was in danger, to save that at all hazards. Their practical vision is spacious, and they can hold many threads without entangling them. All the steps they orderly take; but with the high logic of never confounding the minor and major proposition; keeping their eye on their aim, in all the complicity and delay incident to the several series of means they employ. There is room in their minds for this and that, — a science of degrees. In the courts the independence of the judges and the loyalty of the suitors are equally excellent. In Parliament they have hit on that capital invention of freedom, a constitutional opposition. And when courts and parliament are both deaf, the plaintiff is not silenced. Calm, patient, his weapon of defence from year to year is the obstinate reproduction of the grievance, with calculations and estimates. But, meantime, he is drawing numbers and money to his opinion, resolved that if all remedy fails, right of revolution is at the bottom of his charter-box. They are bound to see their measure carried, and stick to it through ages of defeat.

Into this English logic, however, an infusion of justice

enters, not so apparent in other races; — a belief in the existence of two sides, and the resolution to see fair play. There
is on every question an appeal from the assertion of the
parties to the proof of what is asserted. They kiss the dust
before a fact. Is it a machine, is it a charter, is it a boxer in
the ring, is it a candidate on the hustings, — the universe of
Englishmen will suspend their judgment until the trial can
be had. They are not to be led by a phrase, they want a working plan, a working machine, a working constitution, and
will sit out the trial and abide by the issue and reject all
preconceived theories. In politics they put blunt questions,
which must be answered; Who is to pay the taxes? What will
you do for trade? What for corn? What for the spinner?

This singular fairness and its results strike the French
with surprise. Philip de Commines says, "Now, in my opinion, among all the sovereignties I know in the world, that
in which the public good is best attended to, and the least
violence exercised on the people, is that of England." [18] Life
is safe, and personal rights; and what is freedom without
security? whilst, in France, "fraternity," "equality," and
"indivisible unity" are names for assassination.[19] Montesquieu said, "England is the freest country in the world. If
a man in England had as many enemies as hairs on his head,
no harm would happen to him." [20]

Their self-respect, their faith in causation, and their realistic logic or coupling of means to ends, have given them the
leadership of the modern world. Montesquieu said, "No
people have true common-sense but those who are born in
England." [21] This common-sense is a perception of all the
conditions of our earthly existence; of laws that can be stated,
and of laws that cannot be stated, or that are learned only by
practice, in which allowance for friction is made. They are
impious in their skepticism of theory, and in high depart-

ments they are cramped and sterile. But the unconditional surrender to facts, and the choice of means to reach their ends, are as admirable as with ants and bees.

The bias of the nation is a passion for utility. They love the lever, the screw and pulley, the Flanders draught-horse, the waterfall, wind-mills, tide-mills; the sea and the wind to bear their freight ships. More than the diamond Koh-i-noor,[22] which glitters among their crown jewels, they prize that dull pebble which is wiser than a man, whose poles turn themselves to the poles of the world and whose axis is parallel to the axis of the world.[23] Now, their toys are steam and galvanism.[24] They are heavy at the fine arts, but adroit at the coarse; not good in jewelry or mosaics, but the best ironmasters, colliers, wool-combers and tanners in Europe. They apply themselves to agriculture, to draining, to resisting encroachments of sea, wind, travelling sands, cold and wet subsoil; to fishery, to manufacture of indispensable staples, — salt, plumbago, leather, wool, glass, pottery and brick, — to bees and silkworms; — and by their steady combinations they succeed. A manufacturer sits down to dinner in a suit of clothes which was wool on a sheep's back at sunrise. You dine with a gentleman on venison, pheasant, quail, pigeons, poultry, mushrooms and pine-apples, all the growth of his estate. They are neat husbands for ordering all their tools pertaining to house and field. All are well kept. There is no want and no waste. They study use and fitness in their building, in the order of their dwellings and in their dress. The Frenchman invented the ruffle; the Englishman added the shirt. The Englishman wears a sensible coat buttoned to the chin, of rough but solid and lasting texture. If he is a lord, he dresses a little worse than a commoner. They have diffused the taste for plain substantial hats, shoes and coats through Europe. They think him the best dressed man whose dress is so fit for his use that you cannot notice or remember to describe it.

They secure the essentials in their diet, in their arts and manufactures. Every article of cutlery shows, in its shape, thought and long experience of workmen. They put the expense in the right place, as, in their sea-steamers, in the solidity of the machinery and the strength of the boat. The admirable equipment of their arctic ships carries London to the pole. They build roads, aqueducts; warm and ventilate houses. And they have impressed their directness and practical habit on modern civilization.

In trade, the Englishman believes that nobody breaks who ought not to break; and that if he do not make trade every thing, it will make him nothing; and acts on this belief. The spirit of system, attention to details, and the subordination of details, or the not driving things too finely, (which is charged on the Germans), constitute that despatch of business which makes the mercantile power of England.

In war, the Englishman looks to his means. He is the opinion of Civilis, his German ancestor, whom Tacitus reports as holding that "the gods are on the side of the strongest;" [25] — a sentence which Bonaparte unconsciously translated, when he said that "he had noticed that Providence always favored the heaviest battalion." [26] Their military science propounds that if the weight of the advancing column is greater than that of the resisting, the latter is destroyed. Therefore Wellington, when he came to the army in Spain, had every man weighed, first with accoutrements, and then without; believing that the force of an army depended on the weight and power of the individual soldiers, in spite of cannon.[27] Lord Palmerston told the House of Commons that more care is taken of the health and comfort of English troops than of any other troops in the world;[28] and that hence the English can put more men into the rank, on the day of action, on the field of battle, than any other army. Before the bombardment of the Danish forts in the Baltic, Nelson spent day after day, himself, in the boats, on the exhausting service of sounding the channel.[29] Clerk of Eldin's celebrated manœuvre of breaking the line of sea-battle,[30] and Nelson's feat of *doubling*,[31] or stationing his ships one on the outer bow, and another on the outer quarter of each of the enemy's, were only translations into naval tactics of Bonaparte's rule of concentration. Lord Collingwood was accustomed to tell his men that if they could fire three well-directed broadsides in five minutes, no vessel could resist them; and from constant practice they came to do it in three minutes and a half.[32]

But conscious that no race of better men exists, they rely most on the simplest means, and do not like ponderous and difficult tactics, but delight to bring the affair hand to hand; where the victory lies with the strength, courage and endurance of the individual combatants. They adopt every improvement in rig, in motor,[33] in weapons, but they fundamentally believe that the best stratagem in naval war is to lay your ship close alongside of the enemy's ship and bring all your guns to bear on him, until you or he go to the bottom. This is the old fashion, which never goes out of fashion, neither in nor out of England.

It is not usually a point of honor, nor a religious sentiment, and never any whim, that they will shed their blood for; but usually property, and right measured by property, that breeds revolution. They have no Indian taste for a tomahawk-dance, no French taste for a badge or a proclamation. The Englishman is peaceably minding his business and earning his day's wages. But if you offer to lay hand on his day's wages, on his cow, or his right in common,[34] or his shop, he will fight to the Judgment. Magna-charta, jury-trial, *habeas-corpus*, star-chamber,[34a] ship-money, Popery, Plymouth colony, American Revolution, are all questions involving a yeoman's right to his dinner, and except as touching that, would not have lashed the British nation to rage and revolt.

Whilst they are thus instinct with a spirit of order and of calculation, it must be owned they are capable of larger views; but the indulgence is expensive to them, costs great crises, or accumulations of mental power. In common, the horse works best with blinders. Nothing is more in the line of English thought than our unvarnished Connecticut question "Pray, sir, how do you get your living when you are at home?" The questions of freedom, of taxation, of privilege, are money questions. Heavy fellows, steeped in beer and flesh-pots, they are hard of hearing and dim of sight. Their drowsy minds need to be flagellated by war and trade and politics and persecution. They cannot well read a principle, except by the light of fagots and of burning towns.

Tacitus says of the Germans, "Powerful only in sudden efforts, they are impatient of toil and labor." [35] This highly-destined race, if it had not somewhere added the chamber of patience to its brain, would not have built London. I know not from which of the tribes and temperaments that went to the composition of the people this tenacity was supplied, but they clinch every nail they drive. They have no running for luck, and no immoderate speed. They spend largely on their fabric, and await the slow return. Their leather lies tanning seven years in the vat. At Rogers's mills,[36] in Sheffield, where I was shown the process of making a razor and a penknife, I was told there is no luck in making good steel; that they make no mistakes, every blade in the hundred and in the thousand is good. And that is characteristic of all their work, — no more is attempted than is done.

When Thor and his companions arrive at Utgard, he is told that "nobody is permitted to remain here, unless he understand some art, and excel in it all other men." [37] The same question is still put to the posterity of Thor. A nation of laborers, every man is trained to some one art or detail and aims at perfection in that; not content unless he has something in which he thinks he surpasses all other men. He would rather not do any thing at all than not do it well. I suppose no people have such thoroughness; — from the highest to the lowest, every man meaning to be master of his art.

"To show capacity," a Frenchman described as the end of a speech in debate: "No," said an Englishman, "but to set your shoulder at the wheel, — to advance the business." Sir Samuel Romilly refused to speak in popular assemblies, confining himself to the House of Commons, where a measure can be carried by a speech. The business of the House of Commons is conducted by a few persons, but these are hardworked. Sir Robert Peel [38] "knew the Blue Books by heart." [39] His colleagues and rivals carry Hansard in their heads.[40] The high civil and legal offices are not beds of ease, but posts which exact frightful amounts of mental labor. Many of the great leaders, like Pitt, Canning, Castlereagh, Romilly, are soon worked to death.[41] They are excellent judges in England of a good worker, and when they find one, like Clarendon, Sir Philip Warwick, Sir William Coventry, Ashley, Burke, Thurlow, Mansfield, Pitt, Eldon, Peel, or Russell, there is nothing too good or too high for him.[42]

They have a wonderful heat in the pursuit of a public aim. Private persons exhibit, in scientific and antiquarian researches, the same pertinacity as the nation showed in the coalitions in which it yoked Europe against the empire of Bonaparte, one after the other defeated, and still renewed, until the sixth hurled him from his seat.

Sir John Herschel, in completion of the work of his father, who had made the catalogue of the stars of the northern hemisphere, expatriated himself for years at the Cape of

Good Hope, finished his inventory of the southern heaven,
came home, and redacted it in eight years more; — a work
whose value does not begin until thirty years have elapsed,
and thenceforward a record to all ages of the highest import.
The Admiralty sent out the Arctic expeditions year after
year, in search of Sir John Franklin,[43] until at last they have
threaded their way through polar pack and Behring's Straits[44]
and solved the geographical problem. Lord Elgin, at Athens,
saw the imminent ruin of the Greek remains, set up his
scaffoldings, in spite of epigrams, and, after five years' labor
to collect them, got his marbles on ship-board. The ship
struck a rock and went to the bottom. He had them all fished
up by divers, at a vast expense, and brought to London;[45]
not knowing that Haydon, Fuseli and Canova,[46] and all good
heads in all the world, were to be his applauders. In the same
spirit, were the excavation and research by Sir Charles Fellowes for the Xanthian monument, and of Layard for his
Nineveh sculptures.[47]

The nation sits in the immense city they have builded, a
London extended into every man's mind, though he live in
Van Dieman's Land [48] or Capetown.[49] Faithful performance
of what is undertaken to be performed, they honor in themselves, and exact in others, as certificate of equality with
themselves. The modern world is theirs. They have made
and make it day by day. The commercial relations of the
world are so intimately drawn to London, that every dollar
on earth contributes to the strength of the English government. And if all the wealth in the planet should perish by war
or deluge, they know themselves competent to replace it.

They have approved their Saxon blood, by their sea-going
qualities; their descent from Odin's smiths,[50] by their hereditary skill in working in iron; their British birth, by hus-
bandry and immense wheat harvests; and justified their occu-
pancy of the centre of habitable land, by their supreme

ability and cosmopolitan spirit. They have tilled, builded, forged, spun and woven. They have made the island a thoroughfare, and London a shop, a law-court, a record-office and scientific bureau, inviting to strangers; a sanctuary to refugees of every political and religious opinion; and such a city that almost every active man, in any nation, finds himself at one time or other forced to visit it.

In every path of practical activity they have gone even with the best. There is no secret of war in which they have not shown mastery. The steam-chamber of Watt, the locomotive of Stephenson, the cotton-mule of Roberts,[51] perform the labor of the world. There is no department of literature, of science, or of useful art, in which they have not produced a first-rate book. It is England whose opinion is waited for on the merit of a new invention, an improved science. And in the complications of the trade and politics of their vast empire, they have been equal to every exigency, with counsel and with conduct. Is it their luck, or is it in the chambers of their brain, — it is their commercial advantage that whatever light appears in better method or happy invention, breaks out *in their race*. They are a family to which a destiny attaches, and the Banshee[52] has sworn that a male heir shall never be wanting. They have a wealth of men to fill important posts, and the vigilance of party criticism insures the selection of a competent person.

A proof of the energy of the British people is the highly artificial construction of the whole fabric. The climate and geography, I said, were factitious, as if the hands of man had arranged the conditions. The same character pervades the whole kingdom. Bacon said, "Rome was a state not subject to paradoxes;"[53] but England subsists by antagonisms and contradictions. The foundations of its greatness are the rolling waves; and from first to last it is a museum of anomalies.

This foggy and rainy country furnishes the world with astronomical observations. Its short rivers do not afford waterpower, but the land shakes under the thunder of the mills. There is no gold-mine of any importance, but there is more gold in England than in all other countries. It is too far north for the culture of the vine, but the wines of all countries are in its docks. The French Comte de Lauraguais[54] said, "No fruit ripens in England but a baked apple;" but oranges and pine-apples are as cheap in London as in the Mediterranean. The Mark-Lane Express, or the Custom House Returns,[55] bear out to the letter the vaunt of Pope, —

> "Let India boast her palms, nor envy we
> The weeping amber, nor the spicy tree,
> While, by our oaks, those precious loads are borne,
> And realms commanded which those trees adorn." [56]

The native cattle are extinct, but the island is full of artificial breeds. The agriculturist Bakewell [57] created sheep and cows and horses to order, and breeds in which every thing was omitted but what is economical. The cow is sacrificed to her bag, the ox to his sirloin. Stall-feeding makes sperm-mills of the cattle, and converts the stable to a chemical factory. The rivers, lakes and ponds, too much fished, or obstructed by factories, are artificially filled with the eggs of salmon, turbot and herring.

Chat Moss[58] and the fens of Lincolnshire and Cambridgeshire are unhealthy and too barren to pay rent. By cylindrical tiles and guttapercha tubes, five millions of acres of bad land have been drained and put on equality with the best, for rape-culture and grass.[59] The climate too, which was already believed to have become milder and drier by the enormous consumption of coal, is so far reached by this new action, that fogs and storms are said to disappear. In due course, all England will be drained and rise a second time out of the waters.

The latest step was to call in the aid of steam to agricuture. Steam is almost an Englishman. I do not know but they will send him to Parliament next, to make laws. He weaves, forges, saws, pounds, fans, and now he must pump, grind, dig and plough for the farmer. The markets created by the manufacturing population have erected agriculture into a great thriving and spending industry. The value of the houses in Britain is equal to the value of the soil. Artificial aids of all kinds are cheaper than the natural resources. No man can afford to walk, when the parliamentary-train[60] carries him for a penny a mile. Gas-burners are cheaper than daylight in numberless floors in the cities. All the houses in London buy their water. The English trade does not exist for the exportation of native products, but on its manufactures, or the making well every thing which is ill-made elsewhere. They make ponchos for the Mexican, bandannas for the Hindoo, ginseng for the Chinese, beads for the Indian, laces for the Flemings, telescopes for astronomers, cannons for kings.

The Board of Trade caused the best models of Greece and Italy to be placed within the reach of every manufacturing population. They caused to be translated from foreign languages and illustrated by elaborate drawings, the most approved works of Munich, Berlin and Paris. They have ransacked Italy to find new forms, to add a grace to the products of their looms, their potteries and their foundries.[61]

The nearer we look, the more artificial is their social system. Their law is a network of fictions. Their property, a scrip or certificate of right to interest on money that no man ever saw. Their social classes are made by statute. Their ratios of power and representation are historical and legal. The last Reform-bill took away political power from a mound, a ruin and a stone-wall, whilst Birmingham and Manchester, whose mills paid for the wars of Europe, had

no representative. Purity in the elective Parliament is secured by the purchase of seats.[62] Foreign power is kept by
armed colonies; power at home, by a standing army of police.
The pauper lives better than the free laborer, the thief better
than the pauper, and the transported felon better than the
one under imprisonment. The crimes are factitious; as smuggling, poaching, nonconformity, heresy and treason. The
sovereignty of the seas is maintained by the impressment of
seamen. "The impressment of seamen," said Lord Eldon,
"is the life of our navy." Solvency is maintained by means
of a national debt, on the principle, "If you will not lend me
the money, how can I pay you?" For the administration of
justice, Sir Samuel Romilly's expedient for clearing the ar-
rears of business in Chancery was, the Chancellor's staying
away entirely from his court.[63] Their system of education is
factitious. The Universities galvanize dead languages into a
semblance of life. Their church is artificial. The manners
and customs of society are artificial; — made-up men with
made-up manners; — and thus the whole is Birminghamized,
and we have a nation whose existence is a work of art; — a
cold, barren, almost arctic isle being made the most fruitful,
luxurious and imperial land in the whole earth.

Man in England submits to be a product of political
economy. On a bleak moor a mill is built, a banking-house
is opened, and men come in as water in a sluice-way, and
towns and cities rise. Man is made as a Birmingham button.
The rapid doubling of the population dates from Watt's
steam-engine. A landlord who owns a province, says "The
tenantry are unprofitable; let me have sheep." He unroofs the
houses and ships the population to America. The nation is
accustomed to the instantaneous creation of wealth. It is the
maxim of their economists, "that the greater part in value of
the wealth now existing in England has been produced by
human hands within the last twelve months." Meantime,

three or four days' rain will reduce hundreds to starving in London.

One secret of their power is their mutual good understanding. Not only good minds are born among them, but all the people have good minds. Every nation has yielded some good wit, if, as has chanced to many tribes, only one. But the intellectual organization of the English admits a communicableness of knowledge and ideas among them all. An electric touch by any of their national ideas, melts them into one family and brings the hoards of power which their individuality is always hiving, into use and play for all. Is it the smallness of the country, or is it the pride and affection of race, — they have solidarity, or responsibleness, and trust in each other.

Their minds, like wool, admit of a dye which is more lasting than the cloth. They embrace their cause with more tenacity than their life. Though not military, yet every common subject by the poll is fit to make a soldier of. These private, reserved, mute family-men can adopt a public end with all their heat, and this strength of affection makes the romance of their heroes. The difference of rank does not divide the national heart. The Danish poet Oehlenschläger[64] complains that who writes in Danish writes to two hundred readers. In Germany there is one speech for the learned, and another for the masses, to that extent that, it is said, no sentiment or phrase from the works of any great German writer is ever heard among the lower classes. But in England, the language of the noble is the language of the poor. In Parliament, in pulpits, in theatres, when the speakers rise to thought and passion, the language becomes idiomatic; the people in the street best understand the best words. And their language seems drawn from the Bible, the Common Law and the works of Shakspeare, Bacon, Milton, Pope,

Young, Cowper, Burns and Scott. The island has produced two or three of the greatest men that ever existed, but they were not solitary in their own time. Men quickly embodied what Newton found out, in Greenwich observatories[65] and practical navigation. The boys know all that Hutton knew of strata, or Dalton of atoms, or Harvey of blood-vessels; and these studies, once dangerous, are in fashion.[66] So what is invented or known in agriculture, or in trade, or in war, or in art, or in literature and antiquities. A great ability, not amassed on a few giants, but poured into the general mind, so that each of them could at a pinch stand in the shoes of the other; and they are more bound in character than differenced in ability or in rank. The laborer is a possible lord. The lord is a possible basket-maker. Every man carries the English system in his brain, knows what is confided to him and does therein the best he can. The chancellor carries England on his mace, the midshipman at the point of his dirk, the smith on his hammer, the cook in the bowl of his spoon; the postilion cracks his whip for England, and the sailor times his oars to "God save the King!" The very felons have their pride in each other's English stanchness. In politics and in war they hold together as by hooks of steel. The charm in Nelson's history is the unselfish greatness, the assurance of being supported to the uttermost by those whom he supports to the uttermost. Whilst they are some ages ahead of the rest of the world in the art of living; whilst in some directions they do not represent the modern spirit but constitute it; — this vanguard of civility and power they coldly hold, marching in phalanx, lockstep, foot after foot, file after file of heroes, ten thousand deep.

CHAPTER VI

Manners

I find the Englishman to be him of all men who stands firmest in his shoes. They have in themselves what they value in their horses, — mettle and bottom.[1] On the day of my arrival at Liverpool,[2] a gentleman, in describing to me the Lord Lieutenant of Ireland, happened to say, "Lord Clarendon has pluck like a cock and will fight till he dies;"[3] and what I heard first I heard last, and the one thing the English value is *pluck*. The word is not beautiful, but on the quality they signify by it the nation is unanimous. The cabmen have it; the merchants have it; the bishops have it; the women have it; the journals have it; — the Times newspaper they say is the pluckiest thing in England, and Sydney Smith had made it a proverb that little Lord John Russell, the minister, would take the command of the Channel fleet to-morrow.

They require you to dare to be of your own opinion, and they hate the practical cowards who cannot in affairs answer directly yes or no. They dare to displease, nay, they will let you break all the commandments, if you do it natively and with spirit. You must be somebody; then you may do this or that, as you will.

Machinery has been applied to all work, and carried to such perfection that little is left for the men but to mind the engines and feed the furnaces. But the machines require punctual service, and as they never tire, they prove too much for their tenders. Mines, forges, mills, breweries, railroads, steam-pump, steam-plough, drill of regiments, drill of police, rule of court and shop-rule have operated to give a mechanical regularity to all the habit and action of men. A terrible machine has possessed itself of the ground, the air, the men and women, and hardly even thought is free.

The mechanical might and organization requires in the people constitution and answering spirits; and he who goes among them must have some weight of metal. At last, you take your hint from the fury of life you find, and say, one thing is plain, this is no country for fainthearted people: don't creep about diffidently; make up your mind; take your own course, and you shall find respect and furtherance.

It requires, men say, a good constitution to travel in Spain. I say as much of England, for other cause, simply on account of the vigor and brawn of the people. Nothing but the most serious business could give one any counterweight to these Baresarks,[4] though they were only to order eggs and muffins for their breakfast. The Englishman speaks with all his body. His elocution is stomachic, — as the American's is labial. The Englishman is very petulant and precise about his accommodation at inns and on the roads; a quiddle[5] about his toast and his chop and every species of convenience, and loud and pungent in his expressions of impatience at any neglect. His vivacity betrays itself at all points, in his manners, in his respiration, and the inarticulate noises he makes in clearing the throat; — all significant of burly strength. He has stamina; he can take the initiative in emergencies. He has that *aplomb* which results from a good adjustment of the moral and physical nature and the obedience of all the powers to the will; as if the axes of his eyes were united to his backbone, and only moved with the trunk.

This vigor appears in the incuriosity and stony neglect, each of every other. Each man walks, eats, drinks, shaves, dresses, gesticulates, and, in every manner acts and suffers without reference to the bystanders, in his own fashion, only careful not to interfere with them or annoy them; not that he is trained to neglect the eyes of his neighbors, — he is really occupied with his own affair and does not think of them. Every man in this polished country consults only his convenience, as much as a solitary pioneer in Wisconsin. I know not where any personal eccentricity is so freely allowed, and no man gives himself any concern with it. An English-man walks in a pouring rain, swinging his closed umbrella like a walking-stick; wears a wig, or a shawl, or a saddle, or stands on his head, and no remark is made. And as he has been doing this for several generations, it is now in the blood.

In short, every one of these islanders is an island himself, safe, tranquil, incommunicable. In a company of strangers you would think him deaf; his eyes never wander from his table and newspaper. He is never betrayed into any curiosity or unbecoming emotion. They have all been trained in one severe school of manners, and never put off the harness. He does not give his hand. He does not let you meet his eye. It is almost an affront to look a man in the face without being introduced. In mixed or in select companies they do not introduce persons; so that a presentation is a circumstance as valid as a contract. Introductions are sacraments. He with-holds his name. At the hotel, he is hardly willing to whisper it to the clerk at the book-office. If he give you his private address on a card, it is like an avowal of friendship; and his bearing, on being introduced, is cold, even though he is seek-ing your acquaintance and is studying how he shall serve you.

It was an odd proof of this impressive energy, that in my lectures I hesitated to read and threw out for its impertinence many a disparaging phrase which I had been accustomed to spin, about poor, thin, unable mortals; — so much had the fine physique and the personal vigor of this robust race worked on my imagination.

I happened to arrive in England at the moment of a commercial crisis.[6] But it was evident that let who will fail, England will not. These people have sat here a thousand years, and here will continue to sit. They will not break up, or arrive at any desperate revolution, like their neighbors; for they have as much energy, as much continence of character as they ever had. The power and possession which surround them are their own creation, and they exert the same commanding industry at this moment.

They are positive, methodical, cleanly and formal, loving routine and conventional ways; loving truth and religion, to be sure, but inexorable on points of form. All the world praises the comfort and private appointments of an English inn, and of English households. You are sure of neatness and of personal decorum. A Frenchman may possibly be clean; an Englishman is conscientiously clean. A certain order and complete propriety is found in his dress and in his belongings.

Born in a harsh and wet climate, which keeps him in doors whenever he is at rest, and being of an affectionate and loyal temper, he dearly loves his house. If he is rich, he buys a demesne and builds a hall; if he is in middle condition, he spares no expense on his house. Without, it is all planted; within, it is wainscoted, carved, curtained, hung with pictures and filled with good furniture. 'T is a passion which survives all others, to deck and improve it. Hither he brings all that is rare and costly, and with the national tendency to sit fast in the same spot for many generations, it comes to be, in the course of time, a museum of heirlooms, gifts and trophies of the adventures and exploits of the family. He is very fond of silver plate, and though he have no gallery of portraits of his ancestors, he has of their punch-bowls and porringers. Incredible amounts of plate are found in good houses, and the poorest have some spoon or saucepan, gift of a godmother, saved out of better times.

An English family consists of a few persons, who, from youth to age, are found revolving within a few feet of each other, as if tied by some invisible ligature, tense as that cartilage which we have seen attaching the two Siamese.[7] England produces under favorable conditions of ease and culture the finest women in the world. And as the men are affectionate and true-hearted, the women inspire and refine them. Nothing can be more delicate without being fantastical, nothing more firm and based in nature and sentiment, than the courtship and mutual carriage of the sexes. The song of 1596 says, "The wife of every Englishman is counted blest." [8] The sentiment of Imogen in Cymbeline is copied from English nature; and not less the Portia of Brutus, the Kate Percy and the Desdemona.[9] The romance does not exceed the height of noble passion in Mrs. Lucy Hutchinson,[10] or in Lady Russell,[11] or even as one discerns through the plain prose of Pepys's Diary, the sacred habit of an English wife. Sir Samuel Romilly could not bear the death of his wife.[12] Every class has its noble and tender examples.

Domesticity is the taproot which enables the nation to branch wide and high. The motive and end of their trade and empire is to guard the independence and privacy of their homes. Nothing so much marks their manners as the concentration on their household ties. This domesticity is carried into court and camp. Wellington governed India[13] and Spain and his own troops, and fought battles, like a good family-man, paid his debts, and though general of an army in Spain, could not stir abroad for fear of public creditors. This taste for house and parish merits has of course its doting and foolish side. Mr. Cobbett attributes the huge popularity of Perceval, prime minister in 1810, to the fact that he was wont to go to church every Sunday, with a large quarto gilt prayer-book under one arm, his wife hanging on the other, and followed by a long brood of children.[14]

They keep their old customs, costumes, and pomps, their wig and mace, sceptre and crown. The Middle Ages still lurk in the streets of London. The Knights of the Bath take oath to defend injured ladies;[15] the gold-stick-in-waiting survives.[16] They repeated the ceremonies of the eleventh century in the coronation of the present Queen. A hereditary tenure is natural to them. Offices, farms trades and traditions descend so. Their leases run for a hundred and a thousand years. Terms of service and partnership are life-long, or are inherited. "Holdship has been with me," said Lord Eldon, "eight-and-twenty years, knows all my business and books."[17] Antiquity of usage is sanction enough. Wordsworth says of the small freeholders of Westmoreland, "Many of these humble sons of the hills had a consciousness that the land which they tilled had for more than five hundred years been possessed by men of the same name and blood." [18] The ship-carpenter in the public yards, my lord's gardener and porter, have been there for more than a hundred years, grandfather, father, and son.

The English power resides also in their dislike of change. They have difficulty in bringing their reason to act, and on all occasions use their memory first. As soon as they have rid themselves of some grievance and settled the better practice, they make haste to fix it as a finality, and never wish to hear of alteration more.

Every Englishman is an embryonic chancellor: his instinct is to search for a precedent. The favorite phrase of their law is, "a custom whereof the memory of man runneth not back to the contrary." The barons say, *"Nolumus mutari;"* [19] and the cockneys stifle the curiosity of the foreigner on the reason

of any practice with "Lord, sir, it was always so." They hate
innovation. Bacon told them, Time was the right reformer;
Chatham, that "confidence was a plant of slow growth;" Canning,[20] to "advance with the times;" and Wellington, that
"habit was ten times nature." All their statesmen learn the
irresistibility of the tide of custom, and have invented many
fine phrases to cover this slowness of perception and pre-
hensility of tail.

A sea-shell should be the crest of England, not only because it represents a power built on the waves, but also the
hard finish of the men. The Englishman is finished like a
cowry or a murex. After the spire and the spines are formed,
or with the formation, a juice exudes and a hard enamel
varnishes every part. The keeping of the proprieties is as
indispensable as clean linen. No merit quite countervails the
want of this, whilst this sometimes stands in lieu of all. " 'T is
in bad taste," is the most formidable word an Englishman
can pronounce. But this japan costs them dear.[21] There is a
prose in certain Englishmen which exceeds in wooden dead-
ness all rivalry with other countrymen. There is a knell in
the conceit and externality of their voice, which seems to say,
Leave all hope behind.[22] In this Gibraltar of propriety, mediocrity gets intrenched and consolidated and founded in adamant. An Englishman of fashion is like one of those
souvenirs,[23] bound in gold vellum, enriched with delicate
engravings on thick hot-pressed paper, fit for the hands of
ladies and princes, but with nothing in it worth reading or
remembering.

A severe decorum rules the court and the cottage. When
Thalberg the pianist was one evening performing before the
Queen at Windsor, in a private party, the Queen accompanied him with her voice.[24] The circumstance took air, and
all England shuddered from sea to sea. The indecorum was
never repeated. Cold, repressive manners prevail. No enthusi-

asm is permitted except at the opera. They avoid every thing
marked. They require a tone of voice that excites no attention in the room. Sir Philip Sidney is one of the patron
saints of England, of whom Wotton said, "His wit was the
measure of congruity." [25]

Pretension and vaporing are once for all distasteful. They
keep to the other extreme of low tone in dress and manners.
They avoid pretension and go right to the heart of the thing.
They hate nonsense, sentimentalism and highflown expression; they use a studied plainness. Even Brummel, their fop,
was marked by the severest simplicity in dress.[26] They value
themselves on the absence of every thing theatrical in the
public business, and on conciseness and going to the point, in
private affairs.

In an aristocratical country like England, not the Trial by
Jury, but the dinner, is the capital institution. It is the mode
of doing honor to a stranger, to invite him to eat, — and has
been for many hundred years. "And they think," says the
Venetian traveller of 1500, "no greater honor can be con-
ferred or received, than to invite others to eat with them, or
to be invited themselves, and they would sooner give five or
six ducats to provide an entertainment for a person, than a
groat to assist him in any distress." [27] It is reserved to the end
of the day, the family-hour being generally six, in London,
and if any company is expected, one or two hours later. Every
one dresses for dinner, in his own house, or in another man's.
The guests are expected to arrive within half an hour of the
time fixed by card of invitation, and nothing but death or
mutilation is permitted to detain them. The English dinner
is precisely the model on which our own are constructed in
the Atlantic cities. The company sit one or two hours before
the ladies leave the table. The gentlemen remain over their
wine an hour longer, and rejoin the ladies in the drawing-
room and take coffee. The dress-dinner generates a talent of

table-talk which reaches great perfection: the stories are so good that one is sure they must have been often told before, to have got such happy turns. Hither come all manner of clever projects, bits of popular science, of practical invention, of miscellaneous humor; political, literary and personal news; railroads, horses, diamonds, agriculture, horticulture, pisciculture and wine.

English stories, *bon-mots* and the recorded table-talk of their wits, are as good as the best of the French. In America, we are apt scholars, but have not yet attained the same perfection: for the range of nations from which London draws, and the steep contrasts of condition, create the picturesque in society, as broken country makes picturesque landscape; whilst our prevailing equality makes a prairie tameness: and secondly, because the usage of a dress-dinner every day at dark has a tendency to hive and produce to advantage every thing good. Much attrition has worn every sentence into a bullet. Also one meets now and then with polished men who know every thing, have tried every thing, and can do every thing, and are quite superior to letters and science. What could they not, if only they would?

CHAPTER VII

Truth

The Teutonic tribes have a national singleness of heart, which contrasts with the Latin races. The German name has a proverbial significance of sincerity and honest meaning. The arts bear testimony to it. The faces of clergy and laity in old sculptures and illuminated missals are charged with earnest belief. Add to this hereditary rectitude the punctuality and precise dealing which commerce creates, and you have the English truth and credit. The government strictly performs its engagements. The subjects do not understand trifling on its part. When any breach of promise occurred, in the old days of prerogative, it was resented by the people as an intolerable grievance. And in modern times, any slipperiness in the government of political faith, or any repudiation or crookedness in matters of finance, would bring the whole nation to a committee of inquiry and reform. Private men keep their promises, never so trivial. Down goes the flying word on the tablets, and is indelible as Domesday Book.[1]

Their practical power rests on their national sincerity. Veracity derives from instinct, and marks superiority in organization. Nature has endowed some animals with cunning, as a compensation for strength withheld; but it has provoked the malice of all others, as if avengers of public wrong. In the nobler kinds, where strength could be afforded, her races are loyal to truth, as truth is the foundation of the social state. Beasts that make no truce with man, do not break faith with each other. 'T is said that the wolf, who makes a *cache* of his prey and brings his fellows with him to the spot, if, on digging, it is not found, is instantly and unresistingly torn in pieces. English veracity seems to result on a sounder animal structure, as if they could afford it. They are blunt in saying what they think, sparing of promises, and they require plain dealing of others. We will not have to do with a man in a mask. Let us know the truth. Draw a straight line, hit whom and where it will. Alfred, whom the affection of the nation makes the type of their race, is called by a writer at the Norman Conquest, the *truth-speaker; Alueredus veridicus.*[2] Geoffrey of Monmouth says of King Aurelius, uncle of Arthur, that "above all things he hated a lie." [3] The Northman Guttorm said to King Olaf, "It is royal work to fulfil royal words." [4] The mottoes of their families are monitory proverbs, as, *Fare fac, —* Say, do, — of the Fairfaxes; *Say and seal,* of the house of Fiennes; *Vero nil verius,*[5] of the DeVeres. To be king of their word is their pride. When they unmask cant, they say, "The English of this is," &c.; and to give the lie is the extreme insult. The phrase of the lowest of the people is "honor-bright," and their vulgar praise, "His word is as good as his bond." They hate shuffling and equivocation, and the cause is damaged in the public opinion, on which any paltering can be fixed. Even Lord Chesterfield, with his French breeding, when he came to define a gentleman, declared that truth made his distinction;[6] and nothing ever spoken by him would find so hearty a suffrage from his nation. The Duke of Wellington, who had the best right to say so, advises the French General Kellermann that he may rely on the parole of an English officer.[7] The English, of all classes, value themselves on this trait, as distinguishing them from the French, who, in the popular belief, are more polite than true. An Englishman understates, avoids the superlative, checks himself in compliments, alleging that in the French language one cannot speak without lying.

They love reality in wealth, power, hospitality, and do not easily learn to make a show, and take the world as it goes. They are not fond of ornaments, and if they wear them, they must be gems. They read gladly in old Fuller that a lady, in the reign of Elizabeth, "would have as patiently digested a lie, as the wearing of false stones or pendants of counterfeit pearl." [7a] They have the earth-hunger, or preference for property in land, which is said to mark the Teutonic nations. They build of stone: public and private buildings are massive and durable. In comparing their ships' houses and public offices with the American, it is commonly said that they spend a pound where we spend a dollar. Plain rich clothes, plain rich equipage, plain rich finish throughout their house and belongings mark the English truth.

They confide in each other, — English believes in English. The French feel the superiority of this probity. The Englishman is not springing a trap for his admiration, but is honestly minding his business. The Frenchman is vain. Madame de Staël [8] says that the English irritated Napoleon, mainly because they have found out how to unite success with honesty. She was not aware how wide an application her foreign readers would give to the remark. Wellington discovered the ruin of Bonaparte's affairs, by his own probity. He augured ill of the empire, as soon as he saw that it was mendacious and lived by war. [9] If war do not bring in its sequel new trade, better agriculture and manufactures, but only games, fireworks and spectacles, — no prosperity could support it; much less a nation decimated for conscripts and out of pocket, like France. So he drudged for years on his military works at Lisbon, [10] and from this base at last extended his gigantic lines to Waterloo, believing in his countrymen and their syllogisms above all the rhodomontade of Europe.

At a St. George's festival, in Montreal,[11] where I happened to be a guest since my return home, I observed that the chairman complimented his compatriots, by saying, "they confided that wherever they met an Englishman, they found a man who would speak the truth." And one cannot think this festival fruitless, if, all over the world, on the 23d of April, wherever two or three English are found, they meet to encourage each other in the nationality of veracity.

In the power of saying rude truth, sometimes in the lion's mouth, no men surpass them. On the king's birthday, when each bishop was expected to offer the king a purse of gold, Latimer gave Henry VIII. a copy of the Vulgate,[12] with a mark at the passage, "Whoremongers and adulterers God will judge;" and they so honor stoutness in each other that the king passed it over. They are tenacious of their belief and cannot easily change their opinions to suit the hour. They are like ships with too much head on to come quickly about, nor will prosperity or even adversity be allowed to shake their habitual view of conduct. Whilst I was in London, M. Guizot arrived there on his escape from Paris, in February, 1848.[13] Many private friends called on him. His name was immediately proposed as an honorary member of the Athenæum.[14] M. Guizot was blackballed. Certainly they knew the distinction of his name. But the Englishman is not fickle. He had really made up his mind now for years as he read his newspaper, to hate and despise M. Guizot; and the altered position of the man as an illustrious exile and a guest in the country, makes no difference to him, as it would instantly to an American.

They require the same adherence, thorough conviction and reality, in public men. It is the want of character which makes the low reputation of the Irish members. "See them," they said, "one hundred and twenty-seven[15] all voting like sheep, never proposing any thing, and all but four voting the

income tax," — which was an ill-judged concession of the
government, relieving Irish property from the burdens
charged on English.

They have a horror of adventurers in or out of Parliament.
The ruling passion of Englishmen in these days is a terror of
humbug. In the same proportion they value honesty, stoutness, and adherence to your own. They like a man committed
to his objects. They hate the French, as frivolous; they hate
the Irish, as aimless; they hate the Germans, as professors. In
February 1848, they said, Look, the French king and his party
fell for want of a shot;[16] they had not conscience to shoot, so
entirely was the pith and heart of monarchy eaten out.

They attack their own politicians every day, on the same
grounds, as adventurers. They love stoutness in standing for
your right, in declining money or promotion that costs any
concession. The barrister refuses the silk gown of Queen's
Counsel,[17] if his junior have it one day earlier. Lord Collingwood would not accept his medal for victory on 14th February, 1797, if he did not receive one for victory on 1st June,
1794; and the long withholden medal was accorded.[18] When
Castlereagh dissuaded Lord Wellington from going to the
king's levee until the unpopular Cintra business had been
explained, he replied, "You furnish me a reason for going.
I will go to this, or I will never go to a king's levee." [19] The
radical mob at Oxford cried after the tory Lord Eldon,
"There's old Eldon; cheer him; he never ratted." [20] They
have given the parliamentary nickname of *Trimmers* to the
timeservers, whom English character does not love.[21]

They are very liable in their politics to extraordinary delu-
sions; thus to believe what stands recorded in the gravest
books, that the movement of 10 April, 1848,[22] was urged or
assisted by foreigners: which, to be sure, is paralleled by the
democratic whimsy in this country which I have noticed to
be shared by men sane on other points, that the English are

at the bottom of the agitation of slavery, in American politics: and then again by the French popular legends on the subject of *perfidious Albion*.[23] But suspicion will make fools of nations as of citizens.

A slow temperament makes them less rapid and ready than other countrymen, and has given occasion to the observation that English wit comes afterwards, — which the French denote as *esprit d'escalier*.[24] This dulness makes their attachment to home and their adherence in all foreign countries to home habits. The Englishman who visits Mount Etna[25] will carry his teakettle to the top. The old Italian author of the "Relation of England" (in 1500), says, "I have it on the best information, that, when the war is actually raging most furiously, they will seek for good eating and all their other comforts, without thinking what harm might befall them." [26] Then their eyes seem to be set at the bottom of a tunnel, and they affirm the one small fact they know, with the best faith in the world that nothing else exists. And as their own belief in guineas is perfect, they readily, on all occasions, apply the pecuniary argument as final. Thus when the Rochester rappings began to be heard of in England,[27] a man deposited £100 in a sealed box in the Dublin Bank, and then advertised in the newspapers to all somnambulists, mesmerizers and others, that whoever could tell him the number of his note should have the money. He let it lie there six months, the newspapers now and then, at his instance, stimulating the attention of the adepts; but none could ever tell him; and he said, "Now let me never be bothered more with this proven lie." It is told of a good Sir John that he heard a case stated by counsel, and made up his mind; then the counsel for the other side taking their turn to speak, he found himself so unsettled and perplexed that he exclaimed, "So help me God! I will never listen to evidence again." Any number of delightful examples of this English stolidity are the anecdotes

of Europe. I knew a very worthy man, — a magistrate, I believe he was, in the town of Derby,[28] — who went to the
opera to see Malibran.[29] In one scene, the heroine was to rush
across a ruined bridge. Mr. B. arose and mildly yet firmly
called the attention of the audience and the performers to
the fact that, in his judgment, the bridge was unsafe! This
English stolidity contrasts with French wit and tact. The
French, it is commonly said, have greatly more influence in
Europe than the English. What influence the English have
is by brute force of wealth and power; that of the French by
affinity and talent. The Italian is subtle, the Spaniard treach-
erous: tortures, it is said, could never wrest from an Egyptian
the confession of a secret. None of these traits belong to the
Englishman. His choler and conceit force every thing out.
Defoe, who knew his countrymen well, says of them, —

> "In close intrigue, their faculty's but weak,
> For generally whate'er they know, they speak,
> And often their own counsels undermine
> By mere infirmity without design;
> From whence, the learned say, it doth proceed,
> That English treasons never can succeed;
> For they're so open-hearted, you may know
> Their own most secret thoughts, and others' too.[30]

CHAPTER VIII

Character

'The English race are reputed morose. I do not know that they have sadder brows than their neighbors of northern climates. They are sad by comparison with the singing and dancing nations: not sadder, but slow and staid, as finding their joys at home. They, too, believe that where there is no enjoyment of life there can be no vigor and art in speech or thought; that your merry heart goes all the way, your sad one tires in a mile. This trait of gloom has been fixed on them by French travellers, who, from Froissart, Voltaire, Le Sage, Mirabeau, down to the lively journalists of the *feuilletons*, have spent their wit on the solemnity of their neighbors.[1] The French say, gay conversation is unknown in their island. The Englishman finds no relief from reflection, except in reflection. When he wishes for amusement, he goes to work. His hilarity is like an attack of fever. Religion, the theatre and the reading the books of his country all feed and increase his natural melancholy. The police does not interfere with public diversions. It thinks itself bound in duty to respect the pleasures and rare gayety of this inconsolable nation; and their well-known courage is entirely attributable to their disgust of life.

I suppose their gravity of demeanor and their few words have obtained this reputation. As compared with the Americans, I think them cheerful and contented. Young people in

this country are much more prone to melancholy. The English have a mild aspect and a ringing cheerful voice. They are
large-natured and not so easily amused as the southerners,
and are among them as grown people among children, requiring war, or trade, or engineering, or science, instead of
frivolous games. They are proud and private, and even if
disposed to recreation, will avoid an open garden. They
sported sadly; *ils s'amusaient tristement, selon la coutume de
leur pays,* said Froissart;[2] and I suppose never nation built
their party-walls so thick, or their garden-fences so high. Meat
and wine produce no effect on them. They are just as cold,
quiet and composed, at the end, as at the beginning of dinner.

The reputation of taciturnity they have enjoyed for six or
seven hundred years; and a kind of pride in bad public
speaking is noted in the House of Commons, as if they were
willing to show that they did not live by their tongues, or
thought they spoke well enough if they had the tone of gentlemen. In mixed company they shut their mouths. A Yorkshire mill-owner told me he had ridden more than once all
the way from London to Leeds, in the first-class carriage,
with the same persons, and no word exchanged. The club-
houses were established to cultivate social habits, and it is
rare that more than two eat together, and oftenest one eats
alone. Was it then a stroke of humor in the serious Swedenborg,[3] or was it only his pitiless logic, that made him shut up
the English souls in a heaven by themselves?

They are contradictorily described as sour, splenetic and
stubborn, — and as mild, sweet and sensible. The truth is
they have great range and variety of character. Commerce
sends abroad multitudes of different classes. The choleric
Welshman, the fervid Scot, the bilious resident in the East
or West Indies, are wide of the perfect behavior of the educated and dignified man of family. So is the burly farmer; so

is the country squire, with his narrow and violent life. In every inn is the Commercial-Room, in which 'travellers,' or bagmen who carry patterns and solicit orders for the manufacturers, are wont to be entertained. It easily happens that this class should characterize England to the foreigner, who meets them on the road and at every public house, whilst the gentry avoid the taverns, or seclude themselves whilst in them.

But these classes are the right English stock, and may fairly show the national qualities, before yet art and education have dealt with them. They are good lovers, good haters, slow but obstinate admirers, and in all things very much steeped in their temperament, like men hardly awaked from deep sleep, which they enjoy. Their habits and instincts cleave to nature. They are of the earth, earthy; and of the sea, as the sea-kinds, attached to it for what it yields them, and not from any sentiment. They are full of coarse strength, rude exercise, butcher's meat and sound sleep; and suspect any poetic in- sinuation or any hint for the conduct of life which reflects on this animal existence, as if somebody were fumbling at the umbilical cord and might stop their supplies. They doubt a man's sound judgment if he does not eat with appetite, and shake their heads if he is particularly chaste. Take them as they come, you shall find in the common people a surly indifference, sometimes gruffness and ill temper; and in minds of more power, magazines of inexhaustible war, chal- lenging

> "The ruggedest hour that time and spite dare bring
> To frown upon the enraged Northumberland." 4

They are headstrong believers and defenders of their opin- ion, and not less resolute in maintaining their whim and per- versity. Hezekiah Woodward wrote a book against the Lord's Prayer.5 And one can believe that Burton, the Anatomist of

Melancholy, having predicted from the stars the hour of his death, slipped the knot himself round his own neck, not to falsify his horoscope.[6]

Their looks bespeak an invincible stoutness: they have extreme difficulty to run away, and will die game. Wellington said of the young coxcombs of the Life-Guards, delicately brought up, "But the puppies fight well;" and Nelson said of his sailors, "They really mind shot no more than peas." [7] Of absolute stoutness no nation has more or better examples. They are good at storming redoubts, at boarding frigates, at dying in the last ditch, or any desperate service which has daylight and honor in it; but not, I think, at enduring the rack, or any passive obedience, like jumping off a castle-roof at the word of a czar. Being both vascular and highly organized, so as to be very sensible of pain; and intellectual, so as to see reason and glory in a matter.

Of that constitutional force which yields the supplies of the day, they have the more than enough; the excess which creates courage on fortitude, genius in poetry, invention in mechanics, enterprise in trade, magnificence in wealth, splendor in ceremonies, petulance and projects in youth. The young men have a rude health which runs into peccant humors. They drink brandy like water, cannot expend their quantities of waste strength on riding, hunting, swimming and fencing, and run into absurd frolics with the gravity of the Eumenides.[8] They stoutly carry into every nook and corner of the earth their turbulent sense; leaving no lie uncontradicted; no pretension unexamined. They chew hasheesh; cut themselves with poisoned creases; swing their hammock in the boughs of the Bohon Upas; taste every poison; buy every secret; at Naples they put St. Januarius's blood in an alembic; they saw a hole into the head of the "winking Virgin," to know why she winks; measure with an English foot-rule every cell of the Inquisition, every Turkish caaba, every

Holy of holies; translate and send to Bentley the arcanum bribed and bullied away from shuddering Bramins; and measure their own strength by the terror they cause.[9] These travellers are of every class, the best and the worst; and it may easily happen that those of rudest behavior are taken notice of and remembered. The Saxon melancholy in the vulgar rich and poor appears as gushes of ill-humor, which every check exasperates into sarcasm and vituperation. There are multitudes of rude young English who have the self-sufficiency and bluntness of their nation, and who, with their disdain of the rest of mankind and with this indigestion and choler, have made the English traveller a proverb for uncomfortable and offensive manners. It was no bad description of the Briton generically, what was said two hundred years ago of one particular Oxford scholar: "He was a very bold man, uttered any thing that came into his mind, not only among his companions, but in public coffee-houses, and would often speak his mind of particular persons then accidentally present, without examining the company he was in; for which he was often reprimanded and several times threatened to be kicked and beaten."

The common Englishman is prone to forget a cardinal article in the bill of social rights, that every man has a right to his own ears. No man can claim to usurp more than a few cubic feet of the audibilities of a public room, or to put upon the company with the loud statement of his crotchets or personalities.

But it is in the deep traits of race that the fortunes of nations are written, and however derived, — whether a happier tribe or mixture of tribes, the air, or what circumstance that mixed for them the golden mean of temperament, — here exists the best stock in the world, broad-fronted, broad-bottomed, best for depth, range and equability; men of aplomb and reserves, great range and many moods, strong

instincts, yet apt for culture; war-class as well as clerks; earls
and tradesmen; wise minority, as well as foolish majority;
abysmal temperament, hiding wells of wrath, and glooms on
which no sunshine settles, alternated with a common sense
and humanity which hold them fast to every piece of cheerful
duty; making this temperament a sea to which all storms are
superficial; a race to which their fortunes flow, as if they
alone had the elastic organization at once fine and robust
enough for dominion; as if the burly inexpressive, now mute
and contumacious, now fierce and sharp-tongued dragon,
which once made the island light with his fiery breath, had
bequeathed his ferocity to his conqueror. They hide virtues
under vices, or the semblance of them. It is the misshapen
hairy Scandinavian troll again, who lifts the cart out of
the mire, "threshes the corn that ten day-laborers could not
end," [10] but it is done in the dark and with muttered male-
dictions. He is a churl with a soft place in his heart, whose
speech is a brash of bitter waters, but who loves to help you
at a pinch. He says no, and serves you, and your thanks
disgust him. Here was lately a cross-grained miser, odd and
ugly, resembling in countenance the portrait of Punch with
the laugh left out;[11] rich by his own industry; sulking in a
lonely house; who never gave a dinner to any man and dis-
dained all courtesies; yet as true a worshipper of beauty in
form and color as ever existed, and profusely pouring over
the cold mind of his countrymen creations of grace and truth,
removing the reproach of sterility from English art, catching
from their savage climate every fine hint, and importing
into their galleries every tint and trait of sunnier cities and
skies; making an era in painting; and when he saw that the
splendor of one of his pictures in the Exhibition[12] dimmed
his rival's that hung next it, secretly took a brush and black-
ened his own.

They do not wear their heart in their sleeve for daws to

peck at.[13] They have that phlegm or staidness which it is a compliment to disturb. "Great men," said Aristotle, "are always of a nature originally melancholy." [14] 'T is the habit of a mind which attaches to abstractions with a passion which gives vast results. They dare to displease, they do not speak to expectation. They like the sayers of No, better than the sayers of Yes. Each of them has an opinion which he feels it becomes him to express all the more that it differs from yours. They are meditating opposition. This gravity is inseparable from minds of great resources.

There is an English hero superior to the French, the German, the Italian, or the Greek. When he is brought to the strife with fate, he sacrifices a richer material possession, and on more purely metaphysical grounds. He is there with his own consent, face to face with fortune, which he defies. On deliberate choice and from grounds of character, he has elected his part to live and die for, and dies with grandeur. This race has added new elements to humanity and has a deeper root in the world.

They have great range of scale, from ferocity to exquisite refinement. With larger scale, they have great retrieving power. After running each tendency to an extreme, they try another tack with equal heat. More intellectual than other races, when they live with other races they do not take their language, but bestow their own. They subsidize other nations, and are not subsidized. They proselyte, and are not proselyted. They assimilate other races to themselves, and are not assimilated. The English did not calculate the conquest of the Indies. It fell to their character. So they administer, in different parts of the world, the codes of every empire and race; in Canada, old French law; in the Mauritius, the Code Napoleon; in the West Indies, the edicts of the Spanish Cortes; in the East Indies, the Laws of Menu; in the Isle of Man, of the Scandinavian Thing; at the Cape of Good Hope, of the old Netherlands; and in the Ionian Islands, the Pandects of Justinian.[15]

They are very conscious of their advantageous position in history. England is the lawgiver, the patron, the instructor, the ally. Compare the tone of the French and of the English press: the first querulous, captious, sensitive about English opinion; the English press never timorous about French opinion, but arrogant and contemptuous.

They are testy and headstrong through an excess of will and bias; churlish as men sometimes please to be who do not forget a debt, who ask no favors and who will do what they like with their own. With education and intercourse, these asperities wear off and leave the good-will pure. If anatomy is reformed according to national tendencies, I suppose the spleen[16] will hereafter be found in the Englishman, not found in the American, and differencing the one from the other. I anticipate another anatomical discovery, that this organ will be found to be cortical and caducous;[17] that they are superficially morose, but at last tender-hearted, herein differing from Rome and the Latin nations. Nothing savage, nothing mean resides in the English heart. They are subject to panics of credulity and of rage, but the temper of the nation, however disturbed, settles itself soon and easily, as, in this temperate zone, the sky after whatever storms clears again, and serenity is its normal condition.

A saving stupidity masks and protects their perception, as the curtain of the eagle's eye. Our swifter Americans, when they first deal with English, pronounce them stupid; but, later, do them justice as people who wear well, or hide their strength. To understand the power of performance that is in their finest wits, in the patient Newton, or in the versatile transcendent poets, or in the Dugdales, Gibbons, Hallams, Eldons and Peels, one should see how English day-laborers hold out. High and low, they are of an unctuous texture.

There is an adipocere[18] in their constitution, as if they had oil also for their mental wheels and could perform vast amounts of work without damaging themselves.

Even the scale of expense on which people live, and to which scholars and professional men conform, proves the tension of their muscle, when vast numbers are found who can each lift this enormous load. I might even add, their daily feasts argue a savage vigor of body.

No nation was ever so rich in able men; "Gentlemen," as Charles I. said of Strafford, "whose abilities might make a prince rather afraid than ashamed in the greatest affairs of state;" men of such temper, that, like Baron Vere, "had one seen him returning from a victory, he would by his silence have suspected that he had lost the day; and, had he beheld him in a retreat, he would have collected him a conqueror by the cheerfulness of his spirit." [19]

The following passage from the "Heimskringla" might almost stand as a portrait of the modern Englishman: — "Haldor was very stout and strong and remarkably handsome in appearances. King Harold gave him this testimony, that he, among all his men, cared least about doubtful circumstances, whether they betokened danger or pleasure; for, whatever turned up, he was never in higher nor in lower spirits, never slept less nor more on account of them, nor ate nor drank but according to his custom. Haldor was not a man of many words, but short in conversation, told his opinion bluntly and was obstinate and hard: and this could not please the king, who had many clever people about him, zealous in his service. Haldor remained a short time with the king, and then came to Iceland, where he took up his abode in Hiardaholt and dwelt in that farm to a very advanced age." [20]

The national temper, in the civil history, is not flashy or whiffling. The slow, deep English mass smoulders with fire, which at last sets all its borders in flame. The wrath of London is not French wrath, but has a long memory, and, in its hottest heat, a register and rule.

Half their strength they put not forth. They are capable of a sublime resolution, and if hereafter the war of races, often predicted, and making itself a war of opinions also (a question of despotism and liberty coming from Eastern Europe), should menace the English civilization, these sea-kings may take once again to their floating castles and find a new home and a second millennium of power in their colonies.

The stability of England is the security of the modern world. If the English race were as mutable as the French, what reliance? But the English stand for liberty. The conservative, money-loving, lord-loving English are yet liberty-loving; and so freedom is safe: for they have more personal force than any other people. The nation always resist the immoral action of their government. They think humanely on the affairs of France, of Turkey, of Poland, of Hungary, of Schleswig Holstein, though overborne by the statecraft of the rulers at last.[21]

Does the early history of each tribe show the permanent bias, which, though not less potent, is masked as the tribe spreads its activity into colonies, commerce, codes, arts, letters? The early history shows it, as the musician plays the air which he proceeds to conceal in a tempest of variations. In Alfred, in the Northmen, one may read the genius of the English society, namely that private life is the place of honor. Glory, a career, and ambition, words familiar to the longitude of Paris, are seldom heard in English speech. Nelson wrote from their hearts his homely telegraph, "England expects every man to do his duty." [22]

For actual service, for the dignity of a profession, or to appease diseased or inflamed talent, the army and navy may be entered (the worst boys doing well in the navy); and the civil service in departments where serious official work is done; and they hold in esteem the barrister engaged in the severer studies of the law. But the calm, sound and most British Briton shrinks from public life as charlatanism, and respects an economy founded on agriculture, coalmines, manufactures or trade, which secures an independence through the creation of real values.

They wish neither to command nor obey, but to be kings in their own houses. They are intellectual and deeply enjoy literature; they like well to have the world served up to them in books, maps, models, and every mode of exact information, and, though not creators in art, they value its refinement. They are ready for leisure, can direct and fill their own day, nor need so much as others the constraint of a necessity. But the history of the nation discloses, at every turn, this original predilection for private independence, and however this inclination may have been disturbed by the bribes with which their vast colonial power has warped men out of orbit, the inclination endures, and forms and reforms the laws, letters, manners and occupations. They choose that welfare which is compatible with the commonwealth, knowing that such alone is stable; as wise merchants prefer investments in the three per cents.[23]

CHAPTER IX

Cockayne

The English are a nation of humorists.[1] Individual right is pushed to the uttermost bound compatible with public order. Property is so perfect that it seems the craft of that race, and not to exist elsewhere. The king cannot step on an acre which the peasant refuses to sell. A testator endows a dog or a rookery, and Europe cannot interfere with his absurdity. Every individual has his particular way of living, which he pushes to folly, and the decided sympathy of his compatriots is engaged to back up Mr. Crump's whim by statutes and chancellors and horse-guards.[2] There is no freak so ridiculous but some Englishman has attempted to immortalize by money and law. British citizenship is as omnipotent as Roman was. Mr. Cockayne is very sensible of this. The pursy[3] man means by freedom the right to do as he pleases, and does wrong in order to feel his freedom, and makes a conscience of persisting in it.

He is intensely patriotic, for his country is so small. His confidence in the power and performance of his nation makes him provokingly incurious about other nations. He dislikes foreigners. Swedenborg, who lived much in England, notes "the similitude of minds among the English, in consequence of which they contract familiarity with friends who are of that nation, and seldom with others; and they regard foreigners as one looking through a telescope from the top of a palace regards those who dwell or wander about out of the city." [4] A much older traveller, the Venetian who wrote the "Relation of England," [5] in 1500, says: — "The English are great lovers of themselves and of every thing belonging to them. They think that there are no other men than themselves and no other world but England; and whenever they see a handsome foreigner, they say that he looks like an Englishman and it is a great pity he should not be an Englishman; and whenever they partake of any delicacy with a foreigner, they ask him whether such a thing is made in his country." When he adds epithets of praise, his climax is, "So English;" and when he wishes to pay you the highest compliment, he says, I should not know you from an Englishman. France is, by its natural contrast, a kind of blackboard on which English character draws its own traits in chalk. This arrogance habitually exhibits itself in allusions to the French. I suppose that all men of English blood in America, Europe, or Asia, have a secret feeling of joy that they are not French natives. Mr. Coleridge is said to have given public thanks to God, at the close of a lecture, that he had defended him from being able to utter a single sentence in the French language. I have found that Englishmen have such a good opinion of England, that the ordinary phrases in all good society, of postponing or disparaging one's own things in talking with a stranger, are seriously mistaken by them for an insuppressible homage to the merits of their nation; and the New Yorker or Pennsylvanian who modestly laments the disadvantage of a new country, log-huts and savages, is surprised by the instant and unfeigned commiseration of the whole company, who plainly account all the world out of England a heap of rubbish.

The same insular limitation pinches his foreign politics. He sticks to his traditions and usages, and, so help him God! he will force his island bylaws down the throat of great countries, like India, China, Canada, Australia, and not only so, but impose Wapping on the Congress of Vienna and trample down all nationalities with his taxed boots.[6] Lord Chatham goes for liberty and no taxation without representation; — for that is British law; but not a hobnail shall they dare make in America, but buy their nails in England; — for that also is British law; and the fact that British commerce was to be re-created by the independence of America, took them all by surprise.

In short, I am afraid that English nature is so rank and aggressive as to be a little incompatible with every other. The world is not wide enough for two.

But beyond this nationality, it must be admitted, the island offers a daily worship to the old Norse god Brage,[7] celebrated among our Scandinavian forefathers for his eloquence and majestic air. The English have a steady courage that fits them for great attempts and endurance: they have also a petty courage, through which every man delights in showing himself for what he is and in doing what he can; so that in all companies, each of them has too good an opinion of himself to imitate any body. He hides no defect of his form, features, dress, connection, or birthplace, for he thinks every circumstance belonging to him comes recommended to you. If one of them have a bald, or a red, or a green head, or bow legs, or a scar, or mark, or a paunch, or a squeaking or a raven voice, he has persuaded himself that there is something modish and becoming in it, and that it sits well on him.

But nature makes nothing in vain, and this little superfluity of self-regard in the English brain is one of the secrets of their power and history. It sets every man on being and doing what he really is and can. It takes away a dodging, skulking, secondary air, and encourages a frank and manly bearing, so that each man makes the most of himself and loses no opportunity for want of pushing. A man's personal defects will commonly have, with the rest of the world, precisely that importance which they have to himself. If he makes light of them, so will other men. We all find in these a convenient meter of character, since a little man would be ruined by the vexation. I remember a shrewd politician, in one of our western cities, told me that "he had known several successful statesmen made by their foible." And another, an ex-governor of Illinois, said to me, "If the man knew anything, he would sit in a corner and be modest; but he is such an ignorant peacock that he goes bustling up and down and hits on extraordinary discoveries." [8]

There is also this benefit in brag, that the speaker is unconsciously expressing his own ideal. Humor him by all means, draw it all out and hold him to it. Their culture generally enables the travelled English to avoid any ridiculous extremes of this self-pleasing, and to give it an agreeable air. Then the natural disposition is fostered by the respect which they find entertained in the world for English ability. It was said of Louis XIV., that his gait and air were becoming enough in so great a monarch, yet would have been ridiculous in another man; so the prestige of the English name warrants a certain confident bearing, which a Frenchman or Belgian could not carry. At all events, they feel themselves at liberty to assume the most extraordinary tone on the subject of English merits.

An English lady on the Rhine hearing a German speaking of her party as foreigners, exclaimed, "No, we are not foreigners; we are English; it is you that are foreigners." They tell you daily in London the story of the Frenchman and Englishman who quarrelled. Both were unwilling to fight, but their companions put them up to it; at last it was agreed that they should fight alone, in the dark, and with pistols: the candles were put out, and the Englishman, to make sure not to hit any body, fired up the chimney, — and brought down the Frenchman. They have no curiosity about foreigners, and answer any information you may volunteer with "Oh, Oh!" until the informant makes up his mind that they shall die in their ignorance, for any help he will offer. There are really no limits to this conceit, though brighter men among them make painful efforts to be candid.

The habit of brag runs through all classes, from the "Times" newspaper through politicians and poets, through Wordsworth, Carlyle, Mill and Sydney Smith, down to the boys of Eton.[9] In the gravest treatise on political economy, in a philosophical essay, in books of science, one is surprised by the most innocent exhibition of unflinching nationality. In a tract on Corn, a most amiable and accomplished gentleman writes thus: — "Though Britain, according to Bishop Berkeley's idea, were surrounded by a wall of brass ten thousand cubits in height, still she would as far excel the rest of the globe in riches, as she now does both in this secondary quality and in the more important ones of freedom, virtue and science." [10]

The English dislike the American structure of society, whilst yet trade, mills, public education and Chartism are doing what they can to create in England the same social condition. America is the paradise of the economists; is the favorable exception invariably quoted to the rules of ruin; but when he speaks directly of the Americans the islander forgets his philosophy and remembers his disparaging anecdotes.

But this childish patriotism costs something, like all narrowness. The English sway of their colonies has no root of kindness. They govern by their arts and ability; they are more just than kind; and whenever an abatement of their power is felt, they have not conciliated the affection on which to rely.

Coarse local distinctions, as those of nation, province, or

town, are useful in the absence of real ones; but we must not insist on these accidental lines. Individual traits are always triumphing over national ones. There is no fence in metaphysics discriminating Greek, or English, or Spanish science. Æsop and Montaigne, Cervantes and Saadi are men of the world; and to wave our own flag at the dinner table or in the University is to carry the boisterous dulness of a fire-club into a polite circle. Nature and destiny are always on the watch for our follies. Nature trips us up when we strut; and there are curious examples in history on this very point of national pride.

George of Cappadocia, born at Epiphania in Cilicia, was a low parasite who got a lucrative contract to supply the army with bacon.[11] A rogue and informer, he got rich and was forced to run from justice. He saved his money, embraced Arianism, collected a library, and got promoted by a faction to the episcopal throne of Alexandria. When Julian came, A. D. 361, George was dragged to prison; the prison was burst open by the mob and George was lynched, as he deserved. And this precious knave became, in good time, Saint George of England, patron of chivalry, emblem of victory and civility and the pride of the best blood of the modern world.

Strange, that the solid truth-speaking Briton should derive from an impostor. Strange, that the New World should have no better luck, — that broad America must wear the name of a thief. Amerigo Vespucci, the pickledealer at Seville, who went out, in 1499, a subaltern with Hojeda, and whose highest naval rank was boatswain's mate in an expedition that never sailed, managed in this lying world to supplant Columbus and baptize half the earth with his own dishonest name. Thus nobody can throw stones. We are equally badly off in our founders; and the false pickledealer is an offset to the false bacon-seller.[12]

CHAPTER X

Wealth

There is no country in which so absolute a homage is paid to wealth. In America there is a touch of shame when a man exhibits the evidences of large property, as if after all it needed apology. But the Englishman has pure pride in his wealth, and esteems it a final certificate. A coarse logic rules throughout all English souls; — if you have merit, can you not show it by your good clothes and coach and horses? How can a man be a gentleman without a pipe of wine? Haydon says, "There is a fierce resolution to make every man live according to the means he possesses." [1] There is a mixture of religion in it. They are under the Jewish law, and read with sonorous emphasis that their days shall be long in the land, they shall have sons and daughters, flocks and herds, wine and oil. In exact proportion is the reproach of poverty. They do not wish to be represented except by opulent men. An Englishman who has lost his fortune is said to have died of a broken heart. The last term of insult is, "a beggar." Nelson said, "The want of fortune is a crime which I can never get over." [2] Sydney Smith said, "Poverty is infamous in England." [3] And one of their recent writers speaks, in reference to a private and scholastic life, of "the grave moral deterioration which follows an empty exchequer." You shall find this sentiment, if not so frankly put, yet deeply implied in the novels and romances of the present century, and not only in these, but in biography and in the votes of public assemblies, in the tone of the preaching and in the table-talk.

I was lately turning over Wood's *Athenæ Oxonienses,* and looking naturally for another standard in a chronicle of the scholars of Oxford for two hundred years. But I found the two disgraces in that, as in most English books, are, first, disloyalty to Church and State, and second, to be born poor, or to come to poverty. A natural fruit of England is the brutal political economy. Malthus finds no cover laid at nature's table for the laborer's son.[4] In 1809, the majority in Parliament expressed itself by the language of Mr. Fuller in the House of Commons, "If you do not like the country, damn you, you can leave it." [5] When Sir S. Romilly proposed his bill forbidding parish officers to bind children apprentices at a greater distance than forty miles from their home, Peel opposed, and Mr. Wortley said, "though, in the higher ranks, to cultivate family affections was a good thing, it was not so among the lower orders. Better take them away from those who might deprave them. And it was highly injurious to trade to stop binding to manufacturers, as it must raise the price of labor and of manufactured goods." [6]

The respect for truth of facts in England is equalled only by the respect for wealth. It is at once the pride of art of the Saxon, as he is a wealth-maker, and his passion for independence. The Englishman believes that every man must take care of himself, and has himself to thank if he do not mend his condition. To pay their debts is their national point of honor. From the Exchequer and the East India House to the huckster's shop, every thing prospers because it is solvent. The British armies are solvent and pay for what they take. The British empire is solvent; for in spite of the huge national debt, the valuation mounts. During the war from 1789 to 1815,[7] whilst they complained that they were taxed within an inch of their lives, and by dint of enormous taxes were subsidizing all the continent against France, the English were growing rich every year faster than any people ever grew before. It is their maxim that the weight of taxes must be calculated, not by what is taken, but by what is left. Solvency is in the ideas and mechanism of an Englishman. The Crystal Palace is not considered honest until it pays;[8] no matter how much convenience, beauty, or *éclat*, it must be self-supporting. They are contented with slower steamers, as long as they know that swifter boats lose money. They proceed logically by the double method of labor and thrift. Every household exhibits an exact economy, and nothing of that uncalculated headlong expenditure which families use in America. If they cannot pay, they do not buy; for they have no presumption of better fortunes next year, as our people have; and they say without shame, I cannot afford it. Gentlemen do not hesitate to ride in the second-class cars, or in the second cabin. An economist, or a man who can proportion his means and his ambition, or bring the year round with expenditure which expresses his character without embarrassing one day of his future, is already a master of life, and a freeman. Lord Burleigh writes to his son that "one ought never to devote more than two thirds of his income to the ordinary expenses of life, since the extraordinary will be certain to absorb the other third." [9]

The ambition to create value evokes every kind of ability; government becomes a manufacturing corporation, and every house a mill. The headlong bias to utility will let no talent lie in a napkin,[10] — if possible will teach spiders to weave silk stockings. An Englishman, while he eats and drinks no more or not much more than another man, labors three times as many hours in the course of a year as another European; or, his life as a workman is three lives. He works fast. Every thing in England is at a quick pace. They have reinforced their own productivity by the creation of that marvellous machinery which differences this age from any other age.

It is a curious chapter in modern history, the growth of the machine-shop. Six hundred years ago, Roger Bacon explained the precession of the equinoxes, the consequent necessity of the reform of the calendar; measured the length of the year; invented gunpowder; and announced (as if looking from his lofty cell, over five centuries, into ours), that "machines can be constructed to drive ships more rapidly than a whole galley of rowers could do; nor would they need anything but a pilot to steer them. Carriages also might be constructed to move with an incredible speed, without the aid of any animal. Finally, it would not be impossible to make machines which by means of a suit of wings should fly in the air in the manner of birds." But the secret slept with Bacon.[11] The six hundred years have not yet fulfilled his words. Two centuries ago the sawing of timber was done by hand; the carriage wheels ran on wooden axles; the land was tilled by wooden ploughs. And it was to little purpose that they had pit-coal, or that looms were improved, unless Watt and Stephenson had taught them to work force-pumps and power-looms by steam. The great strides were all taken within the last hundred years. The Life of Sir Robert Peel, in his day the model Englishman, very properly has, for a frontispiece, a drawing of the spinning-jenny, which wove the web of his fortunes. Hargreaves invented the spinning-jenny, and died in a workhouse.[12] Arkwright[13] improved the invention, and the machine dispensed with the work of ninety-nine men; that is, one spinner could do as much work as one hundred had done before. The loom was improved further. But the men would sometimes strike for wages and combine against the masters, and, about 1829–30, much fear was felt lest the trade would be drawn away by these interruptions and the emigration of the spinners to

Belgium and the United States. Iron and steel are very obedient. Whether it were not possible to make a spinner that would not rebel, nor mutter, nor scowl, nor strike for wages, nor emigrate? At the solicitation of the masters, after a mob and riot at Staley Bridge, Mr. Roberts of Manchester undertook to create this peaceful fellow, instead of the quarrelsome fellow God had made.[14] After a few trials, he succeeded, and in 1830 procured a patent for his self-acting mule; a creation, the delight of mill-owners, and "destined," they said, "to restore order among the industrious classes;" a machine requiring only a child's hand to piece the broken yarns. As Arkwright had destroyed domestic spinning, so Roberts destroyed the factory spinner. The power of machinery in Great Britain, in mills, has been computed to be equal to 600,000,000 men, one man being able by the aid of steam to do the work which required two hundred and fifty men to accomplish fifty years ago. The production has been commensurate. England already had this laborious race, rich soil, water, wood, coal, iron and favorable climate. Eight hundred years ago commerce had made it rich, and it was recorded, "England is the richest of all the northern nations." The Norman historians[15] recite that "in 1067, William carried with him into Normandy, from England, more gold and silver then had ever before been seen in Gaul." But when, to this labor and trade and these native resources was added this goblin of steam, with his myriad arms, never tired, working night and day everlastingly, the amassing of property has run out of all figures. It makes the motor[16] of the last ninety years. The steampipe has added to her population and wealth the equivalent of four or five Englands. Forty thousand ships are entered in Lloyd's lists. The yield of wheat has gone on from 2,000,000 quarters[17] in the time of the Stuarts, to 13,-000,000 in 1854. A thousand million of pounds sterling are said to compose the floating money of commerce. In 1848,

Lord John Russell [18] stated that the people of this country had laid out £300,000,000 of capital in railways, in the last four years. But a better measure than these sounding figures is the estimate that there is wealth enough in England to support the entire population in idleness for one year.

The wise, versatile, all-giving machinery makes chisels, roads, locomotives, telegraphs. Whitworth divides a bar to a millionth of an inch.[19] Steam twines huge cannon into wreaths, as easily as it braids straw, and vies with the volcanic forces which twisted the strata. It can clothe shingle mountains with ship-oaks,[20] make sword-blades that will cut gun-barrels in two. In Egypt, it can plant forests, and bring rain after three thousand years.[21] Already it is ruddering the balloon, and the next war will be fought in the air. But another machine more potent in England than steam is the Bank. It votes an issue of bills, population is stimulated and cities rise; it refuses loans, and emigration empties the country; trade sinks; revolutions break out; kings are dethroned. By these new agents our social system is moulded. By dint of steam and of money, war and commerce are changed. Nations have lost their old omnipotence; the patriotic tie does not hold. Nations are getting obsolete, we go and live where we will. Steam has enabled men to choose what law they will live under. Money makes place for them. The telegraph is a limp band that will hold the Fenriswolf of war.[22] For now that a telegraph line runs through France and Europe from London,[23] every message it transmits makes stronger by one thread the band which war will have to cut.

The introduction of these elements gives new resources to existing proprietors. A sporting duke may fancy that the state depends on the House of Lords, but the engineer sees that every stroke of the steam-piston gives value to the duke's land, fills it with tenants; doubles, quadruples, centuples the duke's capital, and creates new measures and new necessities for the culture of his children. Of course it draws the nobility into the competition, as stock-holders in the mine, the canal, the railway, in the application of steam to agriculture, and sometimes into trade. But it also introduces large classes into the same competition; the old energy of the Norse race arms itself with these magnificent powers; new men prove an overmatch for the land-owner, and the mill buys out the castle. Scandinavian Thor, who once forged his bolts in icy Hecla and built galleys by lonely fiords, in England has advanced with the times, has shorn his beard, enters Parliament, sits down at a desk in the India House and lends Miollnir to Birmingham for a steam-hammer.[24]

The creation of wealth in England in the last ninety years is a main fact in modern history. The wealth of London determines prices all over the globe. All things precious, or useful, or amusing, or intoxicating, are sucked into this commerce and floated to London. Some English private fortunes reach, and some exceed a million of dollars a year. A hundred thousand palaces adorn the island. All that can feed the senses and passions, all that can succor the talent or arm the hands of the intelligent middle class, who never spare in what they buy for their own consumption; all that can aid science, gratify taste, or soothe comfort, is in open market. Whatever is excellent and beautiful in civil, rural, or ecclesiastic architecture, in fountain, garden, or grounds, — the English noble crosses sea and land to see and to copy at home. The taste and science of thirty peaceful generations; the gardens which Evelyn planted;[25] the temples and pleasure-houses which Inigo Jones and Christopher Wren built;[26] the wood that Gibbons carved;[27] the taste of foreign and domestic artists, Shenstone, Pope, Brown, Loudon, Paxton,[28] — are in the vast auction, and the hereditary principle heaps on the owner of to-day the benefit of ages of owners. The present possessors are to the full as absolute as any of their fathers in choosing and procuring what they like. This comfort and splendor, the breadth of lake and mountain, tillage, pasture and park, sumptuous castle and modern villa, — all consist with perfect order. They have no revolutions; no horse-guards dictating to the crown; no Parisian *poissardes*[29] and barricades; no mob: but drowsy habitude, daily dress-dinners, wine and ale and beer and gin and sleep.

With this power of creation and this passion for independence, property has reached an ideal perfection. It is felt and treated as the national life-blood. The laws are framed to give property the securest possible basis, and the provisions to lock and transmit it have exercised the cunningest heads in a profession which never admits a fool. The rights of property nothing but felony and treason can override. The house is a castle which the king cannot enter. The Bank is a strong box to which the king has no key. Whatever surly sweetness possession can give, is tasted in England to the dregs. Vested rights are awful things, and absolute possession gives the smallest freeholder identity of interest with the duke. High stone fences and padlocked garden-gates announce the absolute will of the owner to be alone. Every whim of exaggerated egotism is put into stone and iron, into silver and gold, with costly deliberation and detail.

An Englishman hears that the Queen Dowager[30] wishes to establish some claim to put her park paling a rod forward into his grounds, so as to get a coachway and save her a mile to the avenue. Instantly he transforms his paling into stone-masonry, solid as the walls of Cuma,[31] and all Europe cannot prevail on him to sell or compound for an inch of the land. They delight in a freak as the proof of their sovereign freedom. Sir Edward Boynton, at Spic Park at Cadenham,[32] on a precipice of incomparable prospect, built a house like a long barn, which had not a window on the prospect side. Strawberry Hill of Horace Walpole,[33] Fonthill Abbey of Mr.

Beckford,[34] were freaks; and Newstead Abbey became one in the hands of Lord Byron.[35]

But the proudest result of this creation has been the great and refined forces it has put at the disposal of the private citizen. In the social world an Englishman to-day has the best lot. He is a king in a plain coat. He goes with the most powerful protection, keeps the best company, is armed by the best education, is seconded by wealth; and his English name and accidents are like a flourish of trumpets announcing him. This, with his quiet style of manners, gives him the power of a sovereign without the inconveniences which belong to that rank. I much prefer the condition of an English gentleman of the better class to that of any potentate in Europe, — whether for travel, or for opportunity of society, or for access to means of science or study, or for mere comfort and easy healthy relation to people at home.

Such as we have seen is the wealth of England; a mighty mass, and made good in whatever details we care to explore. The cause and spring of it is the wealth of temperament in the people. The wonder of Britain is this plenteous nature. Her worthies are ever surrounded by as good men as themselves; each is a captain a hundred strong, and that wealth of men is represented again in the faculty of each individual, — that he has waste strength, power to spare. The English are so rich and seem to have established a tap-root in the bowels of the planet, because they are constitutionally fertile and creative.

But a man must keep an eye on his servants, if he would not have them rule him. Man is a shrewd inventor and is ever taking the hint of a new machine from his own structure, adapting some secret of his own anatomy in iron, wood and leather to some required function in the work of the world. But it is found that the machine unmans the user. What he gains in making cloth, he loses in general power.

There should be temperance in making cloth, as well as in eating. A man should not be a silk-worm, nor a nation a tent of caterpillars. The robust rural Saxon degenerates in the mills to the Leicester stockinger,[36] to the imbecile Manchester spinner, — far on the way to be spiders and needles. The incessant repetition of the same handwork dwarfs the man, robs him of his strength, wit and versatility, to make a pin-polisher, a buckle-maker, or any other specialty; and presently, in a change of industry, whole towns are sacrificed like ant-hills, when the fashion of shoe-strings supersedes buckles, when cotton takes the place of linen, or railways of turn-pikes, or when commons are inclosed by landlords. Then society is admonished of the mischief of the division of labor, and that the best political economy is care and culture of men; for in these crises all are ruined except such as are proper individuals, capable of thought and of new choice and the application of their talent to new labor. Then again come in new calamities. England is aghast at the disclosure of her fraud in the adulteration of food, of drugs and of almost every fabric in her mills and shops; finding that milk will not nourish, nor sugar sweeten, nor bread satisfy, nor pepper bite the tongue, nor glue stick. In true England all is false and forged. This too is the reaction of machinery, but of the larger machinery of commerce. 'T is not, I suppose, want of probity, so much as the tyranny of trade, which necessitates a perpetual competition of underselling, and that again a perpetual deterioration of the fabric.

The machinery has proved, like the balloon, unmanageable, and flies away with the aeronaut. Steam from the first hissed and screamed to warn him; it was dreadful with its explosion, and crushed the engineer. The machinist has wrought and watched, engineers and firemen without number have been sacrificed in learning to tame and guide the monster. But harder still it has proved to resist and rule the dragon Money, with his paper wings. Chancellors and Boards of Trade, Pitt, Peel and Robinson[37] and their Parliaments and their whole generation adopted false principles, and went to their graves in the belief that they were enriching the country which they were impoverishing. They congratulated each other on ruinous expedients. It is rare to find a merchant who knows why a crisis occurs in trade, why prices rise or fall, or who knows the mischief of paper-money. In the culmination of national prosperity, in the annexation of countries; building of ships, depots, towns; in the influx of tons of gold and silver; amid the chuckle of chancellors and financiers, it was found that bread rose to famine prices, that the yeoman was forced to sell his cow and pig, his tools and his acre of land; and the dreadful barometer of the poor-rates was touching the point of ruin. The poor-rate was sucking in the solvent classes and forcing an exodus of farmers and mechanics. What befalls from the violence of financial crises, befalls daily in the violence of artificial legislation.

Such a wealth has England earned, ever new, bounteous and augmenting. But the question recurs, does she take the step beyond, namely to the wise use, in view of the supreme wealth of nations? We estimate the wisdom of nations by seeing what they did with their surplus capital. And, in view of these injuries, some compensation has been attempted in England. A part of the money earned returns to the brain to buy schools, libraries, bishops, astronomers, chemists and artists with; and a part to repair the wrongs of this intemperate weaving, by hospitals, savings-banks, Mechanics' Institutes, public grounds and other charities and amenities. But the antidotes are frightfully inadequate, and the evil requires a deeper cure, which time and a simpler social organization must supply. At present she does not rule her wealth. She is simply a good England, but no divinity, or wise and instructed soul. She too is in the stream of fate, one victim more in a common catastrophe.

But being in the fault, she has the misfortune of greatness to be held as the chief offender. England must be held responsible for the despotism of expense. Her prosperity, the splendor which so much manhood and talent and perseverance has thrown upon vulgar aims, is the very argument of materialism. Her success strengthens the hands of base wealth. Who can propose to youth poverty and wisdom, when mean gain has arrived at the conquest of letters and arts; when English success has grown out of the very renunciation of principles, and the dedication to outsides? A civility of trifles, of money and expense, an erudition of sensation takes place, and the putting as many impediments as we can between the man and his objects. Hardly the bravest among them have the manliness to resist it successfully. Hence it has come that not the aims of a manly life, but the means of meeting a certain ponderous expense, is that which is to be considered by a youth in England emerging from his minority. A large family is reckoned a misfortune. And it is a consolation in the death of the young, that a source of expense is closed.

CHAPTER XI

Aristocracy

The feudal character of the English state, now that it is getting obsolete, glares a little, in contrast with the democratic tendencies. The inequality of power and property shocks republican nerves. Palaces, halls, villas, walled parks, all over England, rival the splendor of royal seats. Many of the halls, like Haddon or Kedleston, are beautiful desolations.[1] The proprietor never saw them, or never lived in them. Primogeniture built these sumptuous piles, and I suppose it is the sentiment of every traveller, as it was mine, It was well to come ere these were gone. Primogeniture is a cardinal rule of English property and institutions. Laws, customs, manners, the very persons and faces, affirm it.

The frame of society is aristocratic, the taste of the people is loyal. The estates, names and manners of the nobles flatter the fancy of the people and conciliate the necessary support. In spite of broken faith, stolen charters and the devastation of society by the profligacy of the court, we take sides as we read for the loyal England and King Charles's "return to his right" with his Cavaliers,[2] — knowing what a heartless trifler he is, and what a crew of God-forsaken robbers they are. The people of England knew as much. But the fair idea of a settled government connecting itself with heraldic names, with the written and oral history of Europe, and, at last, with the Hebrew religion and the oldest traditions of the world, was too pleasing a vision to be shattered by a few offensive realities and the politics of shoe-makers and costermongers. The hopes of the commoners take the same direction with the interest of the patricians. Every man who becomes rich buys land and does what he can to fortify the nobility, into which he hopes to rise. The Anglican clergy are identified with the aristocracy. Time and law have made the joining and moulding perfect in every part. The Cathedrals, the Universities, the national music, the popular romances, conspire to uphold the heraldry which the current politics of the day are sapping. The taste of the people is conservative. They are proud of the castles, and of the language and symbol of chivalry. Even the word *lord* is the luckiest style that is used in any language to designate a patrician. The superior education and manners of the nobles recommend them to the country.

The Norwegian pirate got what he could and held it for his eldest son. The Norman noble, who was the Norwegian pirate baptized, did likewise. There was this advantage of Western over Oriental nobility, that this was recruited from below. English history is aristocracy with the doors open. Who has courage and faculty, let him come in. Of course the terms of admission to this club are hard and high. The selfishness of the nobles comes in aid of the interest of the nation to require signal merit. Piracy and war gave place to trade, politics and letters; the war-lord to the law-lord; the law-lord to the merchant and the mill-owner; but the privilege was kept, whilst the means of obtaining it were changed.

The foundations of these families lie deep in Norwegian exploits by sea and Saxon sturdiness on land. All nobility in its beginnings was somebody's natural superiority. The things these English have done were not done without peril of life, nor without wisdom and conduct; and the first hands, it may be presumed, were often challenged to show their right to their honors, or yield them to better men. "He that will be a head, let him be a bridge," said the Welsh chief Benegridran,[3] when he carried all his men over the river on his back. "He shall have the book," said the mother of Alfred,[4] "who can read it;" and Alfred won it by that title: and I make no doubt that feudal tenure was no sinecure, but baron, knight and tenant often had their memories refreshed, in regard to the service by which they held their lands. The De Veres, Bohuns, Mowbrays and Plantagenets were not addicted to contemplation.[5] The Middle Age adorned itself with proofs of manhood and devotion. Of Richard Beauchamp, Earl of Warwick, the Emperor told Henry V. that no Christian king had such another knight for wisdom, nurture and manhood, and caused him to be named, "Father of curtesie." "Our success in France," says the historian, "lived and died with him." [6]

The war-lord earned his honors, and no donation of land was large, as long as it brought the duty of protecting it, hour by hour, against a terrible enemy. In France and in England, the nobles were, down to a late day, born and bred to war: and the duel, which in peace still held them to the risks of war, diminished the envy that in trading and studious nations would else have pried into their title. They were looked on as men who played high for a great stake.

Great estates are not sinecures, if they are to be kept great. A creative economy is the fuel of magnificence. In the same line of Warwick, the successor next but one[7] to Beauchamp was the stout earl of Henry VI. and Edward IV.[8] Few esteemed themselves in the mode, whose heads were not adorned with the black ragged staff, his badge.[9] At his house in London, six oxen were daily eaten at a breakfast, and every tavern was full of his meat, and who had any acquaintance in his family should have as much boiled and roast as he could carry on a long dagger.

The new age brings new qualities into request; the virtues of pirates gave way to those of planters, merchants, senators and scholars. Comity, social talent and fine manners, no doubt, have had their part also. I have met somewhere with a historiette, which, whether more or less true in its particulars, carries a general truth. "How came the Duke of Bedford by his great landed estates? His ancestor having travelled on the continent, a lively, pleasant man, became the companion of a foreign prince wrecked on Dorsetshire coast, where Mr. Russell lived. The prince recommended him to Henry VIII., who, liking his company, gave him a large share of the plundered church lands." [10]

The pretence is that the noble is of unbroken descent from the Norman, and has never worked for eight hundred years. But the fact is otherwise. Where is Bohun? where is De Vere? The lawyer, the farmer, the silkmercer lies *perdu* under the coronet, and winks to the antiquary to say nothing; especially skilful lawyers, nobody's sons, who did some piece of work at a nice moment for government and were rewarded with ermine.

The national tastes of the English do not lead them to the life of the courtier, but to secure the comfort and independence of their homes. The aristocracy are marked by their predilection for country-life. They are called the county-families. They have often no residence in London and only go thither a short time, during the season, to see the opera; but they concentrate the love and labor of many generations on the building, planting and decoration of their homesteads. Some of them are too old and too proud to wear titles, or, as Sheridan said of Coke, "disdain to hide their head in a coronet;" [11] and some curious examples are cited to show the stability of English families. Their proverb is, that fifty miles from London, a family will last a hundred years; at a hundred miles, two hundred years; and so on; but I doubt that steam, the enemy of time as well as of space, will disturb these ancient rules. Sir Henry Wotton says of the first Duke of Buckingham, "He was born at Brookeby in Leicestershire, where his ancestors had chiefly continued about the space of four hundred years, rather without obscurity, than with any great lustre." [12] Wraxall says that in 1781, Lord Surrey, afterwards Duke of Norfolk, told him that when the year 1783 should arrive, he meant to give a grand festival to all the descendants of the body of Jockey of Norfolk, to mark the day when the dukedom should have remained three hundred years in their house, since its creation by Richard III.[13] Pepys tells us, in writing of an Earl Oxford, in 1666, that the honor had now remained in that name and blood six hundred years.[14]

This long descent of families and this cleaving through ages to the same spot of ground, captivates the imagination. It has too a connection with the names of the towns and districts of the country.

The names are excellent, — an atmosphere of legendary melody spread over the land. Older than all epics and histories which clothe a nation, this undershirt sits close to the body. What history too, and what stores of primitive and savage observation it infolds! Cambridge is the bridge of the Cam; Sheffield the field of the river Sheaf; Leicester the *castra*, or camp, of the Lear, or Leir, (now Soar); Rochdale, of the Roch; Exeter or Excester, the *castra* of the Ex; Exmouth, Dartmouth, Sidmouth, Teignmouth, the mouths of the Ex, Dart, Sid and Teign rivers. Waltham is strong town; Radcliffe is red cliff; and so on: — a sincerity and use in naming very striking to an American, whose country is whitewashed all over by unmeaning names, the cast-off clothes of the country from which its emigrants came; or named at a pinch from a psalm-tune. But the English are those "barbarians" of Jamblichus, who "are stable in their manners, and firmly continue to employ the same words, which also are dear to the gods." [15]

'T is an old sneer that the Irish peerage drew their names from playbooks. The English lords do not call their lands after their own names, but call themselves after their lands, as if the man represented the country that bred him; and they rightly wear the token of the glebe that gave them birth, suggesting that the tie is not cut, but that there in London, — the crags of Argyle, the kail of Cornwall, the downs of Devon, the iron of Wales, the clays of Stafford are neither forgetting nor forgotten, but know the man who was born by them and who, like the long line of his fathers, has carried that crag, that shore, dale, fen, or woodland, in his blood and manners. It has, too, the advantage of suggesting responsibleness. A susceptible man could not wear a name which represented in a strict sense a city or a county of England, without hearing in it a challenge to duty and honor.

The predilection of the patricians for residence in the country, combined with the degree of liberty possessed by the peasant, makes the safety of the English hall. Mirabeau wrote prophetically from England, in 1784, "If revolution break out in France, I tremble for the aristocracy: their chateaux will be reduced to ashes and their blood spilt in torrents. The English tenant would defend his lord to the last extremity." [16] The English go to their estates for grandeur. The French live at court, and exile themselves to their estates for economy. As they do not mean to live with their tenants, they do not conciliate them, but wring from them the last *sous*. Evelyn writes from Blois, in 1644: "The wolves are here in such numbers, that they often come and take children out of the streets; yet will not the Duke, who is sovereign here, permit them to be destroyed." [17]

In evidence of the wealth amassed by ancient families, the traveller is shown the palaces in Piccadilly, Burlington House,

Devonshire House, Lansdowne House in Berkshire Square, and lower down in the city, a few noble houses which still withstand in all their amplitude the encroachment of streets. The Duke of Bedford includes or included a mile square in the heart of London, where the British Museum, once Montague House, now stands, and the land occupied by Woburn Square, Bedford Square, Russell Square.[18] The Marquis of Westminster built within a few years the series of squares called Belgravia. Stafford House is the noblest palace in London. Northumberland House holds its place by Charing Cross. Chesterfield House remains in Audley Street. Sion House and Holland House are in the suburbs.[19] But most of the historical houses are masked or lost in the modern uses to which trade or charity has converted them. A multitude of town palaces contain inestimable galleries of art.

In the country, the size of private estates is more impressive. From Barnard Castle[20] I rode on the highway twenty-three miles from High Force, a fall of the Tees, towards Darlington, past Raby Castle, through the estate of the Duke of Cleveland. The Marquis of Breadalbane[21] rides out of his house a hundred miles in a straight line to the sea,[22] on his own property. The Duke of Sutherland owns the county of Sutherland, stretching across Scotland from sea to sea.[23] The Duke of Devonshire, besides his other estates, owns 96,000 acres in the County of Derby. The Duke of Richmond has 40,000 acres at Goodwood and 300,000 at Gordon Castle. The Duke of Norfolk's park in Sussex is fifteen miles in circuit. An agriculturist bought lately the island of Lewes, in Hebrides, containing 500,000 acres. The possessions of the Earl of Lonsdale gave him eight seats in Parliament.[24] This is the Heptarchy again;[25] and before the Reform of 1832, one hundred and fifty-four persons sent three hundred and seven members to Parliament. The borough-mongers governed England.

These large domains are growing larger. The great estates are absorbing the small freeholds. In 1786 the soil of England was owned by 250,000 corporations and proprietors; and in 1822, by 32,000. These broad estates find room in this narrow island. All over England, scattered at short intervals among ship-yards, mills, mines and forges, are the paradises of the nobles, where the livelong repose and refinement are heightened by the contrast with the roar of industry and necessity, out of which you have stepped aside.

I was surprised to observe the very small attendance usually in the House of Lords. Out of 573 peers, on ordinary days only twenty or thirty. Where are they? I asked. "At home on their estates, devoured by *ennui,* or in the Alps, or up the Rhine, in the Harz Mountains, or in Egypt, or in India, on the Ghauts." [26] But, with such interests at stake, how can these men afford to neglect them? "O," replied my friend,[27] "why should they work for themselves, when every man in England works for them and will suffer before they come to harm?" The hardest radical instantly uncovers and changes his tone to a lord. It was remarked, on the 10th April, 1848 (the day of the Chartist demonstration), that the upper classes were for the first time actively interesting themselves in their own defence, and men of rank were sworn special constables with the rest. "Besides, why need they sit out the debate? Has not the Duke of Wellington, at this moment, their proxies, — the proxies of fifty peers — in his pocket, to vote for them if there be an emergency?" [28]

It is however true that the existence of the House of Peers as a branch of the government entitles them to fill half the Cabinet; and their weight of property and station gives them a virtual nomination of the other half; whilst they have their share in the subordinate offices, as a school of training. This monopoly of political power has given them their intellectual and social eminence in Europe. A few law lords[29] and a few political lords take the brunt of public business. In the army, the nobility fill a large part of the high commissions, and give to these a tone of expense and splendor and also of exclusiveness. They have borne their full share of duty and danger in this service, and there are few noble families which have not paid, in some of their members, the debt of life or limb in the sacrifices of the Russian war.[30] For the rest, the nobility have the lead in matters of state and of expense; in questions of taste, in social usages, in convivial and domestic hospitalities. In general, all that is required of them is to sit securely, to preside at public meetings, to countenance charities and to give the example of that decorum so dear to the British heart.

If one asks, in the critical spirit of the day, what service this class have rendered? — uses appear, or they would have perished long ago. Some of these are easily enumerated, others more subtle make a part of unconscious history. Their institution is one step in the progress of society. For a race yields a nobility in some form, however we name the lords, as surely as it yields women.

The English nobles are high-spirited, active, educated men, born to wealth and power, who have run through every country and kept in every country the best company, have seen every secret of art and nature, and, when men of any ability or ambition, have been consulted in the conduct of every important action. You cannot wield great agencies without lending yourself to them, and when it happens that the spirit of the earl meets his rank and duties, we have the best examples of behavior. Power of any kind readily appears in the manners; and beneficent power, *le talent de bien faire*,[31] gives a majesty which cannot be concealed or resisted.

These people seem to gain as much as they lose by their position. They survey society as from the top of St. Paul's,[32] and if they never hear plain truth from men, they see the best of every thing, in every kind, and they see things so grouped and amassed as to infer easily the sum and genius, instead of tedious particularities. Their good behavior deserves all its fame, and they have that simplicity and that air of repose which are the finest ornament of greatness.

The upper classes have only birth, say the people here, and not thoughts. Yes, but they have manners, and it is wonderful how much talent runs into manners: — nowhere and never so much as in England. They have the sense of superiority, the absence of all the ambitious effort which disgusts in the aspiring classes, a pure tone of thought and feeling, and the power to command, among their other luxuries, the presence of the most accomplished men in their festive meetings.

Loyalty is in the English a sub-religion. They wear the laws as ornaments, and walk by their faith in their painted May-Fair as if among the forms of gods.[33] The economist of 1855 who asks, Of what use are the lords? may learn of Franklin to ask, Of what use is a baby?[34] They have been a social church proper to inspire sentiments mutually honoring the lover and the loved. Politeness is the ritual of society, as prayers are of the church, a school of manners, and a gentle blessing to the age in which it grew. 'T is a romance adorning English life with a larger horizon; a midway heaven, fulfilling to their sense their fairy tales and poetry. This, just as far as the breeding of the nobleman really made him brave, handsome, accomplished and great-hearted.

On general grounds, whatever tends to form manners or to finish men, has a great value. Every one who has tasted the delight of friendship will respect every social guard which our manners can establish, tending to secure from the intrusion of frivolous and distasteful people. The jealousy of every class to guard itself is a testimony to the reality they have found in life. When a man once knows that he has done justice to himself, let him dismiss all terrors of aristocracy as superstitions, so far as he is concerned. He who keeps the door of a mine, whether of cobalt, or mercury, or nickel, or plumbago, securely knows that the world cannot do without him. Every body who is real is open and ready for that which is also real.

Besides, these are they who make England that strongbox and museum it is; who gather and protect works of art, dragged from amidst burning cities and revolutionary countries, and brought hither out of all the world. I look with respect at houses six, seven, eight hundred, or, like Warwick Castle, nine hundred years old.[35] I pardoned high park-fences, when I saw that besides does and pheasants, these have preserved Arundel marbles, Townley galleries, Howard and Spenserian libraries, Warwick and Portland vases, Saxon manuscripts, monastic architectures, millennial trees and breeds of cattle elsewhere extinct.[36] In these manors, after the frenzy of war and destruction subsides a little, the antiquary finds the frailest Roman jar or crumbling Egyptian mummy-case, without so much as a new layer of dust, keeping the series of history unbroken and waiting for its interpreter, who is sure to arrive. These lords are the treasurers and librarians of mankind, engaged by their pride and wealth to this function.

Yet there were other works for British dukes to do. George Loudon, Quintinye, Evelyn, had taught them to make gardens.[37] Arthur Young, Bakewell and Mechi have made them agricultural.[38] Scotland was a camp until the day of Culloden.[39] The Dukes of Athol, Sutherland, Buccleugh[40] and the Marquis of Breadalbane have introduced the rape-culture, the sheep-farm, wheat, drainage, the plantation of forests, the artificial replenishment of lakes and ponds with fish, the renting of game-preserves. Against the cry of the old tenantry and the sympathetic cry of the English press, they have rooted out and planted anew, and now six millions of people live, and live better, on the same land that fed three millions.

The English barons, in every period, have been brave and great, after the estimate and opinion of their times. The grand old halls scattered up and down in England, are dumb vouchers to the state and broad hospitality of their ancient lords. Shakspeare's portraits of good Duke Humphrey, of Warwick, of Northumberland, of Talbot, were drawn in strict consonance with the traditions.[41] A sketch of the Earl of Shrewsbury, from the pen of Queen Elizabeth's archbishop Parker;[42] Lord Herbert of Cherbury's autobiography;[43] the letters and essays of Sir Philip Sidney;[44] the anecdotes preserved by the antiquaries Fuller and Collins;[45] some glimpses at the interiors of noble houses, which we owe to Pepys and Evelyn; the details which Ben Jonson's masques (performed at Kenilworth, Althorpe, Belvoir[46] and other noble houses), record or suggest; down to Aubrey's passages[47] of the life of Hobbes in the house of the Earl of Devon, are favorable pictures of a romantic style of manners. Penshurst[48] still shines for us, and its Christmas revels, "where logs not burn, but men." At Wilton House[49] the "Arcadia"[50] was written, amidst conversations with Fulke Greville, Lord Brooke,[51] a man of no vulgar mind, as his own poems declare him. I must hold Ludlow Castle an honest house, for which Milton's "Comus" was written, and the company nobly bred which performed it with knowledge and sympathy.[52] In the roll of nobles are found poets, philosophers, chemists, astronomers, also men of solid virtues and of lofty sentiments; often they have been the friends and patrons of genius and learning, and especially of the fine arts; and at this moment, almost every great house has its sumptuous picture-gallery.

Of course there is another side to this gorgeous show.

Every victory was the defeat of a party only less worthy. Castles are proud things, but 't is safest to be outside of them. War is a foul game, and yet war is not the worst part of aristocratic history. In later times, when the baron, educated only for war, with his brains paralyzed by his stomach, found himself idle at home, he grew fat and wanton and a sorry brute. Grammont,[53] Pepys and Evelyn show the kennels to which the king and court went in quest of pleasure. Prostitutes taken from the theatres were made duchesses, their bastards dukes and earls. "The young men sat uppermost, the old serious lords were out of favor." The discourse that the king's companions had with him was "poor and frothy." [54] No man who valued his head might do what these pot-companions familiarly did with the king. In logical sequence of these dignified revels, Pepys can tell the beggarly shifts to which the king was reduced, who could not find paper at his council table, and "no handkerchers" in his wardrobe, "and but three bands to his neck," and the linen-draper and the stationer were out of pocket and refusing to trust him, and the baker will not bring bread any longer. Meantime the English Channel was swept and London threatened by the Dutch fleet, manned too by English sailors, who, having been cheated of their pay for years by the king, enlisted with the enemy.

The Selwyn correspondence,[55] in the reign of George III., discloses a rottenness in the aristocracy which threatened to decompose the state. The sycophancy and sale of votes and honor, for place and title; lewdness, gaming, smuggling, bribery and cheating; the sneer at the childish indiscretion of quarrelling with ten thousand a year; the want of ideas; the splendor of the titles, and the apathy of the nation, are instructive, and make the reader pause and explore the firm bounds which confined these vices to a handful of rich men. In the reign of the Fourth George, things do not seem to have mended, and the rotten debauchee let down from a window by an inclined plane into his coach to take the air, was a scandal to Europe which the ill fame of his queen and of his family did nothing to retrieve.[56]

Under the present reign[57] the perfect decorum of the Court is thought to have put a check on the gross vices of the aristocracy; yet gaming, racing, drinking and mistresses bring them down, and the democrat can still gather scandals, if he will. Dismal anecdotes abound, verifying the gossip of the last generation, of dukes served by bailiffs, with all their plate in pawn; of great lords living by the showing of their houses, and of an old man wheeled in his chair from room to room, whilst his chambers are exhibited to the visitor for money; of ruined dukes and earls living in exile for debt. The historic names of the Buckinghams, Beauforts, Marlboroughs and Hertfords have gained no new lustre,[58] and now and then darker scandals break out, ominous as the new chapters added under the Orleans dynasty[59] to the "Causes Célèbres" [60] in France. Even peers who are men of worth and public spirit are overtaken and embarrassed by their vast expense. The respectable Duke of Devonshire, willing to be the Mecænas and Lucullus of his island, is reported to have said that he cannot live at Chatsworth but one month in the year.[61] Their many houses eat them up. They cannot sell them, because they are entailed. They will not let them, for pride's sake, but keep them empty, aired, and the grounds mown and dressed, at a cost of four or five thousand pounds a year. The spending is for a great part in servants, in many houses exceeding a hundred.

Most of them are only chargeable with idleness, which, because it squanders such vast power of benefit, has the mischief of crime. "They might be little Providences on earth," said my friend,[62] "and they are, for the most part, jockeys and fops." Campbell says,[63] "Acquaintance with the nobility,

I could never keep up. It requires a life of idleness, dressing and attendance on their parties." I suppose too that a feeling of self-respect is driving cultivated men out of this society, as if the noble were slow to receive the lessons of the times and had not learned to disguise his pride of place. A man of wit, who is also one of the celebrities of wealth and fashion, confessed to his friend that he could not enter their houses without being made to feel that they were great lords, and he a low plebeian. With the tribe of *artistes,* including the musical tribe, the patrician morgue keeps no terms, but excludes them. When Julia Grisi and Mario[64] sang at the houses of the Duke of Wellington and other grandees, a cord was stretched between the singer and the company.

When every noble was a soldier, they were carefully bred to great personal prowess. The education of a soldier is a simpler affair than that of an earl in the nineteenth century. And this was very seriously pursued; they were expert in every species of equitation, to the most dangerous practices, and this down to the accession of William of Orange.[65] But graver men appear to have trained their sons for civil affairs. Elizabeth extended her thought to the future; and Sir Philip Sidney in his letter to his brother, and Milton and Evelyn, gave plain and hearty counsel. Already too the English noble and squire were preparing for the career of the country-gentleman and his peaceable expense. They went from city to city, learning receipts to make perfumes, sweet powders, pomanders, antidotes, gathering seeds, gems, coins and divers curiosities, preparing for a private life thereafter, in which they should take pleasure in these recreations.

All advantages given to absolve the young patrician from intellectual labor are of course mistaken. "In the university, noblemen are exempted from the public exercises for the degree, &c., by which they attain a degree called *honorary.* At the same time, the fees they have to pay for matriculation,

and on all other occasions, are much higher." [66] Fuller
records "the observation of foreigners, that Englishmen, by
making their children gentlemen before they are men, cause
they are so seldom wise men." [66a] This cockering justifies Dr.
Johnson's bitter apology for primogeniture, that "it makes
but one fool in a family." [67]

The revolution in society has reached this class. The great
powers of industrial art have no exclusion of name or blood.
The tools of our time, namely steam, ships, printing, money
and popular education, belong to those who can handle
them; and their effect has been that advantages once confined to men of family are now open to the whole middle
class. The road that grandeur levels for his coach, toil can
travel in his cart.

This is more manifest every day, but I think it is true
throughout English history. English history, wisely read, is
the vindication of the brain of that people. Here at last were
climate and condition friendly to the working faculty. Who
now will work and dare, shall rule. This is the charter, or
the chartism, which fogs and seas and rains proclaimed, —
that intellect and personal force should make the law; that
industry and administrative talent should administer; that
work should wear the crown. I know that not this, but something else is pretended. The fiction with which the noble
and the bystander equally please themselves is that the former is of unbroken descent from the Norman, and so has
never worked for eight hundred years. All the families are
new, but the name is old, and they have made a covenant
with their memories not to disturb it. But the analysis of
the peerage and gentry shows the rapid decay and extinction
of old families, the continual recruiting of these from new
blood. The doors, though ostentatiously guarded, are really
open, and hence the power of the bribe. All the barriers to
rank only whet the thirst and enhance the prize. "Now," said

Nelson, when clearing for battle, "a peerage, or Westminster Abbey!" [68] "I have no illusion left," said Sydney Smith, "but the Archbishop of Canterbury." [69] "The lawyers," said Burke, "are only birds of passage in this House of Commons," and then added, with a new figure, "they have their best bower anchor in the House of Lords."

Another stride that has been taken appears in the perishing of heraldry. Whilst the privileges of nobility are passing to the middle class, the badge is discredited and the titles of lordship are getting musty and cumbersome. I wonder that sensible men have not been already impatient of them. They belong, with wigs, powder and scarlet coats, to an earlier age and may be advantageously consigned, with paint and tattoo, to the dignitaries of Australia and Polynesia.

A multitude of English, educated at the universities, bred into their society with manners, ability and the gifts of fortune, are every day confronting the peers on a footing of equality, and outstripping them, as often, in the race of honor and influence. That cultivated class is large and ever enlarging. It is computed that, with titles and without, there are seventy thousand of these people coming and going in London, who make up what is called high society. They cannot shut their eyes to the fact that an untitled nobility possess all the power without the inconveniences that belong to rank, and the rich Englishman goes over the world at the present day, drawing more than all the advantages which the strongest of his kings could command.

CHAPTER XII

Universities

Of British universities, Cambridge has the most illustrious names on its list. At the present day too, it has the advantage of Oxford, counting in its *alumni* a greater number of distinguished scholars. I regret that I had but a single day wherein to see King's College Chapel, the beautiful lawns and gardens of the colleges, and a few of its gownsmen.

But I availed myself of some repeated invitations to Oxford, where I had introductions to Dr. Daubeny, Professor of Botany,[1] and to the Regius Professor of Divinity, as well as to a valued friend,[2] a Fellow of Oriel, and went thither on the last day of March, 1848. I was the guest of my friend in Oriel, was housed close upon that college, and I lived on college hospitalities.

My new friends showed me their cloisters, the Bodleian Library, the Randolph Gallery, Merton Hall and the rest.[3] I saw several faithful, high-minded young men, some of them in the mood of making sacrifices for peace of mind, — a topic, of course, on which I had no counsel to offer. Their affectionate and gregarious ways reminded me at once of the habits of *our* Cambridge men,[4] though I imputed to these English an advantage in their secure and polished manners. The halls are rich with oaken wainscoting and ceiling. The pictures of the founders hang from the walls; the tables glitter with plate.[5] A youth came forward to the upper table[6] and pronounced the ancient form of grace before meals, which, I suppose, has been in use here for ages, *Benedictus benedicat; benedicitur, benedicatur.*[7]

It is a curious proof of the English use and wont, or of their good nature, that these young men are locked up every night at nine o'clock, and the porter at each hall is required to give the name of any belated student who is admitted after that hour. Still more descriptive is the fact that out of twelve hundred young men, comprising the most spirited of the aristocracy, a duel has never occurred.

Oxford is old, even in England, and conservative. Its foundations date from Alfred and even from Arthur, if, as is alleged, the Pheryllt of the Druids had a seminary here.[8] In the reign of Edward I.,[9] it is pretended, here were thirty thousand students; and nineteen most noble foundations were then established. Chaucer found it as firm as if it had always stood; and it is, in British story, rich with great names, the school of the island and the link of England to the learned of Europe. Hither came Erasmus, with delight, in 1497. Albericus Gentilis, in 1580, was relieved and maintained by the university.[10] Albert Alaskie, a noble Polonian, Prince of Sirad, who visited England to admire the wisdom of Queen Elizabeth, was entertained with stage-plays in the Refectory of Christ-church in 1583.[11] Isaac Casaubon, coming from Henri Quatre of France by invitation of James I., was admitted to Christ-Church, in July, 1613.[12] I saw the Ashmolean Museum, whither Elias Ashmole in 1682 sent twelve cart-loads of rarities.[13] Here indeed was the Olympia of all Antony Wood's and Aubrey's games and heroes, and every inch of ground has its lustre.[14] For Wood's *Athenæ Oxonienses,* or calendar of the writers of Oxford for two hundred years, is a lively record of English manners and merits, and as much a national monument as Purchas's Pilgrims[15] or Hansard's Register. On every side, Oxford is redolent of age and authority. Its gates shut of themselves against modern innovation. It is still governed by the statutes of Archbishop Laud.[16] The books in Merton Library are still chained to the wall.[17] Here, on August 27, 1660, John Milton's *Pro Populo Anglicano Defensio* and *Iconoclastes* were committed to the flames.[18] I saw the school-court or quadrangle where, in 1683, the Convocation[19] caused the Leviathan of Thomas Hobbes to be publicly burnt. I do not know whether this learned body have yet heard of the Declaration of American Independence, or whether the Ptolemaic astronomy does not still hold its ground against the novelties of Copernicus.

As many sons, almost so many benefactors. It is usual for a nobleman, or indeed for almost every wealthy student, on quitting college to leave behind him some article of plate; and gifts of all values, from a hall or a fellowship or a library, down to a picture or a spoon, are continually accruing, in the course of a century. My friend Doctor J.,[20] gave me the following anecdote. In Sir Thomas Lawrence's[21] collection at London were the cartoons[22] of Raphael and Michel Angelo. This inestimable prize was offered to Oxford University for seven thousand pounds. The offer was accepted, and the committee charged with the affair had collected three thousand pounds, when, among other friends, they called on Lord Eldon.[23] Instead of a hundred pounds, he surprised them by putting down his name for three thousand pounds. They told him they should now very easily raise the remainder. "No," he said, "your men have probably already contributed all they can spare; I can as well give the rest:" and he withdrew his cheque for three thousand, and wrote four thousand pounds. I saw the whole collection in April, 1848.

In the Bodleian Library, Dr. Bandinel[24] showed me the manuscript Plato, of the date of A. D. 896, brought by Dr. Clarke from Egypt;[25] a manuscript Virgil of the same cen-

tury; the first Bible printed at Mentz[26] (I believe in 1450);
and a duplicate of the same, which had been deficient in
about twenty leaves at the end. But one day, being in Venice,
he bought a room full of books and manuscripts, — every
scrap and fragment, — for four thousand louis d'ors,[27] and
had the doors locked and sealed by the consul. On proceed-
ing afterwards to examine his purchase, he found the twenty
deficient pages of his Mentz Bible, in perfect order; brought
them to Oxford with the rest of his purchase, and placed
them in the volume; but has too much awe for the Providence that appears in bibliography also, to suffer the re-
united parts to be re-bound. The oldest building[28] here is
two hundred years younger than the frail manuscript brought
by Dr. Clarke from Egypt. No candle or fire is ever lighted
in the Bodleian. Its catalogue is the standard catalogue on
the desk of every library in Oxford. In each several college
they underscore in red ink on this catalogue the titles of
books contained in the library of that college, — the theory
being that the Bodleian has all books. This rich library spent
during the last year (1847), for the purchase of books, £1,668.

The logical English train a scholar as they train an engineer. Oxford is a Greek factory, as Wilton mills weave carpet
and Sheffield grinds steel.[29] They know the use of a tutor, as
they know the use of a horse; and they draw the greatest
amount of benefit out of both. The reading men are kept,
by hard walking, hard riding and measured eating and drinking, at the top of their condition, and two days before the
examination, do no work, but lounge, ride, or run, to be
fresh on the college doomsday. Seven years' residence is the
theoretic period for a master's degree. In point of fact, it has
long been three years' residence, and four years more of
standing. This "three years" is about twenty-one months in
all.[30]

"The whole expense," says Professor Sewel, "of ordinary

college tuition at Oxford, is about sixteen guineas a year." [31]
But this plausible statement may deceive a reader unac-
quainted with the fact that the principal teaching relied on
is private tuition. And the expenses of private tuition are
reckoned at from £50 to £70 a year, or $1,000 for the whole
course of three years and a half. At Cambridge, $750 a year is
economical, and $1,500 not extravagant. [32]

The number of students and of residents, the dignity of
the authorities, the value of the foundations, the history and
the architecture, the known sympathy of entire Britain in
what is done there, justify a dedication to study in the undergraduate such as cannot easily be in America, where his college is half suspected by the Freshman to be insignificant in
the scale beside trade and politics. Oxford is a little aristocracy in itself, numerous and dignified enough to rank with
other estates in the realm; and where fame and secular promotion are to be had for study, and in a direction which has
the unanimous respect of all cultivated nations.

This aristocracy, of course, repairs its own losses; fills
places, as they fall vacant, from the body of students. The
number of fellowships at Oxford is 540, averaging £200 a
year, with lodging and diet at the college. If a young American, loving learning and hindered by poverty, were offered a
home, a table, the walks and the library in one of these
academical palaces, and a thousand dollars a year, as long as
he chose to remain a bachelor, he would dance for joy. Yet
these young men thus happily placed, and paid to read, are
impatient of their few checks, and many of them preparing
to resign their fellowships. They shuddered at the prospect
of dying a Fellow, and they pointed out to me a paralytic
old man, who was assisted into the hall. As the number of
undergraduates at Oxford is only about 1,200 or 1,300, and
many of these are never competitors, the chance of a fellow-

ship is very great. The income of the nineteen colleges is conjectured at £150,000 a year.

The effect of this drill is the radical [33] knowledge of Greek and Latin and of mathematics, and the solidity and taste of English criticism. Whatever luck there may be in this or that award, an Eton captain[34] can write Latin longs and shorts, can turn the Court-Guide into hexameters,[35] and it is certain that a Senior Classic can quote correctly from the *Corpus Poetarum*[36] and is critically learned in all the humanities. Greek erudition exists on the Isis and Cam,[37] whether the Maud man or the Brasenose man be properly ranked or not;[38] the atmosphere is loaded with Greek learning; the whole river has reached a certain height, and kills all that growth of weeds which this Castalian water kills.[39] The English nature takes culture kindly. So Milton thought. It refines the Norseman. Access to the Greek mind lifts his standard of taste. He has enough to think of, and, unless of an impulsive nature, is indisposed from writing or speaking, by the fulness of his mind and the new severity of his taste. The great silent crowd of thorough-bred Grecians[40] always known to be around him, the English writer cannot ignore. They prune his orations and point his pen. Hence the style and tone of English journalism. The men have learned accuracy and comprehension, logic, and pace, or speed of working. They have bottom, endurance, wind. When born with good constitutions, they make those eupeptic studying-mills, the cast-iron men, the *dura ilia*,[41] whose powers of performance compare with ours as the steam-hammer with the music-box; — Cokes, Mansfields, Seldens and Bentleys, and when it happens that a superior brain puts a rider on this admirable horse, we obtain those masters of the world who combine the highest energy in affairs with a supreme culture.

It is contended by those who have been bred at Eton,

Harrow, Rugby and Westminster, that the public sentiment within each of those schools is high-toned and manly; that, in their playgrounds, courage is universally admired, meanness despised, manly feelings and generous conduct are encouraged: that an unwritten code of honor deals to the spoiled child of rank and to the child of upstart wealth, an even-handed justice, purges their nonsense out of both and does all that can be done to make them gentlemen.

Again, at the universities, it is urged that all goes to form what England values as the flower of its national life, — a well-educated gentleman. The German Huber, in describing to his countrymen the attributes of an English gentleman, frankly admits that "in Germany, we have nothing of the kind. A gentleman must possess a political character, an independent and public position, or at least the right of assuming it. He must have average opulence, either of his own, or in his family. He should also have bodily activity and strength, unattainable by our sedentary life in public offices. The race of English gentlemen presents an appearance of manly vigor and form not elsewhere to be found among an equal number of persons. No other nation produces the stock. And in England, it has deteriorated. The university is a decided presumption in any man's favor. And so eminent are the members that a glance at the calendars will show that in all the world one cannot be in better company than on the books of one of the larger Oxford or Cambridge colleges." [42]

These seminaries are finishing schools for the upper classes, and not for the poor. The useful is exploded. The definition of a public school is "a school which excludes all that could fit a man for standing behind a counter." [43]

No doubt, the foundations have been perverted. Oxford, which equals in wealth several of the smaller European states, shuts up the lectureships which were made "public for all men thereunto to have concourse;" [44] mis-spends the revenues bestowed for such youths "as should be most meet for towardness, poverty and painfulness;" there is gross favoritism; many chairs and many fellowships are made beds of ease; and it is likely that the university will know how to resist and make inoperative the terrors of parliamentary inquiry; no doubt their learning is grown obsolete; — but Oxford also has its merits, and I found here also proof of the national fidelity and thoroughness. Such knowledge as they prize they possess and impart. Whether in course or by indirection, whether by a cramming tutor or by examiners with prizes and foundation scholarships, education, according to the English notion of it, is arrived at. I looked over the Examination Papers of the year 1848, for the various scholarships and fellowships, the Lusby, the Hertford, the Dean-Ireland and the University (copies of which were kindly given me by a Greek professor), containing the tasks which many competitors had victoriously performed, and I believed they would prove too severe tests for the candidates for a Bachelor's degree in Yale or Harvard. And in general, here was proof of a more searching study in the appointed directions, and the knowledge pretended to be conveyed was conveyed. Oxford sends out yearly twenty or thirty very able men and three or four hundred well-educated men.

The diet and rough exercise secure a certain amount of old Norse power. A fop will fight, and in exigent circumstances will play the manly part. In seeing these youths I believed I saw already an advantage in vigor and color and general habit, over their contemporaries in the American colleges. No doubt much of the power and brilliancy of the reading-men is merely constitutional or hygienic. With a hardier habit and resolute gymnastics, with five miles more walking,[45] or five ounces less eating, or with a saddle and gallop of twenty miles a day, with skating and rowing-matches, the American would arrive at as robust exegesis and cheery and hilarious tone. I should readily concede these advantages, which it would be easy to acquire, if I did not find also that they read better than we, and write better.

English wealth falling on their school and university train- ing, makes a systematic reading of the best authors, and to the end of a knowledge how the things whereof they treat really stand: whilst pamphleteer or journalist, reading for an argument for a party, or reading to write, or at all events for some by-end imposed on them, must read meanly and frag- mentarily. Charles I. said that he understood English law as well as a gentleman ought to understand it.

Then they have access to books; the rich libraries collected at every one of many thousands of houses, give an advantage not to be attained by a youth in this country, when one thinks how much more and better may be learned by a scholar who, immediately on hearing of a book, can consult it, than by one who is on the quest, for years, and reads inferior books because he cannot find the best.

Again, the great number of cultivated men keep each other up to a high standard. The habit of meeting well-read and knowing men teaches the art of omission and selection.

Universities are of course hostile to geniuses, which seeing and using ways of their own, discredit the routine: as churches and monasteries persecute youthful saints. Yet we all send our sons to college, and though he be a genius, the youth must take his chance. The university must be retro- spective. The gale that gives direction to the vanes on all its towers blows out of antiquity. Oxford is a library, and the professors must be librarians. And I should as soon think of quarrelling with the janitor for not magnifying his office by hostile sallies into the street, like the Governor of Kertch or Kinburn,[46] as of quarrelling with the professors for not admiring the young neologists who pluck the beards of

Euclid and Aristotle, or for not attempting themselves to fill their vacant shelves as original writers.

It is easy to carp at colleges, and the college, if we will wait for it, will have its own turn. Genius exists there also, but will not answer a call of a committee of the House of Commons. It is rare, precarious, eccentric and darkling. England is the land of mixture and surprise, and when you have settled it that the universities are moribund, out comes a poetic influence from the heart of Oxford,[47] to mould the opinions of cities, to build their houses as simply as birds their nests, to give veracity to art and charm mankind, as an appeal to moral order always must. But besides this restorative genius, the best poetry of England of this age, in the old forms, comes from two graduates of Cambridge.[48]

CHAPTER XIII

Religion

No people at the present day can be explained by their national religion. They do not feel responsible for it; it lies far outside of them. Their loyalty to truth and their labor and expenditure rest on real foundations, and not on a national church. And English life, it is evident, does not grow out of the Athanasian creed, or the Articles, or the Eucharist. It is with religion as with marriage. A youth marries in haste; afterwards, when his mind is opened to the reason of the conduct of life, he is asked what he thinks of the institution of marriage and of the right relations of the sexes? 'I should have much to say,' he might reply, 'if the question were open, but I have a wife and children, and all question is closed for me.' In the barbarous days of a nation, some *cultus* is formed or imported; altars are built, tithes are paid, priests ordained. The education and expenditure of the country take that direction, and when wealth, refinement, great men, and ties to the world supervene, its prudent men say, Why fight against Fate, or lift these absurdities which are now mountainous? Better find some niche or crevice in this mountain of stone which religious ages have quarried and carved, wherein to bestow yourself, than attempt any thing ridiculously and dangerously above your strength, like removing it.

In seeing old castles and cathedrals, I sometimes say, as to-day in front of Dundee Church tower,[1] which is eight hundred years old, 'This was built by another and a better race than any that now look on it.' And plainly there has been great power of sentiment at work in this island, of which these buildings are the proofs; as volcanic basalts show the work of fire which has been extinguished for ages. England felt the full heat of the Christianity which fermented Europe, and drew, like the chemistry of fire, a firm line between barbarism and culture. The power of the religious sentiment put an end to human sacrifices, checked appetite, inspired the crusades, inspired resistance to tyrants, inspired self-respect, set bounds to serfdom and slavery, founded liberty, created the religious architecture, — York, Newstead, Westminster, Fountains Abbey, Ripon, Beverley and Dundee,[2] — works to which the key is lost, with the sentiment which created them; inspired the English Bible, the liturgy, the monkish histories, the chronicle of Richard of Devizes.[3] The priest translated the Vulgate,[4] and translated the sanctities of old hagiology into English virtues on English ground. It was a certain affirmative or aggressive state of the Caucasian races. Man awoke refreshed by the sleep of ages. The violence of the northern savages exasperated Christianity into power. It lived by the love of the people. Bishop Wilfrid manumitted two hundred and fifty serfs, whom he found attached to the soil.[5] The clergy obtained respite from labor for the boor[6] on the Sabbath and on church festivals. "The lord who compelled his boor to labor between sunset on Saturday and sunset on Sunday, forfeited him altogether." The priest came out of the people and sympathized with his class. The church was the mediator, check and democratic principle, in Europe. Latimer, Wicliffe, Arundel, Cobham, Antony Parsons, Sir Harry Vane, George Fox, Penn, Bunyan are the democrats, as well as the saints of their times.[7] The Catholic church, thrown on this toiling, serious people, has made in fourteen centuries a massive system, close fitted to the manners and genius of the country, at once domestical and stately. In the long time, it has blended with every thing in heaven above and the earth beneath. It moves through a zodiac of feasts and fasts, names every day of the year, every town and market and headland and monument, and has coupled itself with the almanac, that no court can be held, no field ploughed, no horse shod, without some leave from the church. All maxims of prudence or shop or farm are fixed and dated by the church. Hence its strength in the agricultural districts. The distribution of land into parishes enforces a church sanction to every civil privilege; and the gradation of the clergy, — prelates for the rich and curates for the poor, — with the fact that a classical education has been secured to the clergyman, makes them "the link which unites the sequestered peasantry with the intellectual advancement of the age." [8]

The English church has many certificates to show of humble effective service in humanizing the people, in cheering and refining men, feeding, healing and educating. It has the seal of martyrs and confessors; the noblest books; a sublime architecture; a ritual marked by the same secular merits, nothing cheap or purchasable.

From this slow-grown church important reactions proceed; much for culture, much for giving a direction to the nation's affection and will to-day. The carved and pictured chapel, — its entire surface animated with image and emblem, — made the parish-church a sort of book and Bible to the people's eye.

Then, when the Saxon instinct had secured a service in the vernacular tongue, it was the tutor and university of the people. In York minster, on the day of the enthronization of the new archbishop,[9] I heard the service of evening prayer read and chanted in the choir. It was strange to hear the pretty pastoral of the betrothal of Rebecca and Isaac,[10] in the morning of the world, read with circumstantiality in York minster, on the 13th January, 1848, to the decorous English audience, just fresh from the Times newspaper and their wine, and listening with all the devotion of national pride. That was binding old and new to some purpose. The reverence for the Scriptures is an element of civilization, for thus has the history of the world been preserved and is preserved. Here in England every day a chapter of Genesis, and a leader[11] in the Times.

Another part of the same service on this occasion was not insignificant. Handel's coronation anthem, *God save the King,*[12] was played by Dr. Camidge on the organ, with sublime effect.[13] The minster and the music were made for each other. It was a hint of the part the church plays as a political engine. From his infancy, every Englishman is accustomed to hear daily prayers for the queen, for the royal family and the Parliament, by name; and this lifelong consecration cannot be without influence on his opinions.

The universities also are parcel of the ecclesiastical system, and their first design is to form the clergy. Thus the clergy for a thousand years have been the scholars of the nation.

The national temperament deeply enjoys the unbroken order and tradition of its church; the liturgy, ceremony, architecture; the sober grace, the good company, the connection with the throne and with history, which adorn it. And whilst it endears itself thus to men of more taste than activity, the stability of the English nation is passionately enlisted to its support, from its inextricable connection with the cause of public order, with politics and with the funds.

Good churches are not built by bad men; at least there must be probity and enthusiasm somewhere in the society. These minsters were neither built nor filled by atheists. No church has had more learned, industrious or devoted men;

plenty of "clerks and bishops, who, out of their gowns, would turn their backs on no man." [14] Their architecture still glows with faith in immortality. Heats and genial periods arrive in history, or, shall we say, plenitudes of Divine Presence, by which high tides are caused in the human spirit, and great virtues and talents appear, as in the eleventh, twelfth, thirteenth, and again in the sixteenth and seventeenth centuries, when the nation was full of genius and piety.

But the age of the Wicliffes, Cobhams, Arundels, Beckets; of the Latimers, Mores, Cranmers; of the Taylors, Leightons, Herberts; of the Sherlocks and Butlers, is gone.[15] Silent revolutions in opinion have made it impossible that men like these should return, or find a place in their once sacred stalls. The spirit that dwelt in this church has glided away to animate other activities, and they who come to the old shrines find apes and players rustling the old garments.

The religion of England is part of good-breeding. When you see on the continent the well-dressed Englishman come into his ambassador's chapel and put his face for silent prayer into his smooth-brushed hat, you cannot help feeling how much national pride prays with him, and the religion of a gentleman. So far is he from attaching any meaning to the words, that he believes himself to have done almost the generous thing, and that it is very condescending in him to pray to God. A great duke said on the occasion of a victory, in the House of Lords, that he thought the Almighty God had not been well used by them, and that it would become their magnanimity, after so great successes, to take order that a proper acknowledgment be made. It is the church of the gentry, but it is not the church of the poor. The operatives do not own it, and gentlemen lately testified in the House of Commons that in their lives they never saw a poor man in a ragged coat inside a church.

The torpidity on the side of religion of the vigorous English understanding shows how much wit and folly can agree in one brain. Their religion is a quotation; their church is a doll; and any examination is interdicted with screams of terror. In good company you expect them to laugh at the fanaticism of the vulgar; but they do not; they are the vulgar.

The English, in common perhaps with Christendom in the nineteenth century, do not respect power, but only performance; value ideas only for an economic result. Wellington esteems a saint only as far as he can be an army chaplain: "Mr. Briscoll, by his admirable conduct and good sense, got the better of Methodism, which had appeared among the soldiers and once among the officers." [16] They value a philosopher as they value an apothecary who brings bark or a drench;[17] and inspiration is only some blowpipe, or a finer mechanical aid.

I suspect that there is in an Englishman's brain a valve that can be closed at pleasure, as an engineer shuts off steam. The most sensible and well-informed men possess the power of thinking just so far as the bishop in religious matters, and as the chancellor of the exchequer in politics. They talk with courage and logic, and show you magnificent results, but the same men who have brought free trade or geology to their present standing, look grave and lofty and shut down their valve as soon as the conversation approaches the English church. After that, you talk with a box-turtle.

The action of the university, both in what is taught and in the spirit of the place, is directed more on producing an English gentleman, than a saint or a psychologist. It ripens a bishop, and extrudes a philosopher. I do not know that there is more cabalism in the Anglican than in other churches, but the Anglican clergy are identified with the aristocracy.[18] They say here, that if you talk with a clergyman, you are sure to find him well-bred, informed and candid: he entertains your thought or your project with sympathy and praise. But if a second clergyman come in, the sympathy is at an end: two together are inaccessible to your thought, and whenever it comes to action, the clergyman invariably sides with his church.

The Anglican church is marked by the grace and good sense of its forms, by the manly grace of its clergy. The gospel it preaches is 'By taste are ye saved.' It keeps the old structures in repair, spends a world of money in music and building, and in buying Pugin and architectural literature.[19] It has a general good name for amenity and mildness. It is not in ordinary a persecuting church; it is not inquisitorial, not even inquisitive; is perfectly well-bred, and can shut its eyes on all proper occasions. If you let it alone, it will let you alone. But its instinct is hostile to all change in politics, literature, or social arts. The church has not been the founder of the London University,[20] of the Mechanics' Institutes, of the Free School,[21] of whatever aims at diffusion of knowledge. The Platonists of Oxford[22] are as bitter against this heresy, as Thomas Taylor.[23]

The doctrine of the Old Testament is the religion of England. The first leaf of the New Testament it does not open. It believes in a Providence which does not treat with levity a pound sterling. They are neither transcendentalists nor Christians. They put up no Socratic prayer,[24] much less any saintly prayer for the queen's mind; ask neither for light nor right, but say bluntly, "Grant her in health and wealth long to live."[25] And one traces this Jewish prayer in all English private history, from the prayers of King Richard, in Richard of Devizes' Chronicle,[26] to those in the diaries of Sir Samuel Romilly and of Haydon the painter.[27] "Abroad with my wife," writes Pepys piously, "the first time that ever I rode in my own coach; which do make my heart rejoice and praise God, and pray him to bless it to me, and continue it."[28] The

bill for the naturalization of the Jews (in 1753) [29] was resisted
by petitions from all parts of the kingdom, and by petition
from the city of London, reprobating this bill, as "tending
extremely to the dishonor of the Christian religion, and extremely injurious to the interests and commerce of the kingdom in general, and of the city of London in particular." [30]

But they have not been able to congeal humanity by act
of Parliament. "The heavens journey still and sojourn not,"
and arts, wars, discoveries and opinion go onward at their
own pace. The new age has new desires, new enemies, new
trades, new charities, and reads the Scriptures with new eyes.
The chatter of French politics, the steam-whistle, the hum of
the mill and the noise of embarking emigrants had quite put
most of the old legends out of mind; so that when you came
to read the liturgy to a modern congregation, it was almost
absurd in its unfitness, and suggested a masquerade of old
costumes.

No chemist has prospered in the attempt to crystallize a
religion. It is endogenous, like the skin and other vital
organs. A new statement every day. The prophet and apostle
knew this,[31] and the nonconformist confutes the conformists,
by quoting the texts they must allow. It is the condition of
a religion to require religion for its expositor. Prophet and
apostle can only be rightly understood by prophet and apostle. The statesman knows that the religious element will not
fail, any more than the supply of fibrine and chyle;[32] but it is
in its nature constructive, and will organize such a church
as it wants. The wise legislator will spend on temples,
schools, libraries, colleges, but will shun the enriching of
priests. If in any manner he can leave the election and pay-
ing of the priest to the people, he will do well. Like the
Quakers, he may resist the separation of a class of priests,
and create opportunity and expectation in the society to run
to meet natural endowment in this kind. But when wealth

accrues to a chaplaincy, a bishopric, or rectorship,[33] it requires moneyed men for its stewards, who will give it another
direction than to the mystics of their day. Of course, money
will do after its kind, and will steadily work to unspiritualize
and unchurch the people to whom it was bequeathed. The
class certain to be excluded from all preferment are the
religious, — and driven to other churches; which is nature's
vis medicatrix.[34]

The curates are ill paid, and the prelates are overpaid.[35]
This abuse draws into the church the children of the nobility
and other unfit persons who have a taste for expense. Thus
a bishop is only a surpliced merchant. Through his lawn[36]
I can see the bright buttons of the shopman's coat glitter.
A wealth like that of Durham makes almost a premium on
felony.[37] Brougham, in a speech in the House of Commons
on the Irish elective franchise, said, "How will the reverend
bishops of the other house be able to express their due ab-
horrence of the crime of perjury, who solemnly declare in
the presence of God that when they are called upon to accept
a living, perhaps of £4,000 a year, at that very instant they
are moved by the Holy Ghost to accept the office and administration thereof, and for no other reason whatever?" [38] The
modes of initiation are more damaging than custom-house
oaths. The Bishop is elected by the Dean and Prebends of
the cathedral.[39] The queen sends these gentlemen a *congé
d'élire*,[40] or leave to elect; but also sends them the name
of the person whom they are to elect. They go into the
cathedral, chant and pray and beseech the Holy Ghost to
assist them in their choice; and, after these invocations, invariably find that the dictates of the Holy Ghost agree with
the recommendations of the Queen.

But you must pay for conformity. All goes well as long
as you run with conformists. But you, who are an honest

man in other particulars, know that there is alive somewhere a man whose honesty reaches to this point also that he shall not kneel to false gods, and on the day when you meet him, you sink into the class of counterfeits. Besides, this succumbing has grave penalties. If you take in a lie, you must take in all that belongs to it. England accepts this ornamented national church, and it glazes the eyes, bloats the flesh, gives the voice a stertorous clang, and clouds the understanding of the receivers.

The English church, undermined by German criticism,[41] had nothing left but tradition; and was led logically back to Romanism.[42] But that was an element which only hot heads could breathe: in view of the educated class, generally, it was not a fact to front the sun; and the alienation of such men from the church became complete.

Nature, to be sure, had her remedy. Religious persons are driven out of the Established Church into sects, which instantly rise to credit and hold the Establishment in check. Nature has sharper remedies, also. The English, abhorring change in all things, abhorring it most in matters of religion, cling to the last rag of form, and are dreadfully given to cant. The English (and I wish it were confined to them, but 't is a taint in the Anglo-Saxon blood in both hemispheres), — the English and the Americans cant beyond all other nations. The French relinquish all that industry to them. What is so odious as the polite bows to God, in our books and newspapers? The popular press is flagitious in the exact measure of its sanctimony, and the religion of the day is a theatrical Sinai, where the thunders are supplied by the property-man. The fanaticism and hypocrisy create satire. Punch finds an inexhaustible material. Dickens writes novels on Exeter-Hall humanity.[43] Thackeray exposes the heartless high life. Nature revenges herself more summarily by the heathenism of the lower classes. Lord Shaftesbury calls the poor thieves together and reads sermons to them, and they call it 'gas.' [44] George Borrow summons the Gypsies to hear his discourse on the Hebrews in Egypt, and reads to them the Apostles' Creed in Romany. "When I had concluded," he says, "I looked around me. The features of the assembly were twisted, and the eyes of all turned upon me with a frightful squint: not an individual present but squinted; the genteel Pepa, the good-humored Chicharona, the Cosdami, all squinted; the Gypsy jockey squinted worst of all." [45]

The church at this moment is much to be pitied. She has nothing left but possession. If a bishop meets an intelligent gentleman and reads fatal interrogations in his eyes, he has no resource but to take wine with him. False position introduces cant, perjury, simony and ever a lower class of mind and character into the clergy: and, when the hierarchy is afraid of science and education, afraid of piety, afraid of tradition and afraid of theology, there is nothing left but to quit a church which is no longer one.

But the religion of England, — is it the Established Church? no; is it the sects? no; they are only perpetuations of some private man's dissent, and are to the Established Church as cabs are to a coach, cheaper and more convenient, but really the same thing. Where dwells the religion? Tell me first where dwells electricity, or motion, or thought, or gesture. They do not dwell or stay at all. Electricity cannot be made fast, mortared up and ended, like London Monument or the Tower,[46] so that you shall know where to find it, and keep it fixed, as the English do with their things, forevermore; it is passing, glancing, gesticular; it is a traveller, a newness, a surprise, a secret, which perplexes them and puts them out. Yet, if religion be the doing of all good, and for its sake the suffering of all evil, *souffrir de tout le monde, et ne faire souffrir personne,*[47] that divine secret has existed in England from the days of Alfred to those of Romilly, of Clarkson and of Florence Nightingale, and in thousands who have no fame.[48]

CHAPTER XIV

Literature

A strong common sense, which it is not easy to unseat or disturb, marks the English mind for a thousand years: a rude strength newly applied to thought, as of sailors and soldiers who had lately learned to read. They have no fancy, and never are surprised into a covert or witty word, such as pleased the Athenians and Italians, and was convertible into a fable not long after; but they delight in strong earthy expression, not mistakable, coarsely true to the human body, and, though spoken among princes, equally fit and welcome to the mob. This homeliness, veracity and plain style appear in the earliest extant works and in the latest. It imports into songs and ballads the smell of the earth, the breath of cattle, and, like a Dutch painter, seeks a household charm, though by pails and pans. They ask their constitutional utility in verse. The kail and herrings are never out of sight. The poet nimbly recovers himself from every sally of the imagination. The English muse loves the farmyard, the lane and market. She says, with De Staël, "I tramp in the mire with wooden shoes, whenever they would force me into the clouds." [1] For the Englishman has accurate perceptions; takes hold of things by the right end, and there is no slipperiness in his grasp. He loves the axe, the spade, the oar, the gun, the steampipe: he has built the engine he uses. He is materialist, economical, mercantile. He must be treated with sincerity and reality;

with muffins, and not the promise of muffins; and prefers his hot chop, with perfect security and convenience in the eating of it, to the chances of the amplest and Frenchiest bill of fare, engraved on embossed paper. When he is intellectual, and a poet or a philosopher, he carries the same hard truth and the same keen machinery into the mental sphere. His mind must stand on a fact. He will not be baffled, or catch at clouds, but the mind must have a symbol palpable and resisting. What he relishes in Dante is the vise-like tenacity with which he holds a mental image before the eyes, as if it were a scutcheon painted on a shield. Byron "liked something craggy to break his mind upon." [2] A taste for plain strong speech, what is called a biblical style, marks the English. It is in Alfred and the Saxon Chronicle and in the Sagas of the Northmen. Latimer was homely. Hobbes was perfect in the "noble vulgar speech." Donne, Bunyan, Milton, Taylor, Evelyn, Pepys, Hooker, Cotton[3] and the translators wrote it. How realistic or materialistic in treatment of his subject is Swift. He describes his fictitious persons as if for the police. Defoe has no insecurity or choice. Hudibras has the same hard mentality,[4] — keeping the truth at once to the senses and to the intellect.

It is not less seen in poetry. Chaucer's hard painting of his Canterbury pilgrims satisfies the senses. Shakspeare, Spenser and Milton, in their loftiest ascents, have this national grip and exactitude of mind. This mental materialism makes the value of English transcendental genius; in these writers and in Herbert, Henry More, Donne and Sir Thomas Browne.[5] The Saxon materialism and narrowness, exalted into the sphere of intellect, makes the very genius of Shakspeare and Milton. When it reaches the pure element, it treads the clouds as securely as the adamant. Even in its elevations materialistic, its poetry is common sense inspired; or iron raised to white heat.

The marriage of the two qualities is in their speech. It is a tacit rule of the language to make the frame or skeleton of Saxon words,[6] and, when elevation or ornament is sought, to interweave Roman, but sparingly; nor is a sentence made of Roman words alone, without loss of strength. The children and laborers use the Saxon unmixed. The Latin unmixed is abandoned to the colleges and Parliament. Mixture is a secret of the English island; and, in their dialect, the male principle is the Saxon, the female, the Latin; and they are combined in every discourse. A good writer, if he has indulged in a Roman roundness, makes haste to chasten and nerve his period by English monosyllables.

When the Gothic nations came into Europe they found it lighted with the sun and moon of Hebrew and of Greek genius. The tablets of their brain, long kept in the dark, were finely sensible to the double glory. To the images from this twin source (of Christianity and art), the mind became fruitful as by the incubation of the Holy Ghost. The English mind flowered in every faculty. The common-sense was surprised and inspired. For two centuries England was philosophic, religious, poetic. The mental furniture seemed of larger scale: the memory capacious like the storehouse of the rains. The ardor and endurance of study, the boldness and facility of their mental construction, their fancy and imagination and easy spanning of vast distances of thought, the enterprise or accosting of new subjects, and, generally, the easy exertion of power, — astonish, like the legendary feats of Guy of Warwick.[7] The union of Saxon precision and Oriental soaring,[8] of which Shakspeare is the perfect example, is shared in less degree by the writers of two centuries. I find not only the great masters out of all rivalry and reach, but the whole writing of the time charged with a masculine force and freedom.

There is a hygienic simpleness, rough vigor and closeness

to the matter in hand even in the second and third class of writers; and, I think, in the common style of the people, as one finds it in the citation of wills, letters and public documents; in proverbs and forms of speech. The more hearty and sturdy expression may indicate that the savageness of the Norseman was not all gone. Their dynamic brains hurled off their words as the revolving stone hurls off scraps of grit. I could cite from the seventeenth century sentences and phrases of edge not to be matched in the nineteenth. Their poets by simple force of mind equalized themselves with the accumulated science of ours. The country gentlemen had a posset or drink they called October;[9] and the poets, as if by this hint, knew how to distil the whole season into their autumnal verses: and as nature, to pique the more, sometimes works up deformities into beauty in some rare Aspasia[10] or Cleopatra; and as the Greek art wrought many a vase or column, in which too long or too lithe, or nodes, or pits and flaws are made a beauty of; — so these were so quick and vital that they could charm and enrich by mean and vulgar objects.

A man must think that age well taught and thoughtful, by which masques and poems, like those of Ben Jonson, full of heroic sentiment in a manly style, were received with favor. The unique fact in literary history, the unsurprised reception of Shakspeare; — the reception proved by his making his fortune; and the apathy proved by the absence of all contemporary panegyric, — seems to demonstrate an elevation in the mind of the people. Judge of the splendor of a nation by the insignificance of great individuals in it. The manner in which they learned Greek and Latin, before our modern facilities were yet ready; without dictionaries, grammars, or indexes, by lectures of a professor, followed by their own searchings, — required a more robust memory, and coöperation of all the faculties; and their scholars, Camden,

Usher, Selden, Mede, Gataker, Hooker, Taylor, Burton, Bentley, Brian Walton, acquired the solidity and method of engineers.[11]

The influence of Plato tinges the British genius. Their minds loved analogy; were cognisant of resemblances, and climbers on the staircase of unity. 'T is a very old strife between those who elect to see identity and those who elect to see discrepances; and it renews itself in Britain. The poets, of course, are of one part; the men of the world, of the other. But Britain had many disciples of Plato; — More, Hooker, Bacon, Sidney, Lord Brooke, Herbert, Browne, Donne, Spenser, Chapman, Milton, Crashaw, Norris, Cudworth, Berkeley, Jeremy Taylor.[12]

Lord Bacon has the English duality. His centuries of observations on useful science, and his experiments, I suppose, were worth nothing. One hint of Franklin, or Watt, or Dalton, or Davy,[13] or any one who had a talent for experiment, was worth all his lifetime of exquisite trifles. But he drinks of a diviner stream, and marks the influx of idealism into England. Where that goes, is poetry, health and progress. The rules of its genesis or its diffusion are not known. That knowledge, if we had it, would supersede all that we call science of the mind. It seems an affair of race, or of metachemistry; — the vital point being, how far the sense of unity, or instinct of seeking resemblances, predominated. For wherever the mind takes a step, it is to put itself at one with a larger class, discerned beyond the lesser class with which it has been conversant. Hence, all poetry and all affirmative action comes.

Bacon, in the structure of his mind, held of the analogists, of the idealists, or (as we popularly say, naming from the best example) Platonists. Whoever discredits analogy and requires heaps of facts before any theories can be attempted, has no poetic power, and nothing original or beautiful will be produced by him. Locke is as surely the influx of decomposition and of prose, as Bacon and the Platonists of growth. The Platonic is the poetic tendency; the so-called scientific is the negative and poisonous. 'T is quite certain that Spenser, Burns, Byron and Wordsworth will be Platonists, and that the dull men will be Lockists. Then politics and commerce will absorb from the educated class men of talents without genius, precisely because such have no resistance.

Bacon, capable of ideas, yet devoted to ends, required in his map of the mind, first of all, universality, or *prima philosophia*;[14] the receptacle for all such profitable observations and axioms as fall not within the compass of any of the special parts of philosophy, but are more common and of a higher stage. He held this element essential: it is never out of mind: he never spares rebukes for such as neglect it; believing that no perfect discovery can be made in a flat or level, but you must ascend to a higher science. "If any man thinketh philosophy and universality to be idle studies, he doth not consider that all professions are from thence served and supplied; and this I take to be a great cause that has hindered the progression of learning, because these fundamental knowledges have been studied but in passage."[15] He explained himself by giving various quaint examples of the summary or common laws of which each science has its own illustration. He complains that "he finds this part of learning very deficient, the profounder sort of wits drawing a bucket now and then for their own use, but the spring-head unvisited. This was the *dry light* which did scorch and offend most men's watery natures."[16] Plato had signified the same sense, when he said "All the great arts require a subtle and speculative research into the law of nature, since loftiness of thought and perfect mastery over every subject seem to be derived from some such source as this. This Pericles had, in addition to a great natural genius. For, meeting with Anaxagoras, who was a person of this kind, he attached himself to him, and nourished himself with sublime speculations on the absolute intelligence; and imported thence into the oratorical art whatever could be useful to it." [17]

A few generalizations always circulate in the world, whose authors we do not rightly know, which astonish, and appear to be avenues to vast kingdoms of thought, and these are in the world *constants*, like the Copernican and Newtonian theories in physics. In England these may be traced usually to Shakspeare, Bacon, Milton, or Hooker, even to Van Helmont and Behmen,[18] and do all have a kind of filial retrospect to Plato and the Greeks. Of this kind is Lord Bacon's sentence, that "Nature is commanded by obeying her;" his doctrine of poetry, which "accommodates the shows of things to the desires of the mind," [19] or the Zoroastrian[20] definition of poetry, mystical, yet exact, "apparent pictures of unapparent natures;" [21] Spenser's creed that "soul is form, and doth the body make;" [22] the theory of Berkeley, that we have no certain assurance of the existence of matter; Doctor Samuel Clarke's argument for theism from the nature of space and time;[23] Harrington's political rule that power must rest on land,[24] — a rule which requires to be literally interpreted; the theory of Swedenborg, so cosmically applied by him, that the man makes his heaven and hell; Hegel's[25] study of civil history, as the conflict of ideas and the victory of the deeper thought; the identity-philosophy of Schelling,[26] couched in the statement that "all difference is quantitative." So the very announcement of the theory of gravitation, of Kepler's three harmonic laws,[27] and even of Dalton's doctrine of definite proportions,[28] finds a sudden response in the mind, which remains a superior evidence to empirical demonstrations. I cite these generalizations, some of which are more recent, merely to indicate a class. Not these particulars, but the mental plane or the atmosphere from which they emanate was the home and element of the writers and readers in what we loosely call the Elizabethan age (say, in literary history, the period from 1575 to 1625), yet a period almost short enough to justify Ben Jonson's remark on Lord Bacon, — "About his time, and within his view, were born all the wits that could honor a nation, or help study." [29]

Such richness of genius had not existed more than once before. These heights could not be maintained. As we find stumps of vast trees in our exhausted soils, and have received traditions of their ancient fertility to tillage, so history reckons epochs in which the intellect of famed races became effete. So it fared with English genius. These heights were followed by a meanness and a descent of the mind into lower levels; the loss of wings; no high speculation. Locke, to whom the meaning of ideas was unknown, became the type of philosophy, and his "understanding" [30] the measure, in all nations, of the English intellect.[31] His countrymen forsook the lofty sides of Parnassus, on which they had once walked with echoing steps, and disused the studies once so beloved; the powers of thought fell into neglect. The later English want the faculty of Plato and Aristotle, of grouping men in natural classes by an insight of general laws, so deep that the rule is deduced with equal precision from few subjects, or from one, as from multitudes of lives. Shakspeare is supreme in that, as in all the great mental energies. The Germans generalize: the English cannot interpret the German mind. German science comprehends the English. The absence of the faculty in England is shown by the timidity which accumulates mountains of facts, as a bad general wants myriads of men and miles of redoubts to compensate the inspirations of courage and conduct.

The English shrink from a generalization. "They do not look abroad into universality, or they draw only a bucketful at the fountain of the First Philosophy for their occasion, and do not go to the spring-head." [32] Bacon, who said this, is almost unique among his countrymen in that faculty; at least among the prose-writers. Milton, who was the stair or high table-land to let down the English genius from the summits of Shakspeare, used this privilege sometimes in poetry, more rarely in prose. For a long interval afterwards, it is not found. Burke was addicted to generalizing, but his was a shorter line; as his thoughts have less depth, they have less compass. Hume's abstractions are not deep or wise. He owes his fame to one keen observation, that no copula[33] had been detected between any cause and effect, either in physics or in thought; that the term cause and effect was loosely or gratuitously applied to what we know only as consecutive, not at all as causal. Doctor Johnson's written abstractions have little value; the tone of feeling in them makes their chief worth.

Mr. Hallam, a learned and elegant scholar, has written the history of European literature for three centuries, — a performance of great ambition, inasmuch as a judgment was to be attempted on every book.[34] But his eye does not reach to the ideal standards: the verdicts are all dated from London; all new thought must be cast into the old moulds. The expansive element which creates literature is steadily denied. Plato is resisted, and his school. Hallam is uniformly polite, but with deficient sympathy; writes with resolute generosity, but is unconscious of the deep worth which lies in the mystics, and which often outvalues as a seed of power and a source of revolution all the correct writers and shining reputations of their day. He passes in silence, or dismisses with a kind of contempt, the profounder masters: a lover of ideas is not only uncongenial, but unintelligible. Hallam inspires respect by his knowledge and fidelity, by his manifest love of good books, and he lifts himself to own better than almost any the greatness of Shakspeare, and better than Johnson he appreciates Milton.[35] But in Hallam, or in the firmer intellectual nerve of Mackintosh, one still finds the same type of English genius.[36] It is wise and rich, but it lives on its capital. It is retrospective. How can it discern and hail the new forms that are looming up on the horizon, — new and gigantic thoughts which cannot dress themselves out of any old wardrobe of the past?

The essays, the fiction and the poetry of the day have the like municipal limits. Dickens, with preternatural apprehension of the language of manners and the varieties of street life; with pathos and laughter, with patriotic and still enlarging generosity, writes London tracts. He is a painter of English details, like Hogarth;[37] local and temporary in his tints and style, and local in his aims. Bulwer, an industrious writer, with occasional ability, is distinguished for his reverence of intellect as a temporality, and appeals to the worldly ambition of the student. His romances tend to fan these low flames. Their novelists despair of the heart. Thackeray finds that God has made no allowance for the poor thing in his universe, — more's the pity, he thinks, — but 't is not for us to be wiser; we must renounce ideals and accept London.

The brilliant Macaulay, who expresses the tone of the English governing classes of the day, explicitly teaches that *good* means good to eat, good to wear, material commodity; that the glory of modern philosophy is its direction on "fruit;" [38] to yield economical inventions; and that its merit is to avoid ideas and avoid morals. He thinks it the distinctive merit of the Baconian philosophy in its triumph over the old Platonic, its disentangling the intellect from theories of the all-Fair and all-Good, and pinning it down to the making a better sick chair and a better wine-whey for an invalid; — this not ironically, but in good faith; — that, "solid advantage," as he calls it, meaning always sensual benefit, is the only good.[39] The eminent benefit of astronomy is the better navigation it creates to enable the fruit-ships to bring home their lemons and wine to the London grocer. It was a curious result, in which the civility and religion of England for a thousand years ends in denying morals and reducing the intellect to a sauce-pan. The critic hides his skepticism under the English cant of practical. To convince the reason, to touch the conscience, is romantic pretension. The fine arts fall to the ground. Beauty, except as luxurious commodity, does not exist. It is very certain, I may say in passing, that if Lord Bacon had been only the sensualist his critic pretends, he would never have acquired the fame which now entitles him to this patronage. It is because he had imagination, the leisures of the spirit, and basked in an element of contemplation out of all modern English atmospheric gauges, that he is impressive to the imaginations of men and has become a potentate not to be ignored. Sir David Brewster sees the high place of Bacon, without finding Newton indebted to him, and thinks it a mistake.[40] Bacon occupies it by specific gravity or levity, not by any feat he did, or by any tutoring more or less of Newton &c., but as an effect of the same cause which showed itself more pronounced afterwards in Hooke, Boyle and Halley.[41]

Coleridge, a catholic mind, with a hunger for ideas; with eyes looking before and after to the highest bards and sages, and who wrote and spoke the only high criticism in his time, is one of those who save England from the reproach of no longer possessing the capacity to appreciate what rarest wit the island has yielded. Yet the misfortune of his life, his vast attempts but most inadequate performings, failing to accomplish any one masterpiece, — seems to mark the closing of an era. Even in him, the traditional Englishman was too strong for the philosopher, and he fell into *accommodations;* and as Burke had striven to idealize the English State, so

Coleridge 'narrowed his mind' [42] in the attempt to reconcile the Gothic rule[43] and dogma of the Anglican Church, with eternal ideas. But for Coleridge, and a lurking taciturn minority uttering itself in occasional criticism, oftener in private discourse, one would say that in Germany and in America is the best mind in England rightly respected. It is the surest sign of national decay, when the Bramins can no longer read or understand the Braminical philosophy.

In the decomposition and asphyxia that followed all this materialism, Carlyle was driven by his disgust at the pettiness and the cant, into the preaching of Fate. In comparison with all this rottenness, any check, any cleansing, though by fire, seemed desirable and beautiful. He saw little difference in the gladiators, or the "causes" for which they combated; the one comfort was, that they were all going speedily into the abyss together. And his imagination, finding no nutriment in any creation, avenged itself by celebrating the majestic beauty of the laws of decay. The necessities of mental structure force all minds into a few categories; and where impatience of the tricks of men makes Nemesis amiable, and builds altars to the negative Deity, the inevitable recoil is to heroism or the gallantry of the private heart, which decks its immolation with glory, in the unequal combat of will against fate.

Wilkinson, the editor of Swedenborg, the annotator of Fourier and the champion of Hahnemann, has brought to metaphysics and to physiology a native vigor, with a catholic perception of relations, equal to the highest attempts, and a rhetoric like the armory of the invincible knights of old.[44] There is in the action of his mind a long Atlantic roll not known except in deepest waters, and only lacking what ought to accompany such powers, a manifest centrality. If his mind does not rest in immovable biases, perhaps the orbit is larger and the return is not yet: but a master should inspire a confidence that he will adhere to his convictions and give his present studies always the same high place.

It would be easy to add exceptions to the limitary tone of English thought, and much more easy to adduce examples of excellence in particular veins; and if, going out of the region of dogma, we pass into that of general culture, there is no end to the graces and amenities, wit, sensibility and erudition of the learned class. But the artificial succor which marks all English performance appears in letters also: much of their aesthetic production is antiquarian and manufactured, and literary reputations have been achieved by forcible men, whose relation to literature was purely accidental, but who were driven by tastes and modes they found in vogue into their several careers. So, at this moment, every ambitious young man studies geology: so members of Parliament are made, and churchmen.

The bias of Englishmen to practical skill has reacted on the national mind. They are incapable of an inutility, and respect the five mechanic powers even in their song. The voice of their modern muse has a slight hint of the steam-whistle, and the poem is created as an ornament and finish of their monarchy, and by no means as the bird of a new morning which forgets the past world in the full enjoyment of that which is forming. They are with difficulty ideal; they are the most conditioned men, as if, having the best conditions, they could not bring themselves to forfeit them. Every one of them is a thousand years old and lives by his memory: and when you say this, they accept it as praise.

Nothing comes to the book-shops but politics, travels, statistics, tabulation and engineering; and even what is called philosophy and letters is mechanical in its structure, as if inspiration had ceased, as if no vast hope, no religion, no song of joy, no wisdom, no analogy existed any more. The tone of colleges and of scholars and of literary society has this mortal air. I seem to walk on a marble floor, where nothing will grow. They exert every variety of talent on the lower ground and may be said to live and act in a sub-mind. They have lost all commanding views in literature, philosophy and science. A good Englishman shuts himself out of three fourths of his mind and confines himself to one fourth. He has learning, good sense, power of labor, and logic; but a faith in the laws of the mind like that of Archimedes; a belief like that of Euler[45] and Kepler, that experience must follow and not lead the laws of the mind; a devotion to the theory of politics like that of Hooker and Milton and Harrington, the modern English mind repudiates.

I fear the same fault lies in their science, since they have known how to make it repulsive and bereave nature of its charm; — though perhaps the complaint flies wider, and the vice attaches to many more than to British physicists. The eye of the naturalist must have a scope like nature itself, a susceptibility to all impressions, alive to the heart as well as to the logic of creation. But English science puts humanity to the door. It wants the connection which is the test of genius. The science is false by not being poetic. It isolates the reptile or mollusk it assumes to explain; whilst reptile or mollusk only exists in system, in relation. The poet only sees it as an inevitable step in the path of the Creator. But, in England, one hermit finds this fact, and another finds that, and lives and dies ignorant of its value. There are great exceptions, of John Hunter, a man of ideas,[46] perhaps of Robert Brown, the botanist; and of Richard Owen, who has imported into Britain the German homologies,[47] and enriched science with contributions of his own, adding sometimes the divination of the old masters to the unbroken power of labor in the English mind. But for the most part the natural science in England is out of its loyal alliance with morals, and is as

void of imagination and free play of thought as conveyanc-
ing. It stands in strong contrast with the genius of the Germans, those semi-Greeks, who love analogy, and, by means of
their height of view, preserve their enthusiasm and think for
Europe.

No hope, no sublime augury cheers the student, no secure
striding from experiment onward to a foreseen law, but only
a casual dipping here and there, like diggers in California
"prospecting for a placer" that will pay.[48] A horizon of brass
of the diameter of his umbrella shuts down around his senses.
Squalid contentment with conventions, satire at the names
of philosophy and religion, parochial and shop-till politics,
and idolatry of usage, betray the ebb of life and spirit. As
they trample on nationalities to reproduce London and Lon-
doners in Europe and Asia, so they fear the hostility of ideas,
of poetry, of religion, — ghosts which they cannot lay; and,
having attempted to domesticate and dress the Blessed Soul [49]
itself in English broadcloth and gaiters, they are tormented
with fear that herein lurks a force that will sweep their system away. The artists say, "Nature puts them out"; the
scholars have become un-ideal. They parry earnest speech
with banter and levity; they laugh you down, or they change
the subject. "The fact is," say they over their wine, "all that
about liberty, and so forth, is gone by; it won't do any
longer." The practical and comfortable oppress them with
inexorable claims, and the smallest fraction of power remains
for heroism and poetry. No poet dares murmur of beauty
out of the precinct of his rhymes. No priest dares hint at a
Providence which does not respect English utility. The island
is a roaring volcano of fate, of material values, of tariffs and
laws of repression, glutted markets and low prices.

In the absence of the highest aims, of the pure love of
knowledge and the surrender to nature, there is the suppression of the imagination, the priapism of the senses and the

understanding; we have the factitious instead of the natural; tasteless expense, arts of comfort, and the rewarding as an illustrious inventor whosoever will contrive one impediment more to interpose between the man and his objects.

Thus poetry is degraded and made ornamental. Pope and his school wrote poetry fit to put round frosted cake. What did Walter Scott write without stint? a rhymed traveller's guide to Scotland.[50] And the libraries of verses they print have this Birmingham character.[51] How many volumes of well-bred metre we must jingle through, before we can be filled, taught, renewed! We want the miraculous; the beauty which we can manufacture at no mill, — can give no account of; the beauty of which Chaucer and Chapman had the secret. The poetry of course is low and prosaic; only now and then, as in Wordsworth, conscientious; or in Byron, passional; or in Tennyson, factitious. But if I should count the poets who have contributed to the Bible of existing England sentences of guidance and consolation which are still glowing and effective, — how few! Shall I find my heavenly bread in the reigning poets? Where is great design in modern English poetry? The English have lost sight of the fact that poetry exists to speak the spiritual law, and that no wealth of description or of fancy is yet essentially new and out of the limits of prose, until this condition is reached. Therefore the grave old poets, like the Greek artists, heeded their designs, and less considered the finish. It was their office to lead to the divine sources, out of which all this and much more, readily springs; and, if this religion is in the poetry, it raises us to some purpose and we can well afford some staidness or hardness, or want of popular tune in the verses.

The exceptional fact of the period is the genius of Wordsworth. He had no master but nature and solitude. "He wrote a poem," says Landor, "without the aid of war."[52] His verse is the voice of sanity in a worldly and ambitious age. One regrets that his temperament was not more liquid and musical. He has written longer than he was inspired. But for the rest, he has no competitor.

Tennyson is endowed precisely in points where Wordsworth wanted. There is no finer ear, nor more command of the keys of language. Color, like the dawn, flows over the horizon from his pencil, in waves so rich that we do not miss the central form. Through all his refinements, too, he has reached the public, — a certificate of good sense and general power, since he who aspires to be the English poet must be as large as London, not in the same kind as London, but in his own kind. But he wants a subject, and climbs no mount of vision to bring its secrets to the people. He contents himself with describing the Englishman as he is, and proposes no better. There are all degrees in poetry and we must be thankful for every beautiful talent. But it is only a first success, when the ear is gained. The best office of the best poets has been to show how low and uninspired was their general style, and that only once or twice they have struck the high chord.

That expansiveness which is the essence of the poetic element, they have not. It was no Oxonian, but Hafiz, who said, "Let us be crowned with roses, let us drink wine, and break up the tiresome old roof of heaven into new forms." [53] A stanza of the song of nature the Oxonian has no ear for, and he does not value the salient and curative influence of intellectual action, studious of truth without a by-end.

By the law of contraries, I look for an irresistible taste for Orientalism in Britain. For a self-conceited modish life, made up of trifles, clinging to a corporeal civilization, hating ideas, there is no remedy like the Oriental largeness. That astonishes and disconcerts English decorum. For once, there is thunder it never heard, light it never saw, and power which trifles with time and space. I am not surprised then to find an Englishman like Warren Hastings,[54] who had been struck with the grand style of thinking in the Indian writings, deprecating the prejudices of his countrymen while offering them a translation of the Bhagvat. "Might I, an unlettered man, venture to prescribe bounds to the latitude of criticism, I should exclude, in estimating the merit of such a production, all rules drawn from the ancient or modern literature of Europe, all references to such sentiments or manners as are become the standards of propriety for opinion and action in our own modes, and, equally, all appeals to our revealed tenets of religion and moral duty."[55] He goes to bespeak indulgence to "ornaments of fancy unsuited to our taste, and passages elevated to a tract of sublimity into which our habits of judgment will find it difficult to pursue them."[56]

Meantime, I know that a retrieving power lies in the English race which seems to make any recoil possible; in other words, there is at all times a minority of profound minds existing in the nation, capable of appreciating every soaring of intellect and every hint of tendency. While the constructive talent seems dwarfed and superficial, the criticism is often in the noblest tone and suggests the presence of the invisible gods. I can well believe what I have often heard, that there are two nations in England; but it is not the Poor and the Rich, nor is it the Normans and Saxons, nor the Celt and the Goth. These are each always becoming the other; for Robert Owen does not exaggerate the power of circumstance.[57] But the two complexions, or two styles of mind, — the perceptive class, and the practical finality class, — are ever in counterpoise, interacting mutually, one in hopeless minorities; the other in huge masses; one studious, contemplative, experimenting; the other, the ungrateful pupil, scornful of the source whilst availing itself of the knowledge for gain; these two nations, of genius and of animal force, though the first consist of only a dozen souls and the second of twenty millions, forever by their discord and their accord yield the power of the English State.

CHAPTER XV

The *"Times"*

The power of the newspaper is familiar in America and in accordance with our political system. In England, it stands in antagonism with the feudal institutions, and it is all the more beneficent succor against the secretive tendencies of a monarchy. The celebrated Lord Somers[1] "knew of no good law proposed and passed in his time, to which the public papers had not directed his attention." There is no corner and no night. A relentless inquisition drags every secret to the day, turns the glare of this solar microscope on every malfaisance, so as to make the public a more terrible spy than any foreigner; and no weakness can be taken advantage of by an enemy, since the whole people are already fore-warned. Thus England rids herself of those incrustations which have been the ruin of old states. Of course, this inspec-tion is feared. No antique privilege, no comfortable monop-oly, but sees surely that its days are counted; the people are familiarized with the reason of reform, and, one by one, take away every argument of the obstructives. "So your grace likes the comfort of reading the newspapers," said Lord Mansfield to the Duke of Northumberland; "mark my words; you and I shall not live to see it, but this young gentleman (Lord Eldon) may, or it may be a little later; but a little sooner or later, these newspapers will most assuredly write the dukes of Northumberland out of their titles and possessions, and the country out of its king." [2] The tendency in England towards social and political institutions like those of America, is inevitable, and the ability of its journals is the driving force.

England is full of manly, clever, well-bred men who possess the talent of writing off-hand pungent paragraphs, expressing with clearness and courage their opinion on any person or performance. Valuable or not, it is a skill that is rarely found, out of the English journals. The English do this, as they write poetry, as they ride and box, by being educated to it. Hundreds of clever Praeds and Freres and Froudes and Hoods and Hooks and Maginns and Mills and Macaulays, make poems, or short essays for a journal, as they make speeches in Parliament and on the hustings, or as they shoot and ride.[3] It is a quite accidental and arbitrary direction of their general ability. Rude health and spirits, an Oxford education and the habits of society are implied, but not a ray of genius. It comes of the crowded state of professions, the violent interest which all men take in politics, the facility of experimenting in the journals, and high pay.

The most conspicuous result of this talent is the "Times" newspaper.[4] No power in England is more felt, more feared, or more obeyed. What you read in the morning in that journal, you shall hear in the evening in all society. It has ears everywhere, and its information is earliest, completest and surest. It has risen, year by year, and victory by victory, to its present authority. I asked one of its old contributors whether it had once been abler than it is now? "Never," he said; "these are its palmiest days." It has shown those qualities which are dear to Englishmen, unflinching adherence to its objects, prodigal intellectual ability and a towering assurance, backed by the perfect organization in its printing-house and its world-wide network of correspondence and reports. It has its own history and famous trophies. In 1820, it adopted the cause of Queen Caroline, and carried it against the king.[5] It adopted a poor-law system, and almost alone lifted it through.[6] When Lord Brougham was in power, it decided against him, and pulled him down.[7] It declared war against Ireland, and conquered it.[8] It adopted the League against the Corn Laws, and, when Cobden had begun to despair, it announced his triumph.[9] It denounced and discredited the French Republic of 1848, and checked every sympathy with it in England, until it had enrolled 200,000 special constables to watch the Chartists and make them ridiculous on the 10th April.[10] It first denounced and then adopted the new French Empire, and urged the French Alliance and its results.[11] It has entered into each municipal, literary and social question, almost with a controlling voice. It has done bold and seasonable service in exposing frauds which threatened the commercial community. Meanwhile, it attacks its rivals by perfecting its printing machinery, and will drive them out of circulation: for the only limit to the circulation of the "Times" is the impossibility of printing copies fast enough; since a daily paper can only be new and seasonable for a few hours. It will kill all but that paper which is diametrically in opposition; since many papers, first and last, have lived by their attacks on the leading journal.

The late Mr. Walter[12] was printer of the "Times," and had gradually arranged the whole *materiel* of it in perfect system. It is told that when he demanded a small share in the proprietary and was refused, he said, "As you please, gentlemen; and you may take away the 'Times' from this office when you will; I shall publish the 'New Times,' next Monday morning." The proprietors, who had already complained that his charges for printing were excessive, found that they were in his power, and gave him whatever he wished.

I went one day with a good friend to the "Times" office, which was entered through a pretty garden-yard in Printing-

House Square.[13] We walked with some circumspection, as if we were entering a powder-mill; but the door was opened by a mild old woman, and, by dint of some transmission of cards, we were at last conducted into the parlor of Mr. Morris, a very gentle person, with no hostile appearances.[14] The statistics are now quite out of date, but I remember he told us that the daily printing was then 35,000 copies; that on the 1st March, 1848, the greatest number ever printed, — 54,000 — were issued; that, since February, the daily circulation had increased by 8000 copies. The old press they were then using printed five or six thousand sheets per hour; the new machine, for which they were then building an engine, would print twelve thousand per hour. Our entertainer confided us to a courteous assistant to show us the establishment, in which, I think, they employed a hundred and twenty men. I remember I saw the reporters' room, in which they redact their hasty stenographs, but the editor's room, and who is in it, I did not see, though I shared the curiosity of mankind respecting it.

The staff of the "Times" has always been made up of able men. Old Walter, Sterling, Bacon, Barnes, Alsiger, Horace Twiss, Jones Lloyd, John Oxenford, Mr. Mosely, Mr. Bailey, have contributed to its renown in their special departments.[15] But it has never wanted the first pens for occasional assistance. Its private information is inexplicable, and recalls the stories of Fouché's police, whose omniscience made it believed that the Empress Josephine must be in his pay.[16] It has mercantile and political correspondents in every foreign city, and its expresses outrun the despatches of the government. One hears anecdotes of the rise of its servants, as of the functionaries of the India House. I was told of the dexterity of one of its reporters, who, finding himself, on one occasion, where the magistrates had strictly forbidden reporters, put his hands into his coat-pocket, and with pencil in one hand and tablet in the other, did his work.

The influence of this journal is a recognized power in Europe, and, of course, none is more conscious of it than its conductors. The tone of its articles has often been the occasion of comment from the official organs of the continental courts, and sometimes the ground of diplomatic complaint. 'What would the "Times" say?' is a terror in Paris, in Berlin, in Vienna, in Copenhagen and in Nepaul.[17] Its consummate discretion and success exhibit the English skill of combination. The daily paper is the work of many hands, chiefly, it is said, of young men recently from the University, and perhaps reading law in chambers in London. Hence the academic elegance and classic allusion which adorn its columns. Hence, too, the heat and gallantry of its onset. But the steadiness of the aim suggests the belief that this fire is directed and fed by older engineers; as if persons of exact information, and with settled views of policy, supplied the writers with the basis of fact and the object to be attained, and availed themselves of their younger energy and eloquence to plead the cause. Both the council and the executive departments gain by this division. Of two men of equal ability, the one who does not write but keeps his eye on the course of public affairs, will have the higher judicial wisdom. But the parts are kept in concert, all the articles appear to proceed from a single will. The "Times" never disapproves of what itself has said, or cripples itself by apology for the absence of the editor, or the indiscretion of him who held the pen. It speaks out bluff and bold, and sticks to what it says. It draws from any number of learned and skilful contributors; but a more learned and skilful person supervises, corrects, and co-ordinates. Of this closet, the secret does not transpire. No writer is suffered to claim the authorship of any paper; every thing good, from whatever quarter, comes out editorially; and thus, by making the paper everything and those who write it nothing, the character and the awe of the journal gain.

The English like it for its complete information. A state-ment of fact in the "Times" is as reliable as a citation from Hansard. Then they like its independence; they do not know, when they take it up, what their paper is going to say: but, above all, for the nationality and confidence of its tone. It thinks for them all; it is their understanding and day's ideal daguerreotyped. When I see them reading its columns, they seem to me becoming every moment more British. It has the national courage, not rash and petulant, but consid-erate and determined. No dignity or wealth is a shield from its assault. It attacks a duke as readily as a policeman, and with the most provoking airs of condescension. It makes rude work with the Board of Admiralty. The Bench of Bishops[18] is still less safe. One bishop fares badly for his rapacity, and another for his bigotry, and a third for his courtliness. It addresses occasionally a hint to Majesty itself, and sometimes a hint which is taken. There is an air of free-dom even in their advertising columns, which speaks well for England to a foreigner. On the days when I arrived in London in 1847, I read, among the daily announcements, one offering a reward of fifty pounds to any person who would put a nobleman, described by name and title, late a member of Parliament, into any county jail in England, he having been convicted of obtaining money under false pre-tences.

Was never such arrogancy as the tone of this paper. Every slip of an Oxonian or Cantabrigian who writes his first leader assumes that we subdued the earth before we sat down to write this particular "Times." One would think the world was on its knees to the "Times" Office for its daily breakfast. But this arrogance is calculated. Who would care for it, if it "surmised," or "dared to confess," or "ventured to predict," &c? No; *it is so,* and so it shall be.

The morality and patriotism of the "Times" claim only to be representative, and by no means ideal. It gives the argument, not of the majority, but of the commanding class. Its editors know better than to defend Russia, or Austria, or English vested rights, on abstract grounds. But they give a voice to the class who at the moment take the lead; and they have an instinct for finding where the power now lies, which is eternally shifting its banks. Sympathizing with, and speaking for the class that rules the hour, yet being apprised of every ground-swell, every Chartist resolution, every Church squabble, every strike in the mills, they detect the first tremblings of change. They watch the hard and bitter struggles of the authors of each liberal movement, year by year; watching them only to taunt and obstruct them, — until, at last, when they see that these have established their fact, that power is on the point of passing to them, they strike in with the voice of a monarch, astonish those whom they succor as much as those whom they desert, and make victory sure. Of course the aspirants see that the "Times" is one of the goods of fortune, not to be won but by winning their cause.

"Punch" [19] is equally an expression of English good sense, as the "London Times." It is the comic version of the same sense. Many of its caricatures are equal to the best pamphlets, and will convey to the eye in an instant the popular view which was taken of each turn of public affairs. Its sketches are usually made by masterly hands, and sometimes with genius; the delight of every class, because uniformly guided by that taste which is tyrannical in England. It is a new trait of the nineteenth century, that the wit and humor of England, — as in Punch, so in the humorists, Jerrold,[20] Dickens, Thackeray, Hood, — have taken the direction of humanity and freedom.

The "Times," like every important institution, shows the way to a better. It is a living index of the colossal British power. Its existence honors the people who dare to print all they know, dare to know all the facts and do not wish to be flattered by hiding the extent of the public disaster. There is always safety in valor. I wish I could add that this journal aspired to deserve the power it wields, by guidance of the public sentiment to the right. It is usually pretended, in Parliament and elsewhere, that the English press has a high tone, — which it has not. It has an imperial tone, as of a powerful and independent nation. But, as with other empires, its tone is prone to be official, and even officinal.[21] The "Times" shares all the limitations of the governing classes, and wishes never to be in a minority. If only it dared to cleave to the right, to show the right to be the only expedient, and feed its batteries from the central heart of humanity, it might not have so many men of rank among its contributors, but genius would be its cordial and invincible ally; it might now and then bear the brunt of formidable combinations, but no journal is ruined by wise courage. It would be the natural leader of British reform; its proud function, that of being the voice of Europe, the defender of the exile and patriot against despots, would be more effectually discharged; it would have the authority which is claimed for that dream of good men not yet come to pass, an International Congress; and the least of its victories would be to give to England a new millennium of beneficent power.

CHAPTER XVI

Stonehenge[1]

It had been agreed between my friend Mr. Carlyle and me, that before I left England we should make an excursion together to Stonehenge,[2] which neither of us had seen; and the project pleased my fancy with the double attraction of the monument and the companion. It seemed a bringing together of extreme points, to visit the oldest religious monument in Britain in company with her latest thinker, and one whose influence may be traced in every contemporary book. I was glad to sum up a little my experiences, and to exchange a few reasonable words on the aspects of England with a man on whose genius I set a very high value, and who had as much penetration and as severe a theory of duty as any person in it. On Friday, 7th July, we took the South Western Railway through Hampshire to Salisbury,[3] where we found a carriage to convey us to Amesbury.[4] The fine weather and my friend's local knowledge of Hampshire, in which he is wont to spend a part of every summer, made the way short. There was much to say, too, of the travelling Americans and their usual objects in London. I thought it natural that they should give some time to works of art collected here which they cannot find at home, and a little to scientific clubs and museums, which, at this moment, make London very attractive. But my philosopher was not contented. Art and 'high art' is a favorite target for his wit. "Yes, *Kunst*[5] is a great delusion, and Goethe and Schiller wasted a great deal of good time on it:" [6] — and he thinks he discovers that old Goethe[7] found this out, and, in his later writings, changed his tone. As soon as men begin to talk of art, architecture and antiquities, nothing good comes of it. He wishes to go through the British Museum in silence, and thinks a sincere man will see something and say nothing. In these days, he thought, it would become an architect to consult only the grim necessity, and say, 'I can build you a coffin for such dead persons as you are, and for such dead purposes as you have, but you shall have no ornament.' For the science, he had if possible even less tolerance, and compared the *savans*[8] of Somerset House[9] to the boy who asked Confucius "how many stars in the sky?" Confucius replied, "he minded things near him:" then said the boy, "how many hairs are there in your eyebrows?" Confucius said, "he did n't know and did n't care." [10]

Still speaking of the Americans, Carlyle complained that they dislike the coldness and exclusiveness of the English, and run away to France and go with their countrymen and are amused, instead of manfully staying in London, and confronting Englishmen and acquiring their culture, who really have much to teach them.

I told Carlyle that I was easily dazzled, and was accustomed to concede readily all that an Englishman would ask; I saw everywhere in the country proofs of sense and spirit, and success of every sort: I like the people; they are as good as they are handsome; they have everything and can do everything; but meantime, I surely know that as soon as I return to Massachusetts I shall lapse at once into the feeling, which the geography of America inevitably inspires, that we play the game with immense advantage; that there and not here is the seat and centre of the British race; and that no skill or activity can long compete with the prodigious natural advantages of that country, in the hands of the same race; and that England, an old and exhausted island, must one day be contented, like other parents, to be strong only in her children. But this was a proposition which no Englishman of whatever condition can easily entertain.

We left the train at Salisbury and took a carriage to Amesbury, passing by Old Sarum, a bare, treeless hill, once containing the town which sent two members to Parliament, — now, not a hut; and, arriving at Amesbury, stopped at the George Inn. After dinner we walked to Salisbury Plain. On the broad downs, under the gray sky, not a house was visible, nothing but Stonehenge, which looked like a group of brown dwarfs in the wide expanse, — Stonehenge and the barrows, which rose like green bosses about the plain, and a few hayricks. On the top of a mountain, the old temple would not be more impressive. Far and wide a few shepherds with their flocks sprinkled the plain, and a bagman[11] drove along the road. It looked as if the wide margin given in this crowded isle to this primeval temple were accorded by the veneration of the British race to the old egg out of which all their ecclesiastical structures and history had proceeded.[12] Stonehenge is a circular colonnade with a diameter of a hundred feet, and enclosing a second and a third colonnade within. We walked round the stones and clambered over them, to wont ourselves with their strange aspect and groupings, and found a nook sheltered from the wind among them, where Carlyle lighted his cigar. It was pleasant to see that just this simplest of all simple structures, — two upright stones and a lintel laid across, — had long outstood all later churches and all history, and were like what is most permanent on the face of the planet: these, and the barrows, — mere mounds (of which there are a hundred and sixty within a circle of three miles about Stonehenge), like the same mound on the plain of Troy,[13] which still makes good to the passing mariner on

Hellespont,[14] the vaunt of Homer and the fame of Achilles. Within the enclosure grow buttercups, nettles, and all around, wild thyme, daisy, meadowsweet, goldenrod, thistle and the carpeting grass. Over us, larks were soaring and singing; — as my friend said, "the larks which were hatched last year, and the wind which was hatched many thousand years ago." We counted and measured by paces the biggest stones, and soon knew as much as any man can suddenly know of the inscrutable temple. There are ninety-four stones, and there were once probably one hundred and sixty. The temple is circular and uncovered, and the situation fixed astronomically, — the grand entrances, here and at Abury,[15] being placed exactly northeast, "as all the gates of the old cavern temples are." How came the stones here? for these *sarsens*,[16] or Druidical sandstones, are not found in this neighborhood. The *sacrificial stone,* as it is called, is the only one in all these blocks that can resist the action of fire, and as I read in the books, must have been brought one hundred and fifty miles.

On almost every stone we found the marks of the mineralogist's hammer and chisel. The nineteen smaller stones of the inner circle are of granite. I, who had just come from Professor Sedgwick's Cambridge Museum of megatheria[17] and mastodons, was ready to maintain that some cleverer elephants or mylodonta[18] had borne off and laid these rocks one on another. Only the good beasts must have known how to cut a well-wrought tenon and mortise,[19] and to smooth the surface of some of the stones. The chief mystery is, that any mystery should have been allowed to settle on so remarkable a monument, in a country on which all the muses have kept their eyes now for eighteen hundred years. We are not yet too late to learn much more than is known of this structure. Some diligent Fellowes or Layard will arrive, stone by stone, at the whole history, by that exhaustive British sense and perseverance, so whimsical in its choice of objects, which leaves its own Stonehenge or Choir Gaur[20] to the rabbits, whilst it opens pyramids and uncovers Nineveh.[21] Stonehenge, in virtue of the simplicity of its plan and its good preservation, is as if new and recent; and, a thousand years hence, men will thank this age for the accurate history. We walked in and out and took again and again a fresh look at the uncanny stones. The old sphinx put our petty differences of nationality out of sight. To these conscious stones we two pilgrims were alike known and near. We could equally well revere their old British meaning. My philosopher was subdued and gentle. In this quiet house of destiny he happened to say, "I plant cypresses wherever I go, and if I am in search of pain, I cannot go wrong." The spot, the gray blocks and their rude order, which refuses to be disposed of, suggested to him the flight of ages and the succession of religions. The old times of England impress Carlyle much: he reads little, he says, in these last years, but *"Acta Sanctorum,"* [22] the fifty-three volumes of which are in the London Library.[23] He finds all English history therein. He can see, as he reads, the old Saint of Iona sitting there and writing, a man to men.[24] The *Acta Sanctorum* show plainly that the men of those times believed in God and in the immortality of the soul, as their abbeys and cathedrals testify: now, even the puritanism is all gone. London is pagan. He fancied that greater men had lived in England than any of her writers; and, in fact, about the time when those writers appeared, the last of these were already gone.

We left the mound in the twilight, with the design to return the next morning, and coming back two miles to our inn we were met by little showers, and late as it was, men and women were out attempting to protect their spread windrows. The grass grows rank and dark in the showery England. At the inn, there was only milk for one cup of tea.

When we called for more, the girl brought us three drops. My friend was annoyed, who stood for the credit of an English inn, and still more the next morning, by the dog-cart, sole procurable vehicle, in which we were to be sent to Wilton. I engaged the local antiquary, Mr. Brown,[25] to go with us to Stonehenge, on our way, and show us what he knew of the "astronomical" and "sacrificial" stones.[26] I stood on the last, and he pointed to the upright, or rather, inclined stone, called the "astronomical," and bade me notice that its top ranged with the sky-line. "Yes." Very well. Now, at the summer solstice, the sun rises exactly over the top of that stone, and, at the Druidical temple at Abury, there is also an astronomical stone, in the same relative position.

In the silence of tradition, this one relation to science becomes an important clew; but we were content to leave the problem with the rocks. Was this the "Giants' Dance," which Merlin brought from Killaraus, in Ireland, to be Uther Pendragon's monument to the British nobles whom Hengist slaughtered here, as Geoffrey of Monmouth relates?[27] or was it a Roman work, as Inigo Jones explained to King James,[28] or identical in design and style with the East Indian temples of the sun, as Davies in the Celtic Researches maintains?[29] Of all the writers, Stukeley is the best.[30] The heroic antiquary, charmed with the geometric perfections of his ruin, connects it with the oldest monuments and religion of the world, and with the courage of his tribe, does not stick to say, "the Deity who made the world by the scheme of Stonehenge." He finds that the *cursus*[31] on Salisbury Plain stretches across the downs like a line of latitude upon the globe, and the meridian line of Stonehenge passes exactly through the middle of this *cursus*. But here is the high point of the theory: the Druids had the magnet;[32] laid their courses by it; their cardinal points in Stonehenge, Ambresbury,[33] and elsewhere, which vary a little from true east

and west, followed the variations of the compass. The Druids
were Phœnicians.³⁴ The name of the magnet is *lapis Hera-
cleus,*³⁵ and Hercules was the god of the Phœnicians. Hercules, in the legend, drew his bow at the sun, and the sun-god
gave him a golden cup, with which he sailed over the ocean.
What was this, but a compass-box? This cup or little boat, in
which the magnet was made to float on water and so show the
north, was probably its first form, before it was suspended
on a pin. But science was an *arcanum,*³⁶ and, as Britain was
a Phœnician secret, so they kept their compass a secret, and
it was lost with the Tyrian commerce.³⁷ The golden fleece
again, of Jason, was the compass, — a bit of loadstone, easily
supposed to be the only one in the world, and therefore
naturally awakening the cupidity and ambition of the young
heroes of a maritime nation to join in an expedition to
obtain possession of this wise stone. Hence the fable that the
ship Argo was loquacious and oracular. There is also some
curious coincidence in the names. Apollodorus makes *Magnes*
the son of *Æolus,* who married *Nais.*³⁸ On hints like these,
Stukeley builds again the grand colonnade into historic harmony, and computing backward by the known variations of
the compass, bravely assigns the year 406 before Christ for the
date of the temple.

For the difficulty of handling and carrying stones of this
size, the like is done in all cities, every day, with no other
aid than horse-power. I chanced to see, a year ago, men at
work on the substructure of a house in Bowdoin Square,³⁹
in Boston, swinging a block of granite of the size of the
largest of the Stonehenge columns, with an ordinary derrick.
The men were common masons, with paddies to help, nor
did they think they were doing anything remarkable. I suppose there were as good men a thousand years ago. And we
wonder how Stonehenge was built and forgotten. After spending half an hour on the spot, we set forth in our dog-cart over

the downs for Wilton, Carlyle not suppressing some threats
and evil omens on the proprietors, for keeping these broad
plains a wretched sheep-walk when so many thousands of
English men were hungry and wanted labor. But I heard
afterwards that it is not an economy to cultivate this land,
which only yields one crop on being broken up, and is then
spoiled.

We came to Wilton and to Wilton Hall, — the renowned
seat of the Earls of Pembroke, a house known to Shakspeare
and Massinger, the frequent home of Sir Philip Sidney,
where he wrote the Arcadia; where he conversed with Lord
Brooke, a man of deep thought, and a poet, who caused to
be engraved on his tombstone, "Here lies Fulke Greville,
Lord Brooke, the friend of Sir Philip Sidney." [40] It is now
the property of the Earl of Pembroke,[41] and the residence of
his brother, Sidney Herbert, Esq.,[42] and is esteemed a noble
specimen of the English manor-hall. My friend had a letter
from Mr. Herbert to his housekeeper, and the house was
shown. The state drawing-room is a double cube, 30 feet
high, by 30 feet wide, by 60 feet long: the adjoining room is
a single cube, of 30 feet every way. Although these apartments and the long library were full of good family portraits,
Vandykes and other;[43] and though there were some good pictures, and a quadrangle cloister full of antique and modern
statuary, — to which Carlyle, catalogue in hand, did all too
much justice, — yet the eye was still drawn to the windows,
to a magnificent lawn, on which grew the finest cedars in
England. I had not seen more charming grounds. We went
out, and walked over the estate. We crossed a bridge built
by Inigo Jones, over a stream of which the gardener did not
know the name (*Qu.* Alph?);[44] watched the deer; climbed to
the lonely sculptured summer-house, on a hill backed by a
wood; came down into the Italian garden and into a French
pavilion garnished with French busts; and so again to the

house, where we found a table laid for us with bread, meats, peaches, grapes and wine.

On leaving Wilton House, we took the coach for Salisbury. The Cathedral,[45] which was finished six hundred years ago, has even a spruce and modern air, and its spire is the highest in England. I know not why, but I had been more struck with one of no fame, at Coventry,[46] which rises three hundred feet from the ground, with the lightness of a mullein plant, and not at all implicated with the church. Salisbury is now esteemed the culmination of the Gothic art in England, as the buttresses are fully unmasked and honestly detailed from the sides of the pile. The interior of the Cathedral is obstructed by the organ in the middle, acting like a screen. I know not why in real architecture the hunger of the eye for length of line is so rarely gratified. The rule of art is that a colonnade is more beautiful the longer it is, and that *ad infinitum*. And the nave of a church is seldom so long that it need be divided by a screen.

We loitered in the church, outside the choir, whilst service was said. Whilst we listened to the organ, my friend remarked, The music is good, and yet not quite religious, but somewhat as if a monk were panting to some fine Queen of Heaven. Carlyle was unwilling, and we did not ask to have the choir shown us, but returned to our inn, after seeing another old church of the place. We passed in the train Clarendon Park,[47] but could see little but the edge of a wood, though Carlyle had wished to pay closer attention to the birthplace of the Decrees of Clarendon.[48] At Bishopstoke[49] we stopped, and found Mr. H.,[50] who received us in his carriage, and took us to his house at Bishops Waltham.[51]

On Sunday we had much discourse, on a very rainy day. My friends asked, whether there were any Americans? — any with an American idea, — any theory of the right future of that country? Thus challenged, I bethought myself neither of caucuses nor congress, neither of presidents nor of cabinet-ministers, nor of such as would make of America another Europe. I thought only of the simplest and purest minds; I said, "Certainly yes; — but those who hold it are fanatics of a dream which I should hardly care to relate to your English ears, to which it might be only ridiculous, — and yet it is the only true." So I opened the dogma of no-government and non-resistance, and anticipated the objections and the fun, and procured a kind of hearing for it. I said, it is true that I have never seen in any country a man of sufficient valor to stand for this truth, and yet it is plain to me that no less valor than this can command my respect. I can easily see the bankruptcy of the vulgar musket-worship, — though great men be musket-worshippers; — and 't is certain as God liveth, the gun that does not need another gun, the law of love and justice alone, can effect a clean revolution. I fancied that one or two of my anecdotes made some impression on Carlyle, and I insisted that the manifest absurdity of the view to English feasibility could make no difference to a gentleman; that as to our secure tenure of our mutton-chop and spinach in London or in Boston, the soul might quote Talleyrand, *"Monsieur, je n'en vois pas la nécessité."* [52] As I had thus taken in the conversation the saint's part, when dinner was announced, Carlyle refused to go out before me, — "he was altogether too wicked." I planted my back against the wall, and our host wittily rescued us from the dilemma, by saying he was the wickedest and would walk out first, then Carlyle followed, and I went last.

On the way to Winchester,[53] whither our host accompanied us in the afternoon, my friends asked many questions respecting American landscape, forests, houses, — my house, for example. It is not easy to answer these queries well. There, I thought, in America, lies nature sleeping, overgrowing, almost conscious, too much by half for man in the picture, and so giving a certain *tristesse*, like the rank vegetation of swamps and forests seen at night, steeped in dews and rains, which it loves; and on it man seems not able to make much impression. There, in that great sloven continent, in high Alleghany pastures, in the sea-wide sky-skirted prairie, still sleeps and murmurs and hides the great mother, long since driven away from the trim hedge-rows and over-cultivated garden of England. And, in England, I am quite too sensible of this. Every one is on his good behavior and must be dressed for dinner at six. So I put off my friends with very inadequate details, as best I could.

Just before entering Winchester we stopped at the Church of Saint Cross,[54] and after looking through the quaint antiquity, we demanded a piece of bread and a draught of beer, which the founder, Henry de Blois,[55] in 1136, commanded should be given to every one who should ask it at the gate. We had both, from the old couple who take care of the church. Some twenty people every day, they said, make the same demand. This hospitality of seven hundred years' standing did not hinder Carlyle from pronouncing a malediction on the priest who receives £2,000 a year, that were meant for the poor, and spends a pittance on this small-beer and crumbs.

In the Cathedral [56] I was gratified, at least by the ample dimensions. The length of line exceeds that of any other English church; being 556 feet, by 250 in breadth of transept. I think I prefer this church to all I have seen, except Westminster and York. Here was Canute buried,[57] and here Alfred the Great was crowned and buried,[58] and here the Saxon kings; and, later, in his own church, William of Wykeham.[59] It is very old: part of the crypt into which we went down and saw the Saxon and Norman arches[60] of the old church on which the present stands, was built fourteen or fifteen hundred years ago. Sharon Turner says, "Alfred was buried at Winchester, in the Abbey he had founded there, but his remains were removed by Henry I. to the new Abbey in the meadows at Hyde, on the northern quarter of the city, and laid under the high altar. The building was destroyed at the Reformation, and what is left of Alfred's body now lies covered by modern buildings, or buried in the ruins of the old." [61] William of Wykeham's shrine tomb was unlocked for us, and Carlyle took hold of the recumbent statue's marble hands and patted them affectionately, for he rightly values the brave man who built Windsor and this Cathedral and the School here and New College at Oxford.[62] But it was growing late in the afternoon. Slowly we left the old house, and parting with our host, we took the train for London.

CHAPTER XVII

Personal

In these comments on an old journey, now revised after seven busy years have much changed men and things in England, I have abstained from reference to persons, except in the last chapter and in one or two cases where the fame of the parties seemed to have given the public a property in all that concerned them. I must further allow myself a few notices, if only as an acknowledgment of debts that cannot be paid. My journeys were cheered by so much kindness from new friends, that my impression of the island is bright with agreeable memories both of public societies and of households: and, what is nowhere better found than in England, a cultivated person fitly surrounded by a happy home, "with honor, love, obedience, troops of friends," [1] is of all institutions the best. At the landing in Liverpool I found my Manchester correspondent[2] awaiting me, a gentleman whose kind reception was followed by a train of friendly and effective attentions which never rested whilst I remained in the country. A man of sense and of letters, the editor of a powerful local journal,[3] he added to solid virtues an infinite sweetness and *bonhommie*. There seemed a pool of honey about his heart which lubricated all his speech and action with fine jets of mead. An equal good fortune attended many later accidents of my journey, until the sincerity of English kindness ceased to surprise. My visit fell in the fortunate days when Mr. Bancroft was the American Minister in London,[4] and at his house, or through his good offices, I had easy access to excellent persons and to privileged places. At the house of Mr. Carlyle, I met persons eminent in society and in letters. The privileges of the Athenæum and of the Reform Clubs were hospitably opened to me, and I found much advantage in the circles of the "Geologic," the "Antiquarian" and the "Royal" Societies.[5] Every day in London gave me new opportunities of meeting men and women who give splendor to society. I saw Rogers, Hallam, Macaulay, Milnes, Milman, Barry Cornwall, Dickens, Thackeray, Tennyson, Leigh Hunt, D'Israeli, Helps, Wilkinson, Bailey, Kenyon and Forster: the younger poets, Clough, Arnold and Patmore; and among the men of science, Robert Brown, Owen, Sedgwick, Faraday, Buckland, Lyell, De la Beche, Hooker, Carpenter, Babbage and Edward Forbes.[6] It was my privilege also to converse with Miss Baillie, with Lady Morgan, with Mrs. Jameson and Mrs. Somerville.[7] A finer hospitality made many private houses not less known and dear. It is not in distinguished circles that wisdom and elevated characters are usually found, or, if found, they are not confined thereto; and my recollections of the best hours go back to private conversations in different parts of the kingdom, with persons little known. Nor am I insensible to the courtesy which frankly opened to me some noble mansions, if I do not adorn my page with their names. Among the privileges of London, I recall with pleasure two or three signal days, one at Kew,[8] where Sir William Hooker showed me all the riches of the vast botanic garden; one at the Museum, where Sir Charles Fellowes explained in detail the history of his Ionic trophy-monument; and still another, on which Mr. Owen accompanied my countryman Mr. H. and myself through the Hunterian Museum.[9]

The like frank hospitality, bent on real service, I found

among the great and the humble, wherever I went; in Birmingham, in Oxford, in Leicester, in Nottingham, in Sheffield, in Manchester, in Liverpool. At Edinburgh, through the kindness of Dr. Samuel Brown,[10] I made the acquaintance of De Quincey, of Lord Jeffrey, of Wilson, of Mrs. Crowe, of the Messrs. Chambers, and of a man of high character and genius, the short-lived painter, David Scott.[11]

At Ambleside in March, 1848, I was for a couple of days the guest of Miss Martineau, then newly returned from her Egyptian tour.[12] On Sunday afternoon I accompanied her to Rydal Mount.[13] And as I have recorded a visit to Wordsworth, many years before, I must not forget this second interview. We found Mr. Wordsworth asleep on the sofa. He was at first silent and indisposed, as an old man suddenly waked before he had ended his nap; but soon became full of talk on the French news.[14] He was nationally bitter on the French; bitter on Scotchmen, too. No Scotchman, he said, can write English. He detailed the two models, on one or the other of which all the sentences of the historian Robertson are framed.[15] Nor could Jeffrey, nor the Edinburgh Reviewers write English, nor can * * *,[16] who is a pest to the English tongue. Incidentally he added, Gibbon cannot write English. The Edinburgh Review wrote what would tell and what would sell. It had however changed the tone of its literary criticism from the time when a certain letter was written to the editor by Coleridge. Mrs. W. had the Editor's answer in her possession. Tennyson he thinks a right poetic genius, though with some affectation. He had thought an elder brother of Tennyson[17] at first the better poet, but must now reckon Alfred the true one. . . . In speaking of I know not what style, he said, "to be sure, it was the manner, but then you know the matter always comes out of the manner." . . . He thought Rio Janeiro[18] the best place in the world for a great capital city. . . . We talked of English national character. I told him it was not creditable that no one in all the country knew anything of Thomas Taylor, the Platonist,[19] whilst in every American library his translations are found. I said, if Plato's Republic were published in England as a new book to-day, do you think it would find any readers? — he confessed, it would not: "And yet," he added after a pause, with that complacency which never deserts a true-born Englishman, "and yet we have embodied it all."

His opinions of French, English, Irish and Scotch, seemed rashly formulized from little anecdotes of what had befallen himself and members of his family, in a diligence or stage-coach. His face sometimes lighted up, but his conversation was not marked by special force or elevation. Yet perhaps it is a high compliment to the cultivation of the English generally, when we find such a man not distinguished. He had a healthy look, with a weather-beaten face, his face corrugated, especially the large nose.

Miss Martineau, who lived near him, praised him to me not for his poetry, but for thrift and economy; for having afforded to his country-neighbors an example of a modest household where comfort and culture were secured without any display. She said that in his early housekeeping at the cottage where he first lived, he was accustomed to offer his friends bread and plainest fare; if they wanted anything more, they must pay him for their board. It was the rule of the house. I replied that it evinced English pluck more than any anecdote I knew. A gentleman in the neighborhood told the story of Walter Scott's staying once for a week with Wordsworth, and slipping out every day, under pretence of a walk, to the Swan Inn for a cold cut and porter; and one day passing with Wordsworth the inn, he was betrayed by the landlord's asking him if he had come for his porter. Of course this trait would have another look in London, and there you will hear from different literary men that Wordsworth had

no personal friend, that he was not amiable, that he was par-
simonious, &c. Landor, always generous, says that he never
praised any body. A gentleman in London showed me a
watch that once belonged to Milton, whose initials are
engraved on its face. He said he once showed this to Wordsworth, who took it in one hand, then drew out his own
watch and held it up with the other, before the company,
but no one making the expected remark, he put back his own
in silence. I do not attach much importance to the disparage-
ment of Wordsworth among London scholars.[20] Who reads
him well will know that in following the strong bent of his
genius, he was careless of the many, careless also of the few,
self-assured that he should "create the taste by which he is
to be enjoyed." He lived long enough to witness the revolution he had wrought, and "to see what he foresaw." [21] There
are torpid places in his mind, there is something hard and
sterile in his poetry, want of grace and variety, want of due
catholicity and cosmopolitan scope: he had conformities to
English politics and traditions; he had egotistic puerilities
in the choice and treatment of his subjects; but let us say of
him that, alone in his time, he treated the human mind well,
and with an absolute trust. His adherence to his poetic creed
rested on real inspirations. The Ode on Immortality[22] is the
high-water-mark which the intellect has reached in this age.
New means were employed, and new realms added to the
empire of the muse, by his courage.

CHAPTER XVIII

Result

England is the best of actual nations. It is no ideal framework, it is an old pile built in different ages, with repairs, additions and makeshifts; but you see the poor best you have got. London is the epitome of our times, and the Rome of to-day. Broad-fronted, broad-bottomed Teutons,[1] they stand in solid phalanx foursquare to the points of compass; they constitute the modern world, they have earned their vantage ground and held it through ages of adverse possession. They are well marked and differing from other leading races. England is tender-hearted. Rome was not. England is not so public in its bias; private life is its place of honor. Truth in private life, untruth in public, marks these home-loving men. Their political conduct is not decided by general views, but by internal intrigues and personal and family interest. They cannot readily see beyond England. The history of Rome and Greece, when written by their scholars, degenerates into English party pamphlets. They cannot see beyond England, nor in England can they transcend the interests of the governing classes. "English principles" mean a primary regard to the interests of property. England, Scotland and Ireland combine to check the colonies. England and Scotland combine to check Irish manufactures and trade. England rallies at home to check Scotland. In England, the strong classes check the weaker. In the home population of near thirty millions, there are but one million voters. The Church punishes dissent, punishes education. Down to a late day, marriages performed by dissenters were illegal. A bitter class-legislation gives power to those who are rich enough to buy a law. The game-laws are a proverb of oppression. Pauperism incrusts and clogs the state, and in hard times becomes hideous. In bad seasons, the porridge was diluted. Multitudes lived miserably by shell-fish and sea-ware. In cities, the children are trained to beg, until they shall be old enough to rob. Men and women were convicted of poisoning scores of children for burial-fees. In Irish districts, men deteriorated in size and shape, the nose sunk, the gums were exposed, with diminished brain and brutal form. During the Australian emigration,[2] multitudes were rejected by the commissioners as being too emaciated for useful colonists. During the Russian war,[3] few of those that offered as recruits were found up to the medical standard, though it had been reduced.

The foreign policy of England, though ambitious and lavish of money, has not often been generous or just. It has a principal regard to the interest of trade, checked however by the aristocratic bias of the ambassador, which usually puts him in sympathy with the continental Courts. It sanctioned the partition of Poland, it betrayed Genoa, Sicily, Parga, Greece, Turkey, Rome and Hungary.[4]

Some public regards they have. They have abolished slavery in the West Indies[5] and put an end to human sacrifices in the East. At home they have a certain statute hospitality. England keeps open doors, as a trading country must, to all nations. It is one of their fixed ideas, and wrathfully supported by their laws in unbroken sequence for a thousand years. In *Magna Charta* it was ordained that all "merchants shall have safe and secure conduct to go out and come into England, and to stay there, and to pass as well by land as by water, to buy and sell by the ancient allowed customs, without any evil toll, except in time of war, or when they shall be of any nation at war with us." [6] It is a statute and obliged hospitality and peremptorily maintained. But this shop-rule had one magnificent effect. It extends its cold unalterable courtesy to political exiles of every opinion, and is a fact which might give additional light to that portion of the planet seen from the farthest star. But this perfunctory hospitality puts no sweetness into their unaccommodating manners, no check on that puissant nationality which makes their existence incompatible with all that is not English.

What we must say about a nation is a superficial dealing with symptoms. We cannot go deep enough into the biography of the spirit who never throws himself entire into one hero, but delegates his energy in parts or spasms to vicious and defective individuals. But the wealth of the source is seen in the plenitude of English nature. What variety of power and talent; what facility and plenteousness of knighthood, lordship, ladyship, royalty, loyalty; what a proud chivalry is indicated in "Collins's Peerage," through eight hundred years! [7] What dignity resting on what reality and stoutness! What courage in war, what sinew in labor, what cunning workmen, what inventors and engineers, what seamen and pilots, what clerks and scholars! No one man and no few men can represent them. It is a people of myriad personalities. Their many-headedness is owing to the advantageous position of the middle class, who are always the source of letters and science. Hence the vast plenty of their æsthetic production. As they are many-headed, so they are many-nationed: their colonization annexes archipelagoes and continents, and their speech seems destined to be the universal language of men. I have noted the reserve of power in the English temperament. In the island, they never let out all the length of the reins, there is no Berserkir rage, no abandonment or ecstasy of will or intellect, like that of the Arabs in the time of Mahomet, or like that which intoxicated France in 1789. But who would see the uncoiling of that tremendous spring, the explosion of their well-husbanded forces, must follow the swarms which pouring now for two hundred years from the British islands, have sailed and rode and traded and planted through all climates, mainly following the belt of empire, the temperate zones, carrying the Saxon seed, with its instinct for liberty and law, for arts and for thought, — acquiring under some skies a more electric energy than the native air allows, — to the conquest of the globe. Their colonial policy, obeying the necessities of a vast empire, has become liberal. Canada and Australia have been contented with substantial independence.[8] They are expiating the wrongs of India by benefits;[9] first, in works for the irrigation of the peninsula, and roads, and telegraphs; and secondly, in the instruction of the people, to qualify them for self-government, when the British power shall be finally called home.

Their mind is in a state of arrested development, — a divine cripple like Vulcan;[10] a blind *savant* like Huber and Sanderson.[11] They do not occupy themselves on matters of general and lasting import, but on a corporeal civilization, on goods that perish in the using. But they read with good intent, and what they learn they incarnate. The English mind turns every abstraction it can receive into a portable utensil, or a working institution. Such is their tenacity and such their practical turn, that they hold all they gain. Hence we say that only the English race can be trusted with freedom, — freedom which is double-edged and dangerous to any but the wise and robust. The English designate the kingdoms emulous of free institutions, as the sentimental nations. Their culture is not an outside varnish, but is thorough and secular in families and the race. They are oppressive with their temperament, and all the more that they are refined. I have sometimes seen them walk with my countrymen when

I was forced to allow them every advantage, and their companions seemed bags of bones.

There is cramp limitation in their habit of thought, sleepy routine, and a tortoise's instinct to hold hard to the ground with his claws, lest he should be thrown on his back. There is a drag of inertia which resists reform in every shape; — law-reform, army-reform, extension of suffrage, Jewish franchise, Catholic emancipation, — the abolition of slavery, of impressment, penal code and entails. They praise this drag, under the formula that it is the excellence of the British constitution that no law can anticipate the public opinion. These poor tortoises must hold hard, for they feel no wings sprouting at their shoulders. Yet somewhat divine warms at their heart and waits a happier hour. It hides in their sturdy will. "Will," said the old philosophy, "is the measure of power," and personality is the token of this race. *Quid vult valde vult*. What they do they do with a will. You cannot account for their success by their Christianity, commerce, character, common law, Parliament, or letters, but by the contumacious sharptongued energy of English *naturel*,[12] with a poise impossible to disturb, which makes all these its instruments. They are slow and reticent, and are like a dull good horse which lets every nag pass him, but with whip and spur will run down every racer in the field. They are right in their feeling, though wrong in their speculation.

The feudal system survives in the steep inequality of property and privilege, in the limited franchise, in the social barriers which confine patronage and promotion to a caste, and still more in the submissive ideas pervading these people. The fagging of the schools is repeated in the social classes. An Englishman shows no mercy to those below him in the social scale, as he looks for none from those above him; any forbearance from his superiors surprises him, and they suffer in his good opinion. But the feudal system can be seen with

less pain on large historical grounds. It was pleaded in miti-
gation of the rotten borough, that it worked well, that substantial justice was done. Fox, Burke, Pitt, Erskine,[13] Wilberforce, Sheridan, Romilly, or whatever national man, were
by this means sent to Parliament, when their return by large
constituencies would have been doubtful. So now we say that
the right measures of England are the men it bred; that it has
yielded more able men in five hundred years than any other
nation; and, though we must not play Providence and balance the chances of producing ten great men against the
comfort of ten thousand mean men, yet retrospectively, we
may strike the balance and prefer one Alfred, one Shakspeare, one Milton, one Sidney, one Raleigh, one Wellington, to a million foolish democrats.

The American system is more democratic, more humane;
yet the American people do not yield better or more able
men, or more inventions or books or benefits than the English. Congress is not wiser or better than Parliament. France
has abolished its suffocating old *régime,* but is not recently
marked by any more wisdom or virtue.

The power of performance has not been exceeded, — the
creation of value. The English have given importance to individuals, a principal end and fruit of every society. Every
man is allowed and encouraged to be what he is, and is
guarded in the indulgence of his whim. "Magna Charta,"
said Rushworth, "is such a fellow that he will have no sovereign." [14] By this general activity and by this sacredness of
individuals, they have in seven hundred years evolved the
principles of freedom. It is the land of patriots, martyrs, sages
and bards, and if the ocean out of which it emerged should
wash it away, it will be remembered as an island famous for
immortal laws, for the announcements of original right
which make the stone tables of liberty.

CHAPTER XIX

Speech at Manchester

A few days after my arrival at Manchester, in November, 1847, the Manchester Athenæum gave its annual Banquet in the Free-Trade Hall.[1] With other guests, I was invited to be present and to address the company. In looking over recently a newspaper-report of my remarks, I incline to reprint it, as fitly expressing the feeling with which I entered England, and which agrees well enough with the more deliberate results of better acquaintance recorded in the foregoing pages. Sir Archibald Alison, the historian, presided, and opened the meeting with a speech.[2] He was followed by Mr. Cobden, Lord Brackley[3] and others, among whom was Mr. Cruikshank,[4] one of the contributors to "Punch." Mr. Dickens's letter of apology for his absence was read. Mr. Jerrold, who had been announced, did not appear. On being introduced to the meeting I said: —

Mr. Chairman and Gentlemen: It is pleasant to me to meet this great and brilliant company, and doubly pleasant to see the faces of so many distinguished persons on this platform. But I have known all these persons already. When I was at home, they were as near to me as they are to you. The arguments of the League[5] and its leader[6] are known to all the friends of free trade. The gayeties and genius, the political the social, the parietal wit[7] of "Punch" go duly every fortnight to every boy and girl in Boston and New York. Sir, when I came to sea, I found the "History of Europe" [8] on the ship's cabin table, the property of the captain; — a sort of programme or play-bill to tell the seafaring New Englander what he shall find on his landing here. And as for Dombey,[9] sir, there is no land where paper exists to print on, where it is not found; no man who can read, that does not read it, and, if he cannot, he finds some charitable pair of eyes that can, and hears it.

But these things are not for me to say; these compliments, though true, would better come from one who felt and understood these merits more. I am not here to exchange civilities with you, but rather to speak of that which I am sure interests these gentlemen more than their own praises; of that which is good in holidays and working-days, the same in one century and in another century. That which lures a solitary American in the woods with the wish to see England, is the moral peculiarity of the Saxon race, — its commanding sense of right and wrong, the love and devotion to that, — this is the imperial trait, which arms them with the sceptre of the globe. It is this which lies at the foundation of that aristocratic character, which certainly wanders into strange vagaries, so that its origin is often lost sight of, but which, if it should lose this, would find itself paralyzed; and in trade and in the mechanic's shop, gives that honesty in performance, that thoroughness and solidity of work which is a national characteristic. This conscience is one element, and the other is that loyal adhesion, that habit of friendship, that homage of man to man, running through all classes, — the electing of worthy persons to a certain fraternity, to acts of kindness and warm and staunch support, from year to year, from youth to age, — which is alike lovely and honorable to those who render and those who receive it; which stands in strong contrast with the superficial attachments of other races, their excessive courtesy and short-lived connection.

You will think me very pedantic, gentlemen, but holiday though it be, I have not the smallest interest in any holiday except as it celebrates real and not pretended joys; and I think it just, in this time of gloom and commercial disaster,[10] of affliction and beggary in these districts, that, on these very accounts I speak of, you should not fail to keep your literary anniversary. I seem to hear you say, that for all that is come and gone yet, we will not reduce by one chaplet or one oak-leaf [11] the braveries of our annual feast. For I must tell you, I was given to understand in my childhood that the British island from which my forefathers came was no lotus-garden, no paradise of serene sky and roses and music and merriment all the year round, no, but a cold, foggy, mournful country, where nothing grew well in the open air but robust men and virtuous women, and these of a wonderful fibre and endurance; that their best parts were slowly revealed; their virtues did not come out until they quarrelled; they did not strike twelve the first time; good lovers, good haters, and you could know little about them till you had seen them long, and little good of them till you had seen them in action; that in prosperity they are moody and dumpish, but in adversity they were grand. Is it not true, sir, that the wise ancients did not praise the ship parting with flying colors from the port, but only that brave sailer which came back with torn sheets and battered sides, stript of her banners, but having ridden out the storm? And so, gentlemen, I feel in regard to this aged England, with the possessions, honors and trophies, and also with the infirmities of a thousand years gathering around her, irretrievably committed as she now is to many old customs which cannot be suddenly changed; pressed upon by the transitions of trade and new and all incalculable modes, fabrics, arts, machines and competing populations. I see her not dispirited, not weak, but well remembering that she has seen dark days before; — indeed with a kind of instinct that she sees a little better in a cloudy day, and that in storm of battle and calamity she has a secret vigor and a pulse like a cannon. I see her in her old age, not decrepit, but young and still daring to believe in her power of endurance and expansion. Seeing this, I say, All hail! mother of nations, mother of heroes, with strength still equal to the time; still wise to entertain and swift to execute the policy which the mind and heart of mankind requires in the present hour, and thus only hospitable to the foreigner and truly a home to the thoughtful and generous who are born in the soil. So be it! so let it be! If it be not so, if the courage of England goes with the chances of a commercial crisis, I will go back to the capes of Massachusetts and my own Indian stream,[12] and say to my countrymen, the old race are all gone, and the elasticity and hope of mankind must henceforth remain on the Alleghany ranges, or nowhere.

Notes

I. First Visit to England

1. The Centenary edition identifies the artist as Mr. Wall, "a young artist of New Bedford." Wall's copy of Michelangelo's "Fates" hung in Emerson's study.

2. In the first quarter of the nineteenth century the cultural and literary life of southern Scotland was extraordinarily lively. *The Edinburgh Review* (Whig) was founded in October 1802, the *Quarterly Review* (Tory) in February 1809, and these became the leading intellectual magazines in Great Britain. Francis Jeffrey (1773–1850), lawyer, critic, and editor, Sir James Mackintosh (1765–1832), historian and publicist, and Henry Hallam (1777–1859), historian, are associated with the *Edinburgh Review*. Sir Walter Scott (1771–1832), John Playfair (1748–1819), mathematician and geologist, and Thomas De Quincey (1785–1859), essayist, being Tories, were associated with the *Quarterly Review*.

3. Through Horatio Greenough, Emerson received an invitation to visit Thomas Carlyle (1795–1881) and his wife, then living at Craigenputtock. The visit marked the beginning of a friendship recorded among other places in the *Correspondence of Emerson and Carlyle*, of which the best edition is that edited by Joseph Slater (2 vols., New York, 1964).

4. Arthur Wellesley, first Duke of Wellington (1769–1852), the conqueror of Napoleon, British prime minister from 1828 to 1830, foreign secretary, 1834–1835.

5. William Wilberforce (1759–1833), philanthropist and abolitionist.

6. Now available in vol. IV of the *Journals and Miscellaneous Notebooks of Ralph Waldo Emerson*, ed. William H. Gilman, *et al.* (Cambridge, Mass., 1960 ——).

7. Horatio Greenough (1805–1852) first visited Rome in 1825, came home, and returned to Italy in 1828. The "Medora" was suggested by the heroine of Byron's poem *The Corsair*. What has become of the two figures is not clear. On the relation between Emerson and the sculptor see Charles R. Metzger, *Emerson and Greenough* (Berkeley and Los Angeles, 1954).

8. In *The United States Magazine and Democratic Review*, 13:206–210 (August 1843).

9. Presumably a reference to Ruskin's *The Seven Lamps of Architecture* (London and New York, 1849).

10. This letter, dated from Washington, D.C., December 28, 1851, is now in the Houghton Library, Harvard University. There are some mild discrepancies between its text and Emerson's transcription.

11. When *English Traits* was published in London, Landor printed at Bath in 1856 a pamphlet, *Letter from W. S. Landor to R. W. Emerson*, of 67 pages, claiming that Emerson had misrepresented him and going on to talk about Carlyle, Wordsworth, and others. In this he insists that he detests democracy but is a staunch republican. The pamphlet was reprinted under the editorship of Samuel Arthur Jones for The Rowfant Club, Cleveland, Ohio, in 1895, in an edition of 108 copies. The Rowfant Club edition includes an introduction by the editor and in the appendix a reprinting of Emerson's admiring essay on Landor from *The Dial*, 2:262f. (October 1841).

12. Greenough procured an invitation from Landor (who admired his statuary) to Emerson, who visited the poet in May 1833. The Villa Gherardesca, now known as the Villa Landor, is in San Domenica di Fiesole, on the south slope of the Fiesole hills near Florence.

13. A double reference to Landor's famous fits of anger and to the theme of the Iliad: "Sing, Goddess, the wrath of Peleus' son, Achilleus."

14. George Washington, not the city; Philip Massinger (1583–1670), British dramatist; Francis Beaumont (1564?–1616) and John Fletcher (1579–1625), who collaborated on many Jacobean plays.

15. Philip II (382–336 B.C.), king of Macedonia, conqueror of Thessaly and Greece, and father of Alexander the Great (356–323 B.C.)

16. The "Venus" is presumably the "Venus Stooping in the Bath" in the Uffizi gallery in Florence. As Margarete Bieber's *Alexander the Great in Greek and Roman Art* (Chicago, 1964) does not include any head of Alexander in any Florentine gallery, it is a little difficult to know what "head of Alexander" Emerson has in mind. Attributions of "classical" heads shift.

17. Giovanni da Bologna (1524–1608), famous for his "Flying Mercury"; Michelangelo Buonarroti (1475–1565); Raffaele Sanzio (1483–1520); Perugino (1445–1523?). The "early masters" shows a taste for the pre-Raphaelite painters in a man usually thought of as committed to classicism.

18. Voltaire (1694–1778) published, among other books, his *Siècle de Louis XIV* (1751) and his *Essai sur l'histoire générale et sur les moeurs et l'esprit des nations* (1756).

19. Pierre Charron (1541–1603), French skeptic.

20. Joseph Marie de Gérando (1772–1842), French philosopher and statesman.

21. Richard Lucas (1648–1715) published an *Inquiry after Happiness*

in 1685, often reprinted, and *Practical Christianity; or, An Account of the Holiness Which the Gospel Enjoins,* which reached a fifth edition in 1700 and was often reprinted after that.

22. Robert Southey (1774–1843), one of the Lake Poets, made poet laureate in 1813. His later years were marked by loss of memory.

23. The lines are quoted in the Centenary edition. Aelius Donatus (fl. 333) wrote an *Ars Grammatica* (sometimes called *Ars Minor*), the standard grammatical treatise of the Middle Ages, the wide use of which made *donat* a term for any basic treatise.

24. Philip Dormer Stanhope, Earl of Chesterfield (1694–1773), whose *Letters to His Son* (posthumously published, 1774) became a standard treatise on polite conduct in worldly circles.

25. Phocion (402–318 B.C.), Athenian general, who fought against Philip of Macedon with some success. Timoleon (d. 337 B.C.), Corinthian statesman and general, who liberated Sicily from tyrants and fought against the Carthaginians.

26. Giovanni Battista Amici (1786?–1863), Florentine scientist visited by Emerson in May 1833. He designed novel physical apparatus, including an achromatic microscope and a telescope used by Herschel.

27. Presumably Sir William Herschel (1738–1822), the discoverer of the planet Uranus, who established the largest astronomical observatory of his time. Emerson read his *A Preliminary Discourse on the Study of Natural Philosophy* (1821).

28. Zampiere Domenichino (Domenico) (1581–1641), Italian painter.

29. Presumably Julius Charles Hare (1796–1855), author, with his brother Augustus, of *Guesses at Truth* (1827).

30. Coleridge went to Highgate (north of Hampstead Heath) in 1816 to live in the home of Dr. James Gillam in order to cure his addiction to opium. Through his writings Coleridge was one of the primary teachers of Emerson.

31. Washington Allston (1779–1843), American painter, met Coleridge in Rome in 1805. He painted a portrait of Coleridge sometime after 1810.

32. William Ellery Channing (1780–1842), the "apostle of Unitarianism" in America. Coleridge had in his younger years been a Unitarian.

33. Daniel Waterland (1683–1740), British theologian. The book here referred to is his *A Vindication of Christ's Divinity* (London, 1719). On Coleridge's religious views see James D. Boulger, *Coleridge as Religious Thinker* (New Haven, 1961).

34. Emerson knew this book, first published in London 1825, in an American edition edited by James Marsh (Burlington, Vermont, 1829).

35. Alexandrian Jewish philosopher (ca. 20 B.C.–50 A.D.), whose doctrine parallels some parts of the New Testament and draws upon the theories of Plato and the Neo-Platonists.

36. Followers of Joseph Priestley (1733–1804), scientist and theologian, one of the founders of English Unitarianism. He came to live in Philadelphia in 1794.

37. Literally, three-ism and four-ism.

38. Scholars have been unable to identify this pamphlet with certainty, but the editors of the new edition of Emerson's *Journals* (IV, 410) think Emerson is referring to "English Independent Tracts, p. 70."

39. From "My Baptismal Birthday," written by Coleridge in the summer of 1833.

40. Coleridge visited Malta in 1804 to improve his health, and touched at Sicily briefly in 1805. The Bishop of London in 1833 was Charles James Bloomfield (1786–1857), who was translated to London from Chester in 1828. For Emerson's visits to these islands see Rusk, *Life*, pp. 170–175.

41. The melting pot of the Mediterranean, Malta was invaded for the third time by the Arabs in the ninth century A.D. and not regained by a Christian power until the eleventh century.

42. The editors of the new edition of Emerson's *Journals* identify him as Basil Montagu, but this does not seem probable.

43. On the Nith river in Dumfriesshire, Scotland. But a detailed atlas will make clear the relation among the various sites in Scotland involved.

44. The letter was from Gustave d'Eichtal (1804–1886), a young French follower of Saint-Simon. Emerson met him at Rome in April.

45. The household gods of the Romans were the lares and penates; hence, by extension, personal or household effects. The lemurs were the ghosts of the dead in Roman belief; here it is tantamount to memories.

46. The references are to *Blackwood's Edinburgh Magazine*, before October 1817 the *Edinburgh Monthly Magazine;* and *Fraser's Magazine for Town and Country*, founded 1830. In 1833 *Fraser's* accepted Carlyle's *Sartor Resartus* for serial publication, beginning November 1833, but this was broken off in August 1834 because readers found Carlyle unintelligible.

47. "What an artist dies in me!" — the last words of the Emperor Nero, according to Suetonius, *Lives of the Caesars*, VI, 49.

48. James Stuart published at Edinburgh *Three Years in North America*, 2 vols., 1833.

49. Mungo is a generic name for a Negro.

50. Honoré Gabriel Riquetti, Comte de Mirabeau (1749–1791), aristocratic radical in the French Revolution, figures importantly in Carlyle's *The French Revolution*.

51. Laurence Sterne published *The Life and Opinions of Tristram Shandy*, 9 vols., 1759–67. It influenced Carlyle's *Sartor Resartus*.

52. Dr. William Robertson (1721–1793) published his *History of America*, 2 vols., 1777; the third volume, incomplete, appeared in 1796.

53. According to R. S. Craig, *The Making of Carlyle* (New York, 1909), it is not known who first counseled Carlyle to learn German, but he studied it intensively in 1819–20.

54. Jane Welsh Carlyle.

55. "Rick burning" was a form of protest against the unemployment created by the introduction of machinery into spinning.

56. Criffel is a mountain in Kirkcudbrightshire northwest of the Lake District, "Wordsworth's country." "Without his cap" means there was no cloud on its summit.

57. This is either Edward Irving (1792–1834); or John Stuart Mill (1806–1873).

58. Rydal Mount was Wordsworth's home from 1813 until his death in 1850.

59. Colonel Thomas Hamilton (1791–1842), author of *Men and Manners in America* (2 vols., London, 1833).

60. The tax on newspapers was common in England after 1694. In 1836 it was reduced from four pence to one penny.

61. Jean Louis Delolme (1743–1807), Swiss constitutional theorist, emigrated to England as a political refugee. Wordsworth was probably alluding to his *La Constitution de l'Angleterre* (1775), translated into English as *The Constitution of England; or, An Account of the English Government* the same year.

62. William Ellery Channing met both Wordsworth and Coleridge in England in 1823.

63. The reference is to Victor Cousin (1792–1867), French eclectic philosopher. His *Introduction to the History of Philosophy* was translated into English and published at Boston in 1832.

64. Goethe's *Wilhelm Meisters Lehrjahre* (1777–1796) was translated by Carlyle in 1824; *Wilhelm Meisters Wanderjahre* (completed in 1829) was in part translated by Carlyle in *German Romances* (1827).

65. Fingal's Cave is on the island of Staffa, one of the Inner Hebrides off the coast of Argyllshire. Wordsworth's sonnets are: "We saw, but surely, in the motley crowd," "Thanks for the lessons of this sport," "Ye shadowy Beings, that have rights and claims." The fourth one, which Wordsworth recited, is "Hope smiled when your nativity was cast." They form numbers 26–29 of the series of *Sonnets Composed or Suggested during a Tour of Scotland in the Summer of 1833*. As printed the fourth poem is addressed to the flowers (a footnote refers

to the ox-eyed daisy). Both the first and the second contain references to the legend of the "Cave of Music."

66. "Lines Composed above Tintern Abbey on Revisiting the Banks of the Wye During a Tour," part of the *Lyrical Ballads* volume of 1789.

67. *The Excursion* was published in 1814. Wordsworth published innumerable sonnets, sometimes in series.

68. Good to-day and good forever. The Greek phrase is from Thucydides, Jowett trans. (Oxford, 1900), I, 16 (Book I, chapter 22).

69. "On the Indignation of a High-Minded Spaniard," dated 1810.

70. "Thoughts of a Briton on the Subjugation of Switzerland," dated 1802. This begins: "Two voices are there; one is of the sea."

71. Probably the poem beginning "Ethereal minstrel! pilgrim of the sky," dated 1827.

II. Voyage to England

1. Suggested by Josiah Holbrook of Derby, Connecticut, in an article published in 1826 (*Journal of Education*), the lyceum movement was a system of adult education through lectures. An American Lyceum on a national scale was organized in 1831.

2. On the union of British Mechanics' Institutes see James Hole, *An Essay on the History and Management of the Literary, Scientific and Mechanics Institutes* (London, 1853).

3. Among these friends were Alexander Ireland (1810–1894), Philip James Bailey (1816–1902), and George Stephenson (1781–1848). Alexander Ireland particularly arranged for Emerson's fees.

4. Cape Sable is at the southeast "corner" of Nova Scotia.

5. The Grand Banks off the coast of Newfoundland, long a famous resort for fishermen.

6. More commonly, hacklet, a seabird, the American shearwater.

7. By "kites" is meant skysails, carried normally in light breezes only. The studding-sail is a light sail set at the side of a principal square sail. "Rod of way" is a landsman's expression. "Rod" is not used to measure maritime distances.

8. There was an actual Persian poet named Saadi (1184–1291), but Emerson commonly uses this name as a persona through which to speak himself. See, however, two articles by J. D. Yohannan, "Emerson's Translations of Persian Poetry from German Sources," *American Literature*, 14:407–420 (1943) and "The Influence of Persian Poetry upon Emerson's Work," *American Literature*, 15:25–41 (1943).

9. As late as 1847 steamships were regarded as uncertain vessels.

10. In ocean matters a ton has varying meanings. As a unit for merchant vessels it is today about 100 cubic feet of space, but it may

also be reckoned at 40 cubic feet of space, or at some figure between 40 and 100.

11. A top-button is an ornament on top of a mast.

12. The phosphorescence in sea water, created by myriads of the microscopic organisms mentioned later in the paragraph.

13. Sweet potato.

14. Cooking oil.

15. A thick knitted, closely fitting vest or shirt, generally made of blue wool, much worn by seamen.

16. Physical laws governing the composition and behavior of water.

17. One who manages his time prudently.

18. A transom is a couch or seat built at the side of a cabin or stateroom on board a ship.

19. Captain Basil Hall (1788–1844), British traveler to the United States, published *Travels in North America* (3 vols., 1829), highly critical of American life. Alexandre Dumas (1802–1870), French romancer. Charles Dickens (1812–1870), whose *American Notes* (2 vols., 1842), an account of his journeys in the United States, was also critical of American manners. Edward E. G. L. Bulwer-Lytton (1803–1873), British novelist and romancer. Honoré de Balzac (1799–1850), French novelist, and George Sand (1804–1876), French novelist, had considerable vogue in the United States in the 1840's. *English Traits* was influenced by this reading..

20. Emerson presumably refers to the Naval War with Holland fought in the 1660's, though the two countries had other maritime encounters.

21. A vessel from America entering Saint George's Channel and the Irish Sea from the southwest will pass these (and other) Irish towns in order along the eastern coast of Ireland.

22. In 1166, during the reign of Henry II (1133–1189), forces from England first attempted the conquest of Ireland.

III. Land

1. Vittorio Alfieri (1749–1803), Italian poet and dramatist known for his political liberalism. Emerson visited his tomb in Florence in April 1833.

2. The phalanstery is the economic unit or association advocated by Charles Fourier (1772–1837) and in America by Albert Brisbane (1809–1890) in books like *The Social Destiny of Man* (1840).

3. Egbert (ca. 775–839), king of Wessex, the first of the Saxon monarchs to have a claim to rule over substantially all of what is modern England.

4. According to the Centenary edition this was said by the pub-

lisher William Chambers (1800–1883) of the famous publishing firm of R. and W. Chambers in Edinburgh.

5. "Add South Carolina, and you have more than an equivalent for the area of Scotland." (Emerson's note.)

6. The architect Sir John Soane (1753–1837) in 1833 presented to the nation his collection of paintings, sculpture, and so forth, in his house in Lincoln's Inn Fields.

7. A cromlech is an ancient sepulchral monument or altar of un-hewn flat stones. A minster is a monastery church, and the one at York, the Cathedral of St. Peter, is famous as a medieval masterpiece.

8. In *The New Dictionary of Quotations* (1942) this reads: "On a fine day the climate of England is like looking up a chimney; on a foul day, like looking down one"; no source is given.

9. Sir John Herschel (1792–1871), distinguished astronomer, and son of an equally distinguished astronomer, Sir William Herschel.

10. Delphi was the seat of the Pythian oracle, at the foot of Mount Parnassus in Greece. A stone (the Omphalos) was supposed to be the center of the earth.

11. A kratometer (cratometer) is an instrument for measuring power.

12. On the same isothermic line.

13. The passage is in the *Aeneid*, I, 67, "Toto divisos orbe Brit-tanos."

14. Oblique reference to a traditional ceremony in Venice when the doge of that city cast a ring into the sea, signifying Venice's marriage with the sea.

15. The North Sea.

16. One who goes from Kent to Cornwall traverses the whole south-ern rim of Great Britain.

17. The exact words are: "that he might remove his court at his pleasure, but could not remove the river of Thames." This is the last line or two of the opening paragraph of the discussion of London in Thomas Fuller's *The Worthies of England*.

18. Cornwall was long a source of tin. Matlock is in Derbyshire on the River Derwent.

19. The valley of the River Dove in north central England.

20. In Devonshire in southwest England, an inlet opening on the English Channel.

21. Snowdon, the highest mountain in Wales, is noted for the exten-sive view to be had from any one of its five peaks.

22. The "Lake Country" in Northwest England, a "pocket Switzer-land" because of the combination of mountains and lakes in the two counties.

23. Bernard Le Bouvier de Fontenelle (1657–1757), French philos-opher. But Emerson apparently got the ensuing quotation from Thomas

Brown, *Lectures on the Philosophy of the Human Mind* (3 vols., Philadelphia, 1824), I, 92.

24. Birmingham as the center of British industrial development.

25. The theories of Emanuel Swedenborg (1688–1772), Swedish scientist and mystic, were of great interest to Emerson, who included a sketch of him in *Representative Men* (1850). Emerson paraphrases rather than quotes a passage from the translation of Swedenborg's *The True Christian Religion*, paragraph 806.

IV. Race

1. Emerson's own note runs: *"The Races, a Fragment.* By Robert Knox. London, 1850." This title should read: *The Races of Men: A Fragment;* Emerson presumably read the book in a Philadelphia reprint of 1850. Knox (1791–1862) was a brilliant but accentric anatomist at the College of Surgeons in Edinburgh; the book is a reduction to print of lectures he delivered at Newcastle-on-Tyne in 1846, in which he insists that race is a fixed distinction.

2. Johann Friedrich Blumenbach (1752–1840), German physiologist, established five races according to skin color. Alexander von Humboldt (1769–1859), author of *Cosmos* (published in New York in four volumes, 1850–1852, and in London, 1848–1852), discusses the races of men in his "General Review of Natural Phenomena" but seems to waive the problem of their exact number. Charles Pickering (1805–1878), American naturalist, was attached to the Wilkes Expedition to the South Seas of 1838–1842 and published *The Races of Man: Their Geographical Distribution* in 1848 (vol. IX of the *Reports* of the Wilkes Expedition). He does not say there are eleven races, but only that he has seen eleven and is "hardly prepared to fix a positive limit to their number" (p. 10).

3. Among the names likely to be less familiar in this list are William of Wykeham (1324–1404), bishop of Winchester after 1367 and founder of both Winchester School and New College, Oxford; George Herbert (1593–1633), English metaphysical poet; and Sir Henry Vane (1613–1662), governor of Massachusetts Bay Colony, 1636–37, beheaded for treason after his return to England.

4. In *De Germania* the Roman historian Tacitus (ca. 55–ca. 117) described the ancient Germans in terms calculated to rebuke the immorality of the Romans.

5. In 1850.

6. To Roman poets the Hercynian forest was a vast woodland extending north from the Rhine. A Hoosier was (and is) a resident of Indiana; a Sucker, of Illinois; a Badger, of Wisconsin.

7. Cassivelaunus (fl. 54 B.C.), the Celtic chieftain who opposed

Julius Caesar when Caesar invaded Britain in 54 B.C. Ossian, if he existed, was a Gaelic poet of the third century A.D., but the name appears in Emerson's text because Alexander MacPherson (1736–1796) published a series of forgeries supposed to be translated from Ossian, which had an enormous vogue.

8. Possibly Gaelic (Celtic), Anglo-Saxon, and French, or if not Celtic, then Latin.

9. The movement for the adoption by Parliament of the "People's Charter" culminated in 1848. The principal demands were for universal suffrage, vote by ballot, equalized electoral districts, annual parliaments, salaries for members of the House of Commons, and the abolishing of property qualifications for voting.

10. The bishopric of Durham was the wealthiest of the episcopal sees, and is here thrown into contrast with "naked heathen colliers" described in Parliamentary Blue Books that exposed the exploitation of labor in the English coal mines.

11. This particular statement has not been found; but the general doctrine is that set forth in Defoe's *The Compleat English Gentleman*, which, however, was not printed during Emerson's life.

12. In the Concord edition the editors summarize (pp. 336–337) the theory of the "amelioration" of fruits proposed by a Dr. Van Mons of Louvain and described in Andrew Jackson Downing, *Fruits and Fruit Trees of America* (New York, 1845), which ran through many editions.

13. From 1838 to 1869 the annual exhibitions of the Royal Academy of Arts were held in the National Gallery in London.

14. This county adjoins the Scottish border on the east coast.

15. Astronomical time.

16. On the assumption that species are fixed, the Swedish naturalist Karl von Linné (Linnæus) (1707–1778) established a binomial system for designating plants and animals. Each species receives two names; one of the genus to which it belongs and the other of the species.

17. Inhabitants of ancient Sidon, a Phoenician people. Contemporary theory derived the Celts from the Phoenicians or equated the two races.

18. Feudal tenure based on violent conquest.

19. Although Merlin is possibly a fictive character, there is in traditional Welsh literature a group of poems of patriotic nature attributed to a bard Merlin or Myrddhin.

20. Gallia Narbonnensia was the south and southeast part of the former Roman province of Gaul. The anecdote about Charlemagne first appears in a Latin life of Charlemagne by the "Monk of St. Gaul" (nothing is known about him), Book II, chap. 14.

21. According to Herodotus (Book VII, chap. 44), Xerxes, the emperor of Persia, who assembled the largest army known to antiquity in order

to conquer Greece, as his forces were about to cross the Hellespont, wept because in a hundred years all of them would be dead.

22. Emerson's footnote refers to the translation of the *Heimskringla* by Samuel Laing (London, 1844).

23. Bonders are peasants holding land; yeomen; farmers.

24. The *New English Dictionary* indicates that this word is peculiar to Emerson.

25. This anecdote appears in Laing's translation of the *Heimskringla* (3 vols., London, 1844), I, 235.

26. All these anecdotes are found in the *Heimskringla*, I, 234, 232, 233–234, 251, 241, 249, 224, 238–239, in that order.

27. *Heimskringla*, III, 176–180.

28. Norse.

29. That is, the army of William the Conqueror.

30. *Heimskringla*, III, 110.

31. In 1801 a British fleet under Sir Hyde Parker (1739–1807) and Horatio Nelson (1758–1805) entered the Öresund, bombarded the forts defending Copenhagen, and destroyed the Danish fleet (Battle of the Baltic). In 1807 a British force under Lord Cathcart (1755–1843) landed at Vedbaek, north of Copenhagen, occupied the city, and captured the few remaining Danish war vessels.

32. Emerson apparently means Konungahella in the *Heimskringla* saga, whither Scandinavian kings constantly repair, but if he does, I am ignorant why the area is said to be rented to an English gentleman for a hunting ground.

33. According to legend, founded by Edward III (1312–1377) in 1344 when a lady of the court lost her garter and the courtiers began to titter. Its motto is "Honi soit qui mal y pense," and membership is probably the highest distinction in the United Kingdom.

34. The prows, sides, and sterns of Norse war vessels were elaborately decorated.

35. Earlier forms of the evolutionary theory laid stress upon the basic structures of the animal kingdom and of man. "Caucasian man" is here used as the highest type of civilized refinement.

36. This is a translation of part of an Italian sentence found in Byron's letter to John Cam Hobhouse prefacing Canto IV of *Childe Harold's Pilgrimage*: "La pianta uomo e più robusta in Italia che in qualunque altra terra — e chi gli stessi atroci delitti che vi si commettono ne sono una prova."

37. Thomas Medwin, *The Life of Percy Bysshe Shelley* (new ed., London, 1913), p. 31. Emerson of course read the original edition of 1847.

38. In 1237 the Jewish communities were commanded to make a gift of 3000 marks to the Earl of Cornwall, the king's brother, to pay

for a crusade intended by Henry III (1207–1272). On the further extortion of money from the Jews see chapter iii, "The Royal Milch-Cow," in Cecil Roth, *A History of the Jews in England* (Oxford, 1941).

39. Sir Samuel Romilly (1757–1818), reformer, but I have not identified the source of the quotation.

40. The House of Commons, according to Hansard's *Parliamentary Debates,* discussed the flogging of prisoners when debating the Naval Prisons Bill on February 9, 1847, and on April 21 recurred to the general subject of flogging.

41. From the eleventh century to the middle of the seventeenth century English sovereigns levied on all towns, shires, and counties in England, whether they bordered on the sea or not, a tax ostensibly intended to maintain the royal navy.

42. Thomas Fuller, *The Worthies of England* (London, 1662), p. 44 (under Staffordshire).

43. The Temple Church is a twelfth-century church in London in the area known as The Temple between Fleet Street and the Thames. Worcester Cathedral dates from the eleventh century; Salisbury Cathedral, from the thirteenth.

44. According to Bede's *Ecclesiastical History,* St. Gregory (pope after 590), on seeing English slaves in Rome, said they were not Angles but angels.

45. Scarcely an English national legend, since it is found in one form or another all the way from China and India to France.

46. Hermaphroditus, the son of Aphrodite and Hermes, was loved by a nymph who prayed they might be eternally united. Their bodies were therefore fused into each other so that Hermaphroditus had the sexual characters of both male and female.

47. Almost certainly Charles Dickens.

48. This anecdote is standard in all the biographies of Nelson. Lord Collingwood (1750–1810) received a dispatch from Nelson on the eve of the battle of Trafalgar reminding him of the plan of battle and of Nelson's affection for him. After Nelson's death in that battle, Collingwood assumed command. Sir Thomas Masterman Hardy (1769–1839) was the captain of the *Victory,* Nelson's ship, and was made a baronet for his distinguished services in the navy.

49. The distinguished British admiral George Brudes, first Baron Rodney (1719–1792), served in the Seven Years War and defeated the French admiral De Grasse in the West Indies in 1782.

50. For Clarendon's characterization of the Duke of Buckingham, see his *History of the Rebellion and Civil Wars of England,* Book I.

51. Sir William Edward Parry (1790–1885) and Sir John Franklin (1786–1847) were close friends. Both were Arctic explorers. At the age of 59 Sir John Franklin headed an expedition to seek the Northwest

Passage. His little fleet was last seen on July 26, 1845. There is a vast library on the fate of the Sir John Franklin expedition, and I do not know where Emerson got his quotation.

52. Admiral Robert Blake (1599–1657) fought sea battles against the Dutch. John Churchill, first Duke of Marlborough (1650–1722), one of the most renowned British generals, won the decisive battle of Blenheim in 1704. William Pitt the Elder, first Earl of Chatham (1708–1778), was the organizer of victory in the Seven Years' War.

53. Shoreditch, Seven Dials, and Spitalfields are poorer districts or slums in London.

54. Tacitus' opinion of beer is found in chapter 23 of the *Germania*.

55. Father William Lacey (1584–1673) lived in Oxfordshire after 1633. Emerson's quotation comes from *Athenae Oxonienses* by Anthony à Wood, ed. Philip Bliss, vol. III (London, 1817), col. 995. A gawn is a gallon.

56. Henry of Navarre (1553–1610), who became king of France in 1594.

57. Peter Hawker wrote *Instructions to Young Sportsmen*, 1824; William Scrope, *The Art of Deer-Stalking*, 1838, and *Days and Nights of Salmon Fishing in the Tweed*, 1843. I suppose Murray is Eustace C. Grenville Murray (1824–1881), a miscellaneous writer, though his *Sports and Its Pleasures* was not published until 1859; Herbert I take to be the Henry William Herbert (1807–1858), born in England, who came to America and after 1834 wrote sketches and tales of outdoor life under the name of Frank Forester. William Hamilton Maxwell published *Sports of the West* (of Ireland), 1832, and *The Field Book, or Sports and Pastimes of the United Kingdom*, 1833; Roualeyn George Gordon Cumming, *Five Years of a Hunter's Life in the Far Interior of South Africa*, 1855.

58. George Louis Leclerc, Comte de Buffon (1707–1788), compiler of *Histoire Naturelle*, 44 vols., 1749–1804.

59. Hengst and Horsa were the traditional leaders of the Germanic invasion of Britain in the fifth century.

60. The first sentence quoted may be somewhere in Camden, but inasmuch as Emerson immediately refers to the *Anglo-Saxon Chronicle*, and there the passage (E under 1086) of verse says much the same thing about William, it is possible his memory betrayed him.

V. Ability

1. The Phoenicians traded with Britain and may have established colonies. As already noted, the Celts were the "original" inhabitants. By "Goth" Emerson seems to mean the Germanic stock, the term being loosely used. Thus Sir William Temple in 1731 wrote: "The Saxons

were one branch of those Gothick Nations, which swarming from the Northern Hive, had, under the conduct of Odin, possessed themselves anciently of all those mighty tracts of Land that surround the Baltick sea." *Works*, II, 537 (London, 1731).

2. The Roman emperor Claudius (10 B.C.–A.D. 54) undertook the conquest of Britain in A.D. 43. Roman power reached its widest extent under the emperor Hadrian (117–138) and in the fifth century dwindled as the Roman Empire succumbed to the "barbarians." In saying that the Roman "presently" heard bad news from Italy, Emerson telescopes history.

3. That is, complimentary gift, used ironically.

4. In the ninth century A.D. "Danes" means Norsemen in general.

5. The "Northmen" under Rolf took possession of Normandy, gradually amalgamated with the resident Celts or "French," and adopted French as their language.

6. Stamina.

7. Emerson accepted the theory of the "Germanic" origin of free institutions.

8. At Runnymede in 1215 the barons compelled King John (1167?–1216) to accept a charter guaranteeing their feudal rights. "Extort charters from the kings," later in this paragraph, also refers to the Magna Charta.

9. This could be clearer. What Emerson seems to mean is that the Anglo-Saxons were too intelligent to accept feudal or military tenure of land as a permanent form of holding.

10. In the feudal system, in Norman times an unfree peasant; he later became a copyhold tenant.

11. Seven percent was the standard rate on investments in Emerson's time.

12. Sir Marc Isambard Brunel (1769–1849), the engineer of the Thames Tunnel (1824–1843). His son, Isambard Kingdom Brunel (1806–1859), bridge builder and railway builder, created the famous steamer, the "Great Eastern" (1852–1858).

13. Among the names not already identified or less familiar are those of the Venerable Bede (673–735), the first great "English" historian; William Caxton (1421–1491), the first English printer; Henry de Bracton (d. 1268), whose *De Legibus et Consuetudinibus Angliae* preceded Blackstone's *Commentaries* as a comprehensive treatise on law; Sir John Selden (1584–1654), English jurist; Sir William Dugdale (1605–1686), English antiquarian; James Brindley (d. 1716), famous builder of canals and aqueducts; James Watt (1736–1819), inventor of a steam engine patented in 1769; Josiah Wedgwood (1730–1795), English pottery manufacturer.

14. From the *Anglo-Saxon Chronicle*, "Ethelwald remained within

the town . . . saying he would either there live or there die" (A.D. 901). Wimborne in Dorsetshire was once part of the kingdom of Wessex.

15. Here, as earlier, Emerson attributes to the "Goths" the manly virtues.

15a. Until 1872, when the secret ballot was made legal, voting in Great Britain was by show of hands.

16. "Antony Wood." (Emerson's note.) Emerson put this quotation together from various passages in the biographical sketch of Sir Kenelm Digby in Anthony à Wood, *Athenae Oxonienses,* vol. III, cols. 687–695.

17. Emerson's note is *"Man's Soule,* p. 29." I do not know what edition this refers to, but the passage may be found in *Two Treatises . . . The Nature of Bodies; . . . the Nature of Mans Soule . . .* (Paris, 1644), "A Treatise of Mans Soule," chap. iii, p. 377.

18. See *Mémoires de Philippe de Commynes,* ed. Mlle. Dupont (new ed., 3 vols., Paris, 1843), II, 142.

19. The phrase "indivisible unity" is an oblique reference to liberty, equality, and fraternity as the aim of the first French Republic, one and indivisible.

20. Paraphrased from Montesquieu's "Notes sur l'Angleterre." See *Œuvres complètes de Montesquieu* (Paris, 1846), pp. 629–633.

21. The general sense of this passage is found in the *Pensées diverses* of Montesquieu, but I have not located the exact source.

22. The Koh-i-noor diamond, originally weighing 186 carats, was presented to Queen Victoria by the East India Company in 1852.

23. This somewhat obscure sentence seems to refer to the legend that toward the end of his life Sir Isaac Newton felt he had been only a child by the seashore picking up pebbles. The "poles of the world" and "axis" fit into the Newtonian (Copernican) theory, but Emerson is also presenting his theory of polarity.

24. Current electricity arising from chemical action.

25. For an account of the heroic struggle of Civilis at the head of the Batavians (Germans) against the Roman armies see Tacitus, *Histories,* Books IV and V, *passim.*

26. Emerson has confused two statements. The first is Voltaire's "It is said that God is always on the side of the heaviest battalions"; the second is Napoleon's "Providence is always on the side of the last reserve."

27. Wellington returned to Lisbon on April 22, 1809, after his previous recall, and on April 24 wrote the British ministry that he had assumed command of the army. Neither Napier, *History of the War in the Peninsula* (1828–1840), nor Robert Southey, *History of the Peninsular War* (1823–1832), the two standard histories available to Emerson, says that "when he came to the army in Spain" (i.e., the Peninsula) he

undertook the action attributed to him thus early by Emerson. I do not know where Emerson got his information. I do not find it in Gurwood's *Selections from the Dispatches . . . of Wellington* (new ed., London, 1851), though Emerson read some edition of that book.

28. Henry John Temple Palmerston, third Viscount (1784–1865), was from 1809 to 1828 Secretary of War, becoming foreign minister in the government of Earl Grey in 1830.

29. On April 1, 1801, the British fleet under Sir Hyde Parker, Nelson second in command, attacked and destroyed the Danish fleet under the guns of Copenhagen. Emerson got most of his information about Nelson from Southey's *Life of Nelson*, of which there are many editions.

30. John Clerk, *An Essay on Naval Tactics* (Edinburgh, 1782; 1790; third ed., 1797). See especially Part II.

31. Brilliantly illustrated at the Battle of Aboukir Bay (1805).

32. Collingwood was second in command at Trafalgar (1805).

33. The *New English Dictionary* seems to indicate that Emerson is the first to use the word motor in the sense of an apparatus for employing the energy of some natural agent or force for the impulsion of machinery; a machine that supplies the motive power for the propulsion of a carriage or vessel.

34. Any legal right, but more usually a right to the use of land, held in commonalty by any group.

34a. A special court, notable under Henry VIII, for confirming royal domination over the remnants of the feudal system, so-called because it sat in a chamber, the ceiling of which was decorated with stars.

35. For the quoted sentence Emerson united parts of two sentences in the *Germania* in the translation of Tacitus' *Works* by Arthur Murphy (6 vols., Boston, 1822), vol. 5, top line of p. 217.

36. Properly, Joseph Rodgers and Sons, cutlers.

37. From the *Younger Edda* of Snorre, "Thor's Adventures on His Journey to the Land of the Giants."

38. Sir Robert Peel (1788–1850), British prime minister in 1834–35 and again in 1841–45.

39. The Blue Books are official reports from government officials and committees, bound in blue paper covers, intended for the information of Parliament.

40. Hansard is the official record of the proceedings of Parliament, corresponding to the American *Congressional Record*.

41. Presumably William Pitt the younger (1759–1806); George Canning (1770–1827); Robert Stewart Castlereagh, Second Marquis of Londonderry (1769–1822).

42. Presumably Edward Hyde, first Earl of Clarendon (1609–1674); Sir Philip Warwick (1606–1683); Sir William Coventry (1628–1686);

Anthony Ashley Cooper, first Baron Ashley and first Earl of Shaftesbury (1621–1683); Edward Thurlow, first Baron Thurlow (1713–1806); William Murray Mansfield, first Earl of Mansfield (1705–1793); John Scott Eldon, first Earl of Eldon (1751–1838); John Russell, first Earl Russell (1792–1878), all prominent British statesmen or jurists or both.

43. Sir John Franklin and all his men disappeared sometime after 1845 while in search of the Northwest Passage. A series of expeditions (1853, 1854, 1857–58) was sent out to solve the mystery of his disappearance, the last one finding the Franklin ships frozen in the ice between Victoria Island and King William Island.

44. More commonly Bering Strait, which separates Asia and North America.

45. Thomas Bruce, seventh Earl Elgin (1766–1841), seeing that the frieze of the Parthenon was in danger of destruction while Greece was in the hands of the Turks, brought it (and some other pieces of Attic statuary) to London after the difficulties described. They are now in the British Museum. Emerson took over this story from chap. xiv of the *Autobiography* of Benjamin Robert Haydon (1853).

46. Benjamin Robert Haydon (1786–1846), British painter; Henry Fuseli (1741–1825), Anglo-Swiss painter and draftsman; Antonio Canova (1757–1822), Italian sculptor. These three artists launched a campaign of appreciation of the Elgin marbles since, when they were installed, not "all good heads" liked them. See Haydon's *Autobiography,* chap. xvi.

47. Sir Charles Fellowes discovered the sites of some fifteen ancient cities in Asia Minor and brought back to the British Museum not merely the remains of the Xanthian monument (from Xanthus, an ancient city in Lydia) but the group of marbles in the Lycian room in the British Museum. When Emerson was in London, Sir Charles gave him a tour of the Museum. Sir Austen Henry Layard caused some of the monuments discovered at Nineveh to be sent to the British Museum.

48. Now Tasmania.

49. In South Africa, when Emerson wrote, a British possession.

50. Odin was the chief of the Norse gods (the Aesir), but does not seem to have been specially the patron of smiths.

51. Richard Roberts (1789–1854), British inventor. Among his creations was a self-regulating cotton mule or spinning machine which draws, stretches, and twists in one operation.

52. In Celtic folklore the banshee is a female spirit whose wailing forewarns hearers that a death in the family is imminent.

53. This is from *The Advancement of Learning,* part of a long sentence about learning, civility, and poverty which concludes: "what a reverend and honoured thing poverty of fortune was, for some ages, in

the Roman state, which nevertheless was a state without paradoxes."
Bacon, *Works,* ed. Montague (16 vols., London, 1824), II, 24.

54. Louis Leon Felicité, Duc de Brancas (1733–1824), Comte de
Lauraguais, writer and scientist. I suspect the quotation is at second
hand.

55. The *Mark Lane Express,* a London periodical (1832–1924), continued as *The Farmer Express* (1924–1929). By the "Custom House
Returns" Emerson seems to mean the annual reports of that office.

56. Alexander Pope, *Windsor Forest,* ll. 29–32.

57. Robert Bakewell (1725–1795), British cattle-breeder and agrarian
reformer.

58. Chat Moss, a swamp south of Birmingham, offered special prob-
lems to early railway builders.

59. Rape is a plant of the mustard family, the seed of which, crushed,
furnishes oil for cooking and medicinal purposes.

60. A train required, following an act of Parliament in 1844, to run
at a third-class fare of one shilling a mile with seats "duly protected"
against the weather and at a speed of not less than twelve miles per
hour.

61. "See Memorial of H. Greenough, p. 66, New York, 1853." (Emerson's note.)

62. "Sir S. Romilly, purest of English patriots, decided that the only
independent mode of entering Parliament was to buy a seat, and he
bought Horsham." (Emerson's note.)

63. Chancery, before 1873 the highest court in England next to the
House of Lords, and presided over by the Lord High Chancellor, was
notoriously dilatory in reaching decisions.

64. Adam Gottlob Oehlenschläger (1779–1850) was crowned the
Scandinavian poet laureate in 1829.

65. The Royal Observatory in Greenwich Park.

66. James Hutton (1726–1797), Scottish geologist, was one of the
founders of modern geological theory. Sir John Dalton formulated the
atomic theory in chemistry. William Harvey (1578–1657) first successfully formulated the doctrine of the circulation of the blood.

VI. Manners

1. Spirit and endurance.

2. October 22, 1847.

3. George William Frederick Villiers, Earl of Clarendon (1800–
1870), Lord-Lieutenant of Ireland (1847–1852).

4. "Bare-shirts" or wild Norse warriors fighting in their shirts only;
Emerson confuses it with "berserk," a warrior who could take on animal
form and whom neither fire nor iron could harm.

5. Finickiness.

6. In 1847 there was a commercial crisis in Great Britain and the beginning of the potato famine in Ireland.

7. The Siamese twins Chang and Eng (1811–1874).

8. "The Spanish Lady's Love" in Joseph Ritson, *A Select Collection of English Songs* (2nd ed., 3 vols., London, 1813), II, 247.

9. These ladies are in *Cymbeline, Julius Caesar, The Taming of the Shrew,* and *Othello,* respectively.

10. Mrs. Lucy Hutchinson (b. 1620) wrote *The Memoirs of the Life of Colonel Hutchinson,* a leader among the Puritans during the English Civil Wars, which, however, was not published until 1806.

11. The *Letters* of Lady Rachel Russell (1636–1723), first published in 1773, were re-edited by Lord John Russell and published in 1853.

12. Sir Samuel Romilly, from excessive grief over the death of his wife, cut his own throat.

13. Wellington succeeded his brother as Governor-General of India in 1799.

14. This is William Cobbett (1763–1835), British journalist and reformer, and Spencer Perceval (1762–1812), prime minister from 1809 to 1812, when he was assassinated by a man of deranged mind.

15. Ranking second to the Order of the Garter, the Knights of the Bath were established (or re-established) as a "military order" by George I in 1725.

16. The gold-stick-in-waiting is an official of the British royal household who on state occasions bears a gilt rod; by extension, other such attendants.

17. Emerson may have secured this anecdote from the life of Eldon in Lord Campbell's *Lives of the Lord Chancellors* or from Horace Twiss's *The Public and Private Life of Lord Chancellor Eldon,* an edition of which in two volumes appeared in Philadelphia in 1844, but in the absence of an index to either of these vast compilations, it is impossible to find out.

18. From William Wordsworth, *A Guide through the District of the Lakes.* See the edition ed. W. M. Merchant (London, 1951), p. 102.

19. We want nothing changed. The phrase is from the Magna Charta.

20. George Canning (1770–1827), foreign secretary in 1822 and prime minister in 1827.

21. Japan is a process of varnishing or lacquering any object to give it a shining black finish, associated with Japan ware.

22. The famous inscription over the entrance to the Inferno in Dante's *Divine Comedy,* Canto III, l. 9.

23. Here, the "gift books" or "annuals" popular in the mid-nineteenth century, intended to lie on the parlor table.

24. The pianist Sigismond Thalberg (1812–1871) was distinguished for his showy and sentimental style.

25. Wherever Emerson picked up this phrase, it originates in *The Life of Sir Henry Wotton* (London, 1651), and may be found in a collected edition of the lives of Donne, Wotton, Hooker, and Herbert (London, 1670), sign. D4.

26. George Bryan Brummel (1778–1840), known as Beau Brummel, the chief figure in the Regency circle of fashionably dressed men.

27. From *A Relation, or rather a True Account, of the Island of England . . . about the Year 1500 by a Venetian Traveller,* printed by the Camden Society (no. XXXVII, 1847), p. 21. Emerson gives only a simple reference in the original text.

VII. Truth

1. The Domesday Book is the record of the census or survey (1085–86) of England ordered by William the Conqueror.

2. This phrase is applied to Alfred by Asser, a ninth-century writer, in his *De Rebus Gestis Ælfredi.*

3. Geoffrey of Monmouth, *Histories of the Kings of Britain,* Book VIII, chapter iii.

4. This is presumably from the *Heimskringla* but I have not located it.

5. Nothing truer than truth.

6. In his *Letters to His Son* (1774).

7. François Etienne de Kellermann (1770–1835), French cavalry leader, was opposed to Wellington during the Peninsular War. The whole passage about the relations between Wellington and Kellermann is a paraphrase of pages 17–19 of Jules Maurel, *The Duke of Wellington; His Characters, His Actions, and His Writings,* trans. with a preface by Egerton Ellesmere (2nd ed., London, 1853). In a letter to William Emerson, September 2, 1856, Emerson falls into the curious error of calling this writer Fauriel, if Rusk's text is correct.

7a. Fuller, *Worthies,* p. 33 (under Bristol).

8. Anne Louise Germaine Necker, Baronne de Staël-Holstein (1766–1817).

9. This seems to be based on Maurel, pp. 42–43.

10. In a memorandum of October 20, 1809, Wellington outlined the plan for a concentric series of fortifications about Lisbon some twelve months before the French army appeared to attack them.

11. In April 1851. Emerson made a speech at the St. George's Society on the day stipulated.

12. St. Jerome's Latin version of the Bible. The passage is found in the Epistle to the Hebrews, 13:4. Hugh Latimer (ca. 1490–1555) was bishop of Worcester in 1535 and was later martyred.

13. François Guizot (1787–1874), historian and statesman, premier in France in 1847–48 under Louis Philippe, had to flee the country because of the Revolution of 1848.

14. The London Athenaeum Club. Emerson was made an honorary member during his stay in London in 1847–48.

15. Under the Act of Union (1800) Ireland was allotted this number of members of the House of Commons.

16. It is not literally true that there was no shot fired during the Revolution of 1848, but in general the army refused to fire on the populace.

17. Barristers (lawyers) appointed by the Lord Chancellor as counsel to the crown.

18. On February 14, 1797, the British fleet defeated the Spanish fleet off Cape St. Vincent; on June 1, 1794, occurred the climax of a protracted naval action off the British coast, in which the British fleet under Lord Howe destroyed a French fleet. Collingwood felt himself aggrieved because he was not mentioned in Lord Howe's dispatches.

19. The unpopular Convention of Cintra (1808) permitted the withdrawal of the French army under Junot from Portugal. This anecdote is more or less standard in all the biographies of Wellington, but I do not know where Emerson picked it up.

20. The mob is radical in the sense that they had favored the First Reform Bill (1832). According to the biography of Eldon in Lord Campbell's *Lives of the Lord Chancellors,* chapter ccxi, one man in the crowd, when Eldon was given an honorary degree at Oxford, cried out as in the text.

21. "It is an unlucky moment to remember those sparkles of solitary virtue in the face of the honors lately paid in England to the Emperor Louis Napoleon. I am sure that no Englishman whom I had the happiness to know, consented, when the aristocracy and the commons of London cringed like a Neapolitan rabble, before a successful thief. But, — how to resist one step, though odious, in a linked series of state necessities? Governments must always learn too late, that the use of dishonest agents is as ruinous for nations as for single men." (Emerson's note.)

22. On that date a huge demonstration in favor of the People's Charter was held in London.

23. A favorite expression of Napoleon's.

24. *Esprit d'escalier* is the kind of retort one thinks of after one has left a gathering where it would have been apt.

25. An active volcano in Sicily.

26. *A Relation, or rather a True Account, of the Island of England,* p. 37. Emerson's quotation is not quite exact.

27. In 1848 Margaret Fox (1836–1893) and her sister in Rochester,

New York, professed to be possessed by spirits who made them rap with their toes. In 1888 she confessed to fraud.

28. Emerson lectured in Derby in the winter of 1847–48.

29. María Felicia Malibran (1808–1836), operatic contralto. Emerson heard her sing in London in 1833.

30. From "The True Born Englishman" by Daniel Defoe, Part II.

VIII. Character

1. Jean Froissart (1337–1410?) spent almost as much time in England as he did in France, and his *Chroniques* (*Chronicles of the Hundred Years' War*) are filled with observations on the English. Voltaire published his *Lettres Philosophiques* (also known as *Lettres sur les Anglais*) in 1733. Alain René Le Sage (1668–1747), author of *Gil Blas*, visited England but seems to have written no travel book about it. Emerson's fourth reference is presumably to *Mirabeau's Letters during His Residence in England* (2 vols., London, 1832), an anonymous translated collection of his correspondence in part. A section of a French newspaper commonly devoted to light literature is called the *feuilleton*.

2. They amuse themselves sadly according to the manner of their country. Since the Brussels edition (1867–1877) of the *Chroniques* is in twenty-five volumes, it is virtually impossible to locate this characterization.

3. See the section "Of the English in the Spiritual World" in Swedenborg's *The True Christian Religion*.

4. Shakespeare, *Henry IV, Part II,* act I, scene i, ll. 151–152.

5. Hezekiah Woodward (1590–1675), controversial Puritan divine, opposed all formal prayers. But Emerson quotes only a part of a sentence he found in Anthony à Wood, *Athenae Oxonienses*, vol. III, col. 1034, which runs: "it is commonly reported now among the inhabitants of Bray, that he wrote a book against the Lord's prayer; which was answer'd by Brice before mention'd." Mr. Brice is not further identified than as a vicar of Bray who left it in 1649.

6. Robert Burton (1577–1640) published the first edition of *The Anatomy of Melancholy* in 1621. Although the story of his death is common, Emerson apparently took it from the account in Anthony à Wood, *Athenae Oxonienses*, vol. II, col. 653.

7. Southey, *Life of Nelson,* chap. iv.

8. The Furies of Greek mythology.

9. Emerson's list is more picturesque than literal. Hasheesh (hashish) is a narcotic prepared from the hemp plant and is associated with the Orient. Creases (kris) are Malay knives. The Bohon Upas is a Japanese tree secreting an acrid, milky juice containing a poison; tradition was that sleeping under it is fatal. The passage about the blood of St. Januarius and the winking Virgin is based upon Lecture VII of John

Henry Newman, *Lectures on the Present Position of Catholics in England* (1851, often reprinted). In a 1924 edition the significant passage (p. 312) is: "I think it impossible to withstand the evidence which is brought for the liquefaction of the blood of St. Januarius at Naples, and for the motion of the eyes of the pictures of the Madonna in the Roman States." This occasioned a controversial correspondence in the *Morning Chronicle* between Dr. Hinds, Bishop of Norwich, and Newman, that may be followed in Note II of the Appendix of the 1924 edition. Two madonnas in the church of St. Grisgono in Travestere in Rome, one in the church and afterwards one in the open piazza, are supposed to have opened and closed their eyes. See James Grant, *The Mysteries of All Nations* (Leith, Scotland, 1880), p. 630. "Every cell of the Inquisition" is an oblique reference to the supposed torture chambers and secret dungeons of that institution; Newman touches briefly on this belief. The Turkish caaba (kaaba, kaabeh) is the black stone in the great mosque at Mecca, supposed to have been given by Gabriel to Abraham, to which the Moslem turns in prayer. It is an object of pilgrimage in the Islamic world. I cannot make out whether Bentley is Richard Bentley the Master of Trinity College, Cambridge, a great classical scholar whose dates are 1662–1743, or Richard Bentley the publisher (1794–1871). The first brought the distinguished Orientalist Henry Sike from Utrecht to Cambridge; the second brought out books on Indian life and religion.

10. Milton, "L'Allegro," ll. 109–110: "hath thresh'd the Corn/ That ten day-labourers could not end."

11. Punch is of course the Punchinello of the Punch and Judy shows, familiar from the cover of the magazine of that name. The person described is the painter J. M. W. Turner (1775–1851).

12. At the Royal Academy of Arts.

13. From Shakespeare, *Othello,* act I, scene i, ll. 70–71.

14. From the *Problemata* of Aristotle, XXX, 1.

15. After the conquest of Canada in 1763 the British left largely untouched the legal code of Quebec, descending from the days of Louis XIV. Mauritius, an island in the Indian Ocean, was taken from the French in 1810. Until that time, like other French possessions, it was governed under the Napoleonic Code, a digest of laws prepared under Napoleon and completed in 1804. The Spanish Cortes was at one time a representative governing body in Spain and therefore in the Spanish Empire. The Laws of Menu are laws written in Sanskrit and purportedly divinely revealed to Menu (or Manu). They govern the rituals of the Brahmins and were used by Warren Hastings in framing a legal code for India. A Thing was the Icelandic parliament, a form of representative government continued on the Isle of Man as the House of Keys. The Cape of Good Hope once belonged to the Dutch and was con-

quered by the English during the Napoleonic wars. The Emperor Justinian, who reigned from 527 to 565, was the Byzantine emperor under whose reign the Corpus Juris Civilis was compiled — an elaborate code of laws for the later Roman Empire. It is, however, scarcely accurate to say that the Pandects (the second portion of the Corpus) governed the Ionian Islands, which were a British protectorate until 1864.

16. Hypochondria; also the organ in the body supposed to produce melancholy.

17. Cortical here means external, like the bark of a tree. Caducous: falling off, or having a tendency to fall off.

18. A waxy brownish substance generated in dead bodies long buried or immersed in moisture.

19. Thomas Fuller, *The Worthies of England* (1662). The statement about Strafford may be found in the edition ed. John Freeman (London, 1852), p. 373. The quotation about Baron Vere is in the same, p. 180. The Earl of Strafford (1593–1641) was at one time Lord Deputy of Ireland and an adviser to Charles I, but was impeached and beheaded. Sir Horace Vere (Baron Vere of Tilbury, 1565–1635) was the first baron created by Charles I. Emerson's own note is simply: "Fuller, *Worthies of England.*"

20. Emerson's note runs: "*Heimskringla,* Laing's translation, vol. iii, p. 37." In the edition of 1889 the passage is on pp. 392–393 in vol. III, and the word is "appearance," not "appearances" (in the first sentence).

21. The British tended to hail with delight the two French revolutions of 1830 and 1848; popular sentiment was on the side of Poland and Hungary in the attempts of these countries to achieve independence in 1848 (and even earlier); and the Schleswig-Holstein problem was whether either or both of these duchies should belong to Denmark or be absorbed into the German states.

22. Nelson's words to his fleet before going into battle at Trafalgar. Although the sentence is found in every life of Nelson, Emerson presumably picked it up from the last chapter of Southey's biography.

23. The consols (consolidated public debts) of Great Britain paid a regular dividend of 3 percent.

IX. Cockayne

1. Individualists.

2. Mr. Crump is Emerson's invention, possibly from the Scottish verb "to crump," meaning "to brag." Cockayne is also Emerson's invention.

3. Individualistic, arrogant.

4. From paragraph 807 of the section "Of the English in the Spiritual World" in Swedenborg, *The True Christian Religion.*

5. "Printed by the Camden Society." (Emerson's note.) This is the edition already cited (London, 1849); see pp. 20–21.

6. Wapping is a district of Stepney, here used symbolically for true cockney provincialism.

7. Brage, usually Bragi, is Odin's counselor in Norse mythology.

8. Emerson lectured in the Middle West in the fifties, and experienced a severe winter in Wisconsin and Illinois in 1856. A letter to his wife says: "My chamber is a cabin, my fellow boarders are legislators . . . Two or three governors or ex-governors live in the house." This was in Springfield, Illinois. Rusk, *Letters of Ralph Waldo Emerson*, IV, 342.

9. Emerson visited Eton College on July 5, 1848.

10. "William Spence." (Emerson's note.) This is from William Spence, *Britain Independent of Commerce; or, Proofs, Deduced from an Investigation into the True Causes of The Wealth of Nations*, a pamphlet, of which an American edition was printed and sold in Boston in 1808 from the fourth London edition, corrected and enlarged. Emerson's quotation is mildly inaccurate; the original is on p. 91 of the pamphlet.

11. Emerson followed Gibbon in this account of George of Cappadocia. See *The History of the Decline and Fall of the Roman Empire*, chap. xxiii. For a corrected view see Rev. F. G. Holweck, *A Biographical Dictionary of the Saints* (St. Louis and London, 1924), p. 423.

12. Emerson's characterization of Vespucci, more picturesque than sound, may owe something to Alexandre von Humboldt, *Examen critique de l'histoire de la géographie du nouveau continent* (Paris, 1814–1834, and Paris, 1836–1839). Hojeda, more commonly Alonso de Ojeda (1465?–1515), a Spanish conquistador, was at one time governor-general of much of the Spanish territory in South America. He vanished into the wilderness. The new-found continents were named America in the *Cosmographiae Introductio* (1507) by a German geographer, Martin Waldseemüller. There is no evidence that Amerigo Vespucci had anything to do with it.

X. Wealth

1. This sentence is presumably in Haydon's *Autobiography* (1853), but I have been unable to find it.

2. From chap. ii of Southey's *Life of Nelson*.

3. In the index to *The Works of the Rev. Sydney Smith* (3 vols., London, 1854), this phrase occurs under "Poverty," the reference being to III, 331, "First Letter to Archdeacon Singleton on the Ecclesiastical Commission, 1837." But the passage in question does not contain the sentence, so that Emerson seems to have taken his quotation from the index.

4. In Thomas Robert Malthus, *Essay on the Principle of Population*, first published in 1798, the proposition is laid down that population tends to increase faster than the food supply; the laboring population would suffer first from lack of food.

5. A somewhat bellicose Tory, J. Fuller, M.P., uttered this remarkable sentiment in a debate in the House of Commons on March 17, 1809, concerning the conduct of the Duke of York and Mrs. Clarke. See Hansard, *Parliamentary Debates*, 2nd series, vol. 13, col. 674.

6. On June 16, 1805, Sir Robert Peel introduced a bill to restrict the employment of young children in cotton mills, and in the immediate debate in the House of Commons Francis Horner (1778–1817) deplored the sending of young children one, two, or three hundred miles from their birthplaces and their relations. It does not appear from the indexes to Hansard that Stuart Wortley spoke on the bill in the terms Emerson gives.

7. The period of the Napoleonic wars.

8. The Crystal Palace, originally located in Hyde Park, was erected in 1851 for the Great Exhibition of that year. It was under construction when Emerson paid his second visit to England.

9. This is presumably William Cecil, Lord Burleigh (Burghley) (1520–1598), the chief minister of Queen Elizabeth; but if this guess is right, I am ignorant where Emerson found his quotation. The Centenary edition quotes Bacon's essay "On Expense": "Certainly, if a man will keep but of even hand, his ordinary expenses ought to be but half of his receipts; and, if he thinks to wax rich, but to the third part." This is parallel but not what Emerson has.

10. From the parable of the talents. See Luke 19:20.

11. This passage on the achievements of Roger Bacon is factually inaccurate, attributing to him suggestions and achievements that were not his; it must come, I think, from some secondary source.

12. James Hargreaves (d. 1788) invented the spinning jenny, which made possible the simultaneous spinning of eight threads. The machine came into use in the 1760's.

13. Sir Richard Arkwright (1732–1792).

14. Stalybridge or Staleybridge, near Manchester, won something of a reputation in the textile trades as what we would call a company town. Mr. Roberts is Richard Roberts.

15. These include William of Poitiers, whose *Gesta Guillelmi ducis Normannorum et regis Anglorum*, a principal authority on the life of William the Conqueror, contains several chapters in Part II celebrating the riches William brought into Normandy. I am, however, unable to locate the exact sentence, which Emerson may have picked up from a modern writer.

16. Motive power.

17. A quarter is a quarter of a bushel.

18. Russell was prime minister from 1846 to 1852.

19. Sir Joseph Whitworth (1803–1887), engineer and inventor.

20. A beach of shingle is a beach made of small flat rocks. Presumably Emerson had in mind a barren hillside made to bear oaks suitable for ship timbers, but what steam has to do with this is not clear.

21. A passage in the essay "Works and Days" in *Society and Solitude* makes this reference partly clear: "Egypt, where no rain fell for three thousand years, now, it is said, thanks Mehemet Ali's irrigations and planted forests for late-returning showers."

22. In Norse myth the Fenris wolf, somehow the son of Loki, was bound on Niflheim but steadily frays his bond. This will break at last and he will swallow the sun on the Last Day.

23. France and England were connected by cable in 1850.

24. Hecla is an active volcano in Iceland. Miollnir is the hammer of Thor in Norse myth.

25. John Evelyn (1620–1706), diarist, author of *Sylva* (1662), a book on arboriculture, and other works, original or translated, on gardens.

26. Inigo Jones (1573–1652), English architect, remembered, among other reasons, for designing the Banquet Hall at Whitehall and St. Paul's Cathedral, London. Christopher Wren (1632–1723) built many London churches after the Great Fire (1666).

27. Grinling Gibbons (1648–1721), possibly the most famous English woodcarver.

28. William Shenstone (1716–1763), poet and landscape gardener; Lancelot ("Capability") Brown (1715–1783), landscape gardener; John Claudius Loudon (1783–1843), botanist and writer on gardening; Sir Joseph Paxton (1801–1855), horticulturist and designer of the Crystal Palace. Alexander Pope is mentioned here presumably because he had strong views on formal gardens.

29. "Lady fishmongers" possessed special privileges under the Bourbons and under Louis Napoleon, and were prominent in the riots of the French Revolution of 1789.

30. Queen Adelaide, the widow of William IV. She died in 1849.

31. The ancient city of Cuma in southern Italy was notable for the strength of its fortified walls.

32. Cadenham is a small town in Hampshire on the edge of the New Forest, but I do not know that Spic Park still exists.

33. Horace Walpole (1717–1797) built Strawberry Hill at Twickenham, "a little Gothick castle," which had considerable influence on the Gothic revival in later English taste.

34. William Beckford (1759–1844), novelist and collector, whose villa, Fonthill Abbey, was an example of eccentric splendor.

35. Byron inherited Newstead Abbey in a "dismantled and ruinous

state" in 1808, but it cannot be fairly said that he turned it into anything as eccentric as Fonthill Abbey.

36. A stockinger is an operator of a stocking-making machine.

37. Frederick John Robinson (1782–1859), later Viscount Goderich and Earl of Ripon, moderate Tory who supported Peel in his repeal of the Corn Laws.

XI. Aristocracy

1. Haddon Hall is near Rowsley in Derbyshire and was the home of the Vernon family. Kedleston is four miles from Derby, and since it was built in 1759–65 from the designs of James Paine and Robert Adam and was as late as 1924 the home of Marquis Curzon, I do not know that Emerson properly includes it in his "beautiful desolations." He seems to mean only that it was not lived in by its owners.

2. Charles II of the House of Stuart was restored to the throne of England in 1660.

3. Bendigeidfran or "Blessed Bran." The passage may be found in the Everyman Library edition of the *Mabinogion,* p. 34.

4. Osbruh, daughter of Oslac and first wife of Aethelwulf.

5. These are noble or royal families that date back to the eleventh or twelfth centuries.

6. Richard de Beauchamp (1382–1439), first Earl of Warwick. The emperor is Sigismund I (1368–1437), crowned emperor of the Holy Roman Empire of the German People in 1414. Henry V was king of England 1413–1422. The passage quoted may be found in the edition of *The Worthies of England* (1662) by Thomas Fuller, ed. John Freeman, p. 624. This is an abridged edition; Emerson's own note refers to another edition.

7. Richard Neville, Earl of Warwick (1428–1471), the "king-maker."

8. Henry VI (1422–1471), crowned king of England in 1429; Edward IV (1442–1483), proclaimed king of England in 1461. Henry represented the House of Lancaster, Edward that of York.

9. The badge of the Earl of Warwick was a bear and a ragged staff.

10. The founder of the Bedford fortunes was John Russell (1486?–1555), first Earl of Bedford. For the story sketched by Emerson see the proper entry in the *Dictionary of National Biography.* The Duke of Bedford of Emerson's time was the seventh duke, Francis Russell (1788–1861).

11. Sheridan is presumably Richard Brinsley Sheridan (1751–1816), dramatist and politician; Coke is Sir Edward Coke (1552–1634), the rival of Francis Bacon. I do not know where Emerson picked up his quotation.

12. "*Reliquiae Wottonianae,* p. 208." (Emerson's note.) The first Duke of Buckingham was George Villiers (1592–1628).

13. From *Posthumous Memoirs of My Own Time* (1784) in *The Historical Posthumous Memoirs of Sir Nathaniel William Wraxall*, ed. Henry B. Wheatley, 5 vols., III, 364.

14. The entry appears in Pepys's *Diary* under date of Sunday, September 16, 1660, not 1666.

15. From Thomas Taylor's translation of Iamblichus, *De Mysteriis* (The Reply of Abammon to Porphyry's *Letter to Aenbo*), 1821, p. 298: "But the Barbarians are stable in their manners, and firmly continue to employ the same words. Hence they are dear to the Gods, and proffer words which are grateful to them; but which it is not lawful for any man by any means to change." Emerson has obviously condensed and modified the passage.

16. *Mirabeau's Letters during His Residence in England*, I, 111–112. But Emerson condenses and alters the original.

17. See *Diary of John Evelyn*, ed. William Bray (new ed., London, 1850–1852, 4 vols.), I, 78. Emerson rephrases and modernizes the passage.

18. Piccadilly was formerly a more fashionable quarter of London than it is now. Concerning the various great houses listed by Emerson there are occasional passages in Emerson's correspondence. Burlington House on Piccadilly now houses the Royal Society and other organizations. Devonshire House was near Green Park; Lansdowne House in Berkeley Square; Montague House was replaced by the British Museum; and the three squares named can be found on any map of London.

19. Belgravia refers to the area centering on Belgrave Square west of Buckingham Palace. Stafford House was the residence of the Duke of Sutherland. Northumberland House was demolished in 1874; the name survives in Northumberland Avenue. Chesterfield House was on South Audley Street. Sion House is in Islesworth. Holland House stood near Kensington Road but is now a wreck.

20. Barnard Castle, near Darlington, "is a prodigious ruin of an old North country keep," Emerson wrote his wife on February 10, 1848. Emerson's topography in this long paragraph can be followed on any large-scale map of Great Britain.

21. This seems to mean John Campbell (1762–1834), fourth Earl of Breadalbane, created a marquis in 1831.

22. The North Sea.

23. The North Sea to the Irish Sea.

24. Although the Reform Bill of 1832 somewhat alleviated the scandal of the rotten borough or pocket borough system, it left a number of seats controlled by the proprietors of lands or villages who in fact continued to dictate the voting of their tenants.

25. The Heptarchy is a reference to the seven kingdoms into which Anglo-Saxon England was once divided.

26. In the 1840's Germany was still "romantic," and the Rhine River

and the Harz Mountains were fashionable among persons of taste. Ghauts, usually Ghats, are the low mountains in southern India along the eastern and western margins of the Deccan Plateau.

27. Thomas Carlyle.

28. Though he had retired from the cabinet, the Duke of Wellington was entrusted with the organization and command of a special military force designed to be used against rioters during the Chartist agitation of April 1848. As a duke, of course, he continued to be a member of the House of Lords and presumably commanded the votes of a number of the members of that house. I take "the proxies of fifty peers" to be more picturesque than factual.

29. The Lord Chancellor and other members of the nobility distinguished for legal learning.

30. The Crimean War, 1854–55.

31. Capacity to do well. In one language or another the phrase is attributed to Prince Henry the Navigator of Portugal.

32. From the dome of St. Paul's Cathedral in London.

33. Mayfair is a fashionable district in London, north of Piccadilly.

34. This is commonly credited to James Parton, *The Life and Times of Benjamin Franklin* (2 vols., New York, 1864), II, 514–515, which Emerson could not have read in preparation for *English Traits*. Parton credits the anecdote to the *Memoirs of Baron de Grimm,* giving, however, no specific reference.

35. Warwick Castle is near Leamington in Warwickshire.

36. The Arundel marbles is a collection of ancient sculptures given to Oxford University by Thomas Howard (1586–1646), the second Earl of Arundel. The Townley (or Towneley) Gallery in the British Museum contains a collection of classical sculptures given by Charles Towneley (1737–1805). The Howard Library was based on the collections of Lord William Howard (1563–1640), third son of the fourth Duke of Norfolk at Naworth Castle, Cumberland. Sir Charles Spencer (1674–1722) laid the foundation of the library at Blenheim Castle, dispersed by sale in 1881–83. The Warwick Vase was found in Hadrian's villa at Tivoli and transported to Warwick Castle. The Portland Vase (or the Barbarini vase) is now in the British Museum.

37. John (not George) Claudius Loudon. John Evelyn, the diarist and writer on gardening, translated and published in 1693 *The Compleat Gardiner,* 2 vols., from the French of Jean de la Quintinie.

38. Arthur Young (1741–1820), English agriculturist and traveler. Robert Bakewell improved the breeding of domestic animals in Great Britain, particularly sheep and kine. John Joseph Mechi (1802–1880), inventor and agriculturist, published *Letters on Agriculture* in 1844.

39. The battle of Culloden (1746), in which the forces of the Young

Pretender were defeated by the army of the Duke of Cumberland, a conflict which ended the threat of the return of the House of Stuart to the British throne.

40. Emerson's reference is presumably to Walter Francis Scott (1806–1884), fifth Duke of Buccleuch. But the Buccleuch genealogy is somewhat complicated.

41. Duke Humphrey appears in *Henry VI*, Part III; the Earl of Warwick in *Henry IV*, Part II, *Henry V*, and the three parts of *Henry VI*; the Earl of Northumberland in *Richard II* and the three parts of *Henry VI*; Lord Talbot in *Henry VI*, Part I, together with his son.

42. "Dibdin's *Literary Reminiscences*, Vol. I, xii." (Emerson's note); that is, *Reminiscences of Thomas Dibdin* (2 vols., London, 1837).

43. The *Autobiography* of Edward Herbert, Lord Herbert of Cherbury (1583–1648), was first printed in 1764 under the title *The Life of Edward, Lord Herbert of Cherbury, Written by Himself*. There were other editions in London in 1826 and 1830.

44. This seems to refer to *The Miscellaneous Works of Sir Philip Sidney* (Oxford, 1829). Fulke Greville wrote a *Life of the Renowned Philip Sidney* in 1652.

45. The principal antiquarian work of Thomas Fuller was his *History of the Worthies of England* (1662); the chief antiquarian work of Arthur Collins (1690?–1760) is *Letters and Memorials of State* (London, 1746).

46. Kenilworth Castle is near Leamington in Warwickshire and was once given to the Earl of Leicester by Queen Elizabeth; Althorp Park is near Northampton and was the seat of the Earl of Spencer in the seventeenth century; Belvoir Castle, rebuilt in 1816 after a disastrous fire, is in Lincolnshire not far from Grantham.

47. John Aubrey, *Letters Written by Eminent Persons . . . and Lives of Eminent Men* (2 vols., London, 1813), contains a biography of Hobbes in II, 593–637. But see also II, 228f.

48. In Kent, Sir Philip Sidney's birthplace.

49. Near Wilton, the residence of the Countess of Pembroke, Sidney's sister.

50. Prose pastoral romance by Sir Philip Sidney, written in 1590.

51. Fulke Greville (1554–1628), Lord Brooke, poet and patron of letters. His *Life* of Sidney is noted above.

52. Ludlow Castle is in Ludlow, Wales. In the Council Hall of the castle in 1634 Milton's *Comus* was performed in honor of the Earl of Bridgewater, made lord-lieutenant of Wales in 1631. Emerson presumably refers to the castle as an honest house because of the praise of virtue in Milton's masque.

53. Philibert, Chevalier de Grammont (1621–1707), a French visitor

at the court of Charles II, is credited with *Memoirs* (1713), which seems to have been written by his brother-in-law, Anthony Hamilton (1646?–1720).

54. The quoted phrases and sentences are all from Pepys's *Diary*; for example, the passage about the poor and frothy discourse of the king's companions is in the *Diary*, November 24, 1662.

55. Emerson presumably read of George Augustus Selwyn (1719–1791), wit and clergyman, in John Heneage Jesse, *George Selwyn and His Contemporaries* (4 vols., London, 1843–1844).

56. George IV (1762–1830) ruled as Regent after his father, George III, had been declared legally insane in 1810, and as king from 1820 to 1830. In his old age he became so fat he could not enter a carriage except by sliding out of a window. Caroline of Brunswick (1768–1821) was sued for divorce by George IV, a suit that became a party matter besides producing a great deal of scandal. As prince, George had had a commoner wife, Mrs. Fitzherbert, though the question of the legality of the marriage is a problem.

57. That of Queen Victoria, who reigned from 1837 to 1901.

58. It sufficiently illustrates Emerson's point to remember that the character of the Marquis of Steyne in Thackeray's *Vanity Fair*, whose mistress is Becky Sharp, was suggested by the second and third marquises of Hertford.

59. The genealogy of the House of Orleans is somewhat complicated, but it is here sufficient to remember that its representatives in France during the eighteenth century were not noted for high moral principles and that Louis Philippe of the House of Orleans, who reigned as King of the French from 1830 to 1848, was a far from distinguished monarch.

60. Although the title is not uncommon, the Centenary edition suggests that Emerson is referring either to *Causes Célèbres Etrangères, publiées en France pour le première fois, et traduites de l'Espagnol, l'Italien et l'Allemagne* (Paris, 1827–1828) or to *Causes Célèbres, Repertoire générale des causes célèbres anciennes et modernes, rédigé par une Société d'hommes de lettres sous la direction de B. Saint-Edme* (Paris, 1834–1835), or to both.

61. William Cavendish (1808–1891), second Earl of Burlington and seventh Duke of Devonshire, philanthropist and liberal, lived at Chatsworth House, a vast Palladian palace in Derbyshire.

62. Carlyle.

63. I take this to be Thomas Campbell (1777–1844) the poet.

64. Giulia Grisi (1811–1869), the most celebrated operatic soprano, and Mario, Marchese di Camdia (1812–1883), the most celebrated operatic tenor of the mid-century.

65. That is, 1689.

66. "Huber, *History of English Universities*." (Emerson's note.) The actual passage runs: "In the University-arrangements they [the noble classes] are exempted from the public exercises for the Degree, &c.: by which means they attain a Degree, called (forsooth!) Honorary: at the same time the fees they have to pay for matriculation and on all other occasions are much higher." To this the translator appends a footnote which Emerson ignores: "Noblemen by no means always avail themselves of this exemption." *The English Universities. From the German of V. A. Huber. An Abridged Translation* by Francis W. Newman (2 vols. in 3, London, 1843) vol. II, pt. I, p. 202.

66a. Paraphrased from Fuller, *Worthies,* p. 216 (under Yorkshire).

67. The attribution of this to Johnson seems to be unwarranted; at least none of the Johnson scholars I have consulted has been able to locate the reference in Johnson's own works.

68. At the Battle of Cape St. Vincent, Nelson gave orders to board the enemy ship, the San Nicolas. "It was done in an instant, he himself leading the way, and exclaiming — 'Westminster Abbey or victory!'" Southey, *Life of Nelson,* chap. iv.

69. I am not clear where Emerson picked this up, but it is standard in lives of Sydney Smith; see, for example, Stuart J. Reid, *A Sketch of the Life and Times of the Rev. Sydney Smith* (New York, 1885), p. 265.

XII. Universities

1. Charles Giles Bridle Daubeny (1795–1867), Fellow of Magdalen College, elected Regius Professor of Botany in 1834.

2. Arthur Hugh Clough (1819–1861), the poet.

3. The Bodleian Library, one of the most famous libraries in the world, was founded in 1602 by Sir Thomas Bodley (1545–1613). The Randolph Gallery is on the ground floor of the Ashmolean Museum and houses the Arundel marbles. Merton Hall is part of Merton College, founded 1264.

4. That is, Harvard men.

5. Articles of household service made of gold or silver.

6. High table.

7. Let the blessed one bless; he is blessed; let him be blessed.

8. The origins of Oxford are shrouded in mystery. Legend attributes its origin to a mythical king named Memphric, or, somewhat more certainly, to Alfred the Great. It is first mentioned in the twelfth century. Pheryllt (Fferyll, Fferylltiad), worker in metal, refers to the legend that a metal workers' school had been established by the Druids, the religious and learned order among the ancient Celts.

9. Edward I (1230–1307), king of England from 1272 to 1307.

10. Alberico Gentili (1552–1608), who fled to England and at Oxford became a professor of civil law in 1580.

11. "A noble and learned Polonian, named Albertus Alaskie, or Laskie, or de Alasco . . . being come to the English Court to see the fashions, and admire the wisdom of the Queen, Letters, dated the 13th May [1583], came from the Chancellor at the University, by her Majesty's command, that the Members thereof should make provision for the reception of him, according to his quality, being a Prince and Palatine of Sirad." John Nichols, *The Progresses and Public Possessions of Queen Elizabeth* (new ed., 3 vols., London, 1823), II, 406–407. Sirad is, or was, Siradia, in Poland. The play was *Rivales* by Dr. William Gager. Christ Church is one of the Oxford colleges, dating from 1546.

12. Isaac Casaubon (1559–1614), classical scholar and theologian, royal librarian under Henry IV of France and prebendary of Canterbury and Westminster under James I of England.

13. Elias Ashmole (1617–1691), antiquarian. His bequest of "rarities" was housed in the Museum built by Sir Christopher Wren in 1683.

14. What Olympia, the seat of the Olympian games (these included contests in music, poetry, and athletic games) was to ancient Greece, Oxford was to antiquarians like Anthony à Wood and Aubrey. The *Athenae Oxonienses* was first printed in 1691–92.

15. Samuel Purchas (1577–1626) published in 1625 *Haklytus Posthumus; or, Purchas: His Pilgrims,* supplementing Richard Hakluyt's *The Principal Navigations, Voyages, and Discoveries of the English Nation* (2nd ed., 1598–1600).

16. William Laud (1573–1645), Chancellor of Oxford in 1629 and Archbishop of Canterbury in 1633, noted for his hostility to the Puritans. The statutes in question were ratified in 1636 and first printed in 1768.

17. The Merton Library, associated with Merton College, dates from 1377–78 and is notable for its medieval treasures.

18. The *First Defense of the English People* (1651) and *The Image-Breaker* (1649), to give the English translations, were tracts on behalf of the Puritans and the Cromwellian theory of government.

19. The body of Masters of Arts who form the ultimate authority for governing Oxford.

20. Doctor William Jacobson, with whom Emerson breakfasted while visiting Oxford.

21. Sir Thomas Lawrence (1769–1830), portrait painter and collector.

22. Sketches, preliminary drawings.

23. Lord Eldon was notable for his wealth and his conservatism.

24. Rev. Bulkeley Bandinel (1781–1861), librarian from 1813 to 1860.

25. The Bodleian in 1809 purchased from the Rev. Edward Daniel

Clarke (1769–1822) a collection of manuscripts, among them this manuscript of Plato.

26. Mainz, in Rhenish Hesse.

27. Worth about four dollars.

28. This may mean the Cathedral, rebuilt in 1004 by Ethelred II, but I am not clear as to Emerson's exact reference.

29. Wilton in Wiltshire was notable for Wilton carpets. Since the fourteenth century Sheffield in Yorkshire has been a cutlery center.

30. "Huber, ii. 305." (Emerson's note.) *The English Universities from the German of V. A. Huber.* But Emerson quotes a footnote.

31. Possibly James Edward Sewell (1810–1903), warden of New College in 1860, who was said to have filled almost every post in the university during his long life.

32. "Bristed, Five Years at an English University." (Emerson's note.) Charles Astor Bristed, *Five Years in an English University* (2nd ed., New York, 1852). Bristed, however, attended not Oxford but Cambridge. It is not clear whence Emerson derived his money figures.

33. Basic.

34. Eton College (in American terms, prep school; in British terms, a public school) was founded in 1440. The tag that the battles of England are won on the playing fields of Eton points to the importance of being captain of, say, an Eton cricket team.

35. Longs and shorts refers to the quantitative scansion of Latin verse. "Court-Guide," a column in *The Times,* is chosen as thoroughly prosaic, so that Emerson is making an indirect attack on the dullness of most schoolboy Latin hexameters.

36. Standard collection of Latin poets.

37. The Thames at Oxford is known as the Isis. Cambridge stands on the River Cam.

38. A Maud man is a student in Magdalen (pronounced Maudlin) College. Brasenose is another Oxford college, founded in 1509.

39. The Castalian spring near Delphi, on the slopes of Mount Parnassus in Greece, sacred to Apollo and the Muses.

40. That is, students learned in Greek.

41. Men of guts.

42. "Huber, *History of the English Universities,* Newman's Translation." (Emerson's note.) See Huber, II, 320f, for this passage, which Emerson has somewhat freely rearranged.

43. "See Bristed, *Five Years in an English University.* New York, 1852." (Emerson's note.) This is Charles Astor Bristed, and the definition is paraphrased from a passage in a letter to Bristed from a friend who is writing from Shrewsbury. See p. 271.

44. Emerson quotes phrases from various regulations regarding Oxford fellowships, and so forth, the point being "the terrors of parlia-

mentary inquiry." Increasing dissatisfaction with the obsolete and inefficient pattern of university finance and with restrictions that prevented Nonconformists from entering Oxford and Cambridge led Lord John Russell in 1850 to establish a commission of inquiry for each university. On this whole subject see Sir Spencer Walpole, *The History of Twenty-Five Years, 1856–1880* (4 vols., London and New York, 1903), III, 133–161.

45. Emerson learned from Bristed's book that walking was the principal exercise at Cambridge. See *Five Years in an English University*, pp. 328–330.

46. Kertch and Kinburn were Russian outposts captured by the Allies during the Crimean War.

47. The Centenary edition glosses this as a reference to Arthur Hugh Clough, but this seems unlikely; it seems to me rather a cloudy reference to Ruskin. The first volumes of *Modern Painters* bore on their title pages: "By an Oxford Undergraduate."

48. Presumably William Wordsworth, who attended St. John's College, and Alfred Tennyson, a graduate of Trinity College, Cambridge.

XIII. Religion

1. I suppose this to be the Tower of St. Mary's or the Old Steeple, which, however, dates only from the fifteenth century, though the chapel originally on this site dates from the twelfth century. The church was destroyed by fire in 1841 and then rebuilt.

2. Fountains Abbey, a ruined Cistercian abbey, is in the West Riding of Yorkshire, and so is Ripon Abbey. Beverley is in the East Riding of Yorkshire.

3. Richard of Devizes, who flourished in the twelfth century, wrote *Gesta Ricardi* (*Chronicle of the Deeds of Richard I*).

4. Possibly Emerson here means St. Jerome, who translated the Bible into Latin (the Vulgate), but he may refer to earlier versions of the Vulgate (or parts of it) turned into English.

5. St. Wilfrid (634–709?), leading cleric in a turbulent period, was for a time Abbot of Ripon and also Bishop of York and of Ripon. He is buried in Ripon.

6. Peasant, serf.

7. Among names not hitherto identified are the Earl of Arundel (1518–1580), arrested in October 1551, along with the Earl of Somerset, as a "conspirator"; John Oldcastle (d. 1417), Lord Cobham, leader of the Lollards, hanged in 1417, his body being afterwards burned; Antony Parsons, apparently an error for Andrew Parsons (1616–1684), fined and jailed for his religious beliefs; George Fox (1624–1691), founder of the Society of Friends.

8. "Wordsworth." (Emerson's note.) This is from a long footnote

attached to lines 1–3 of Sonnet XVIII, Part III of Wordsworth's *Ecclesiastical Sonnets*.

9. Thomas Musgrave (1788–1860) was consecrated Archbishop of York on January 15, 1848. (January 13 is an error.) Under the crown the archbishops of Canterbury and York are heads of the Anglican Church.

10. Genesis, chap. 24.

11. Editorial.

12. The origin of "God Save the King (Queen)" is wrapped in obscurity, and there is no reason to believe that George Frederick Handel (1685–1759) wrote it. See *Grove's Dictionary of Music and Musicians*, ed. Blum (London, 1954), vol. III, under "God Save the Queen."

13. John Camidge (1790–1859), who succeeded his father as cathedral organist in 1842.

14. "Fuller." (Emerson's note.) Fuller, *Worthies*, p. 199, reads that George Mountaine "was Chaplain to the Earl of Essex, whom he attended in his Voyage to Cales, being indeed one of such personall valour, that out of his gown, he would turn his back to no man." (under Yorkshire).

15. John Wycliffe (ca. 1340–1384), translator of the Bible into English; Thomas de Cobham (d. 1327), bishop of Worcester and benefactor of Oxford; Thomas Arundel (1353–1414), archbishop of Canterbury; Thomas à Becket (1117–1170), archbishop of Canterbury; Sir Thomas More (1478–1535), beheaded for refusing to subscribe to Henry VIII's divorce from Katherine of Aragon; Thomas Cranmer (1489–1556), archbishop of Canterbury and translator of the Bible; Jeremy Taylor (1613–1667), bishop of Down and Connor and Anglican divine; Robert Leighton (1611–1684), archbishop of Glasgow (unless Emerson has some other Leighton in mind); Joseph Butler (1692–1752), author of *The Analogy of Revealed Religion* (1736). A number of prominent persons named Sherlock have been important in English church history.

16. This is the Rev. Samuel Briscall (not Briscoll), who was appointed chaplain to the headquarters of the British army in the Peninsula in 1810, served to the end of the war, was with the British troops in the Low Countries and France from 1815 to 1818, and became curate at Strathfieldsaye. Wellington expressed these opinions, though not in Emerson's *ipsissima verba*, in a letter to Lieutenant General Calvert dated from Cartaxo, February 6, 1811, which may be found in any collection of Wellington's dispatches. In 1811 "Methodism" was a pejorative term.

17. "Jesuit's bark," the bark of the cinchona tree, from which quinine derives; "drench" means any large dose of liquid medicine but is here used in the sense of a purge. Both quinine and "drenches" were once indiscriminately administered.

18. A cabal was originally a group of English politicians (Clifford,

Arlington, Buckingham, Ashley, Lauderdale) supposed to have run the British government by intrigue and secrecy in 1672; their initials spell the word. The word has been confused with Cabbala (qabbalah), a Jewish term for a mystical interpretation of the Scriptures, and Emerson is making a pun. In general the Anglican clergy were confined to the gentlemen class.

19. Augustus Charles Pugin (1762–1832), himself an architect, wrote extensively on the appropriateness of the Gothic style for church architecture; and Ruskin published in 1849 his *Seven Lamps of Architecture* and in 1851–53 his *Stones of Venice*.

20. London University, founded in 1826, was known as the "godless university in Gower Street" because it had no church connections.

21. A school not connected with the Anglican Church.

22. Presumably an oblique reference to Benjamin Jowett (1817–1893), fellow of Balliol College after 1838 and translator of Plato, who had a devoted following of young men, but whose religious views were from the point of view of High-church Anglicanism unorthodox.

23. The Centenary edition says that this reference is to Thomas Taylor (1758–1835), a translator of various Greek authors who called Christianity a "most irrational and gigantic impiety," but this seems to reverse Emerson's meaning. Another Thomas Taylor (1576–1633), known as "a brazen wall against papacy," would seem to be a better example of bitterness against heresy.

24. See the concluding pages of the *Phaedo* of Plato.

25. From the "Prayer for the King's (Queen's) Majesty in the 'Morning Prayer,'" *Book of Common Prayer*.

26. See section 97 of the *Chronicle of Richard of Devizes*, trans. Giles (Bohn Library, 1849).

27. See *Memoirs of the Life of Sir Samuel Romilly, Written by Himself, with a Selection from His Correspondence*, ed. by his sons (3 vols., 2nd ed., London, 1840); the *The Life of Benjamin Robert Haydon from His Autobiography and Journals*, ed. Tom Taylor (3 vols., London, 1853).

28. In his *Diary* Samuel Pepys under date of November 30, 1668, says: "On leaving them I went away by coach home to dinner, and my wife, after dinner, went the first time abroad to take the maidenhead of her coach," but I do not find in this entry the quotation given by Emerson.

29. The act of 1753 was immediately repealed.

30. In *Hansard's Parliamentary Debates*, vol. 14 (1747–1753), col. 1417, under date of May 7, 1753, the London petition is quoted in part, but the passage differs somewhat from Emerson's phrasing.

31. Emerson's meaning becomes clearer if one consults any concordance to the English Bible under the word "new."

32. Fibrin is a white proteid compound obtained when blood is

coagulated; chyle is a nutritive coagulate milky fluid contained in the lacteals of the small intestine during digestion.

33. In the Anglican establishment a rectorship is a freehold of a parsonage and other church property.

34. *Vis naturae medicatrix,* the curative power of nature.

35. The curates are the lower clergy; the prelates, the higher clergy.

36. Lawn sleeves of a bishop's gown.

37. The bishopric of Durham had, when Emerson wrote, the largest income of any bishopric in England.

38. This is a paraphrase of a passage from a speech by Henry Brougham (1778–1868), not yet Lord Brougham, in the House of Commons April 26, 1825, for which see Hansard's *Parliamentary Debates,* 2nd series, vol. 13, col. 202.

39. In the Anglican church the dean is the senior officer of a cathedral or collegiate church. A prebend is a stipend allotted from the revenues of a cathedral or collegiate church to an ecclesiastic who serves in the church, and who is known as a prebendary or prebend.

40. The legal formulary by which the king or queen, titular head of the Church of England, permits the ecclesiastics of a given cathedral or other ecclesiastical unit to nominate (and in effect elect) a bishop or other high officials.

41. German theological scholarship in the forties and fifties devoted itself to the texts of the Bible, treating and studying them as human documents rather than divine.

42. The Oxford movement, which in turn produced the return of Newman and others to the Roman Catholic church.

43. Exeter Hall is a large hall on the north side of The Strand, London, which, after 1831, was especially associated with evangelical religion. In characters like Podsnap and Chadband Dickens satirizes the religious sanctimoniousness he associated with evangelical hypocrisy.

44. According to the account in the *Dictionary of National Biography,* 450 thieves asked Lord Shaftesbury to address them. I do not know whence Emerson derived his version of the episode.

45. In Chapter VIII, part II, of *The Zincali: An Account of the Gypsies of Spain* (London, 1841), George Borrow says he discoursed on the situation of the Jews in Egypt as a parallel to that of the Gypsies in Spain and that he read in "Rommany" "a portion of Scripture, and the Lord's Prayer and Apostles' Creed." The quoted matter in Emerson's text concludes the chapter.

46. The Monument is a tall column erected to commemorate the Great Fire of 1666. The Tower is of course the Tower of London.

47. To suffer from everybody and make no one suffer.

48. Thomas Clarkson (1760–1846), notable abolitionist; Florence Nightingale (1820–1910), influential in modernizing nursing and hospital services during the Crimean War.

XIV. Literature

1. Anne Louise Germaine Necker (1766–1817), Baronne de Staël-Holstein; but neither the most recent editor of the Carlyle-Emerson correspondence nor I have been able to identify the source of the sentence.

2. Writing Thomas Moore from Venice on November 17, 1816, Byron said in a postscript dated December 5 that he was studying Armenian because "I found that my mind wanted something craggy to break upon."

3. Charles Cotton (1630–1687), translator of Montaigne.

4. *Hudibras*, a satirical poem against the Puritans (1663) by Samuel Butler (1612–1680).

5. Henry More (1614–1687), leading Cambridge Platonist. Sir Thomas Browne (1605–1682), author of *Religio Medici* (1643).

6. Emerson indulges the fallacy that all Saxon words are shorter and all words derived from Latin are longer.

7. Guy of Warwick was the hero of a popular verse romance of the fourteenth century.

8. The romantic movement liked to believe that "Oriental" poets had a more sublime style than European ones. Emerson of course had a special penchant for translations from Oriental literature.

9. October ale.

10. Aspasia was the mistress of Pericles (fifth century B.C.).

11. Among the names not previously identified: James Usher (or Ussher) (1581–1656), English prelate and scholar; Joseph Mede (or Mead) (1586–1638), Biblical scholar, author of *Clavis Apocalypica;* Thomas Gataker (1574–1654), Puritan divine and classical scholar; Brian (or Bryan) Walton (1600?–1661), editor of a Polyglot Bible of 1653–57.

12. George Chapman (1559?–1634) translated Homer; Richard Crashaw (?1612–1649) wrote metaphysical verse; John Norris (1657–1711) was a supporter of the philosophy of Malebranche; Ralph Cudworth (1617–1688) wrote *A True Intellectual System of the Universe* (1678); and George Berkeley (1685–1753) was an "idealistic" philosopher.

13. Sir Humphry Davy (1778–1829), chemist and physicist, is remembered for his invention of a miner's safety lamp, among other things.

14. Translated, at least from Emerson's point of view, in the preceding phrase.

15. From Bacon's "The Advancement of Learning" in *Works*, 16 vols., ed. Montague, I, 70. Emerson's interpretation of Bacon as a "platonist" is not universally accepted.

16. Emerson has compounded this out of various phrases in the "The Advancement of Learning." The first half of the quoted matter is a

paraphrase of a passage on page 96 and the second comes from page 131 of Bacon, *Works*, vol. I.

17. Although Emerson used Thomas Taylor's translation of Plato, this passage is not from it. The most convenient translation for the modern reader is Jowett's, and can be found in I, 605.

18. Jan Baptista van Helmont (1577–1644), physicist and mystic; Jakob Boehme (1575–1624), religious mystic.

19. The notion that nature is commanded by obeying her is repeated many times in Bacon; for example, "Aphorism" 3 and 129, *Works*, VIII, 1, 73. The passage about the "shows of things" is from "The Advancement of Learning," *Works*, I, 90.

20. Zoroaster (660–538 B.C.) founded a Persian religion, the scriptures of which are the Zend-Avesta. Emerson means here by "Zoroastrian" little more than "dualistic."

21. "The Advancement of Learning," *Works*, I, 90.

22. Edmund Spenser, "An Hymne in Honour of Beauty," l. 133: "For Soule is forme and doth the bodie make."

23. Samuel Clarke (1675–1729), Cambridge philosopher, who argued for an immutable harmony in certain things and circumstances.

24. James Harrington (1611–1677), author of *The Commonwealth of Oceana* (1656).

25. Georg Wilhelm Friedrich Hegel (1770–1831), who taught that any great force, movement, or idea (thesis) produces a countermovement (antithesis), and that these are in turn resolved into a higher state (synthesis). This is for him the dynamic process of nature.

26. Friedrich Wilhelm Joseph von Schelling (1775–1854), who taught that nature is an organic continuum working toward self-consciousness and self-realization.

27. Johannes Kepler (1571–1630), who taught that the movements of the planets must conform to mathematical order. The three harmonic laws are (1) the planets move about the sun in an ellipse with the sun at one of the foci; (2) the radius vector of each planet sweeps over equal areas in equal times; (3) the square of the time for a complete revolution of any planet is proportional to the cube of its mean distance from the sun.

28. That is, Dalton's doctrine of atomic weights of the elements.

29. Slightly rearranged from Ben Jonson, "Discoveries," in *Works* (7 vols., London, 1756), VII, 100.

30. This is an oblique reference both to the title of Locke's principal work, *Essay Concerning Human Understanding* (1690) and to Locke's denial of the kind of intuitive psychology in which Emerson believed.

31. The seventeenth-century English Platonists seemed to Emerson to preach a "higher" philosophy than the empirical philosophy of Emerson's time.

32. Paraphrased from "The Advancement of Learning," *Works*, I, 96.

33. Link.

34. *Introduction to the Literature of Europe during the Fifteenth, Sixteenth, and Seventeenth Centuries* was published in 1837–39 by Henry Hallam.

35. The reference is to the severe strictures on "Lycidas" in the biography of Milton included in *The Lives of the Poets* (1779–1781) by Dr. Samuel Johnson.

36. Most of Mackintosh's writing was historical; for example, *The History of the Revolution in England in 1688* (1834).

37. William Hogarth (1697–1764), painter, engraver, and social caricaturist.

38. That is, practical result.

39. See in this connection the final section of Macaulay's essay on Bacon in his *Essays*.

40. Sir David Brewster (1781–1868), Scottish physicist, published the *Life of Sir Isaac Newton* in 1828.

41. Robert Hooke (1635–1703), English physicist and mathematician; Robert Boyle (1627–1691), English chemist, the propounder of Boyle's law on the pressure of gases; Edmund Halley (1656–1742), astronomer, who identified the periodic comet which bears his name (1682).

42. From Goldsmith's "Retaliation," the description of Edmund Burke.

43. That is, the government of the Anglican church retains its medieval structure.

44. James John Garth Wilkinson (1812–1899) published a number of books about Swedenborg and Swedenborgianism and advocated the medical theories of Samuel Hahnemann (1755–1843), the founder of homeopathy or the doctrine that "like cures like," and thought the physician should administer minute doses of medicines, but was an "annotator" of Fourier only in the general sense of accepting his theories of society.

45. Leonhard Euler (1707–1783), Swiss mathematician.

46. John Hunter (1728–1793), anatomist and physiologist, founder of the Hunterian Museum in London.

47. German biologists, in some degree anticipating Darwinian evolution, inferred likeness of origin from likeness of use and structure.

48. In placer mining running water is "panned" and the gold remains in the pan.

49. This is apparently an oblique reference to the "schöne Seele" of the German romantic movement. But it may mean only the Christian "Blessed Soul," one that is saved.

50. Scott's verse romances are filled with descriptions of Scotch scenery.

51. Middle-class, un-ideal.

52. Apparently a gleaning from Emerson's conversations with Landor.

53. Emerson's interest in Oriental poetry was great. The passage in quotation marks reflects the Epicureanism of the Persian poet Hafiz (d. 1389?).

54. Warren Hastings (1732–1818), first Governor-General of India (1774); he succeeded in winning the confidence of the priesthood in India if Macaulay is to be believed.

55. "Preface to Wilkins's Translations of the Bhagvat Geeta." (Emerson's note.) This is from a letter by Warren Hastings to Nathaniel Smith, dated October 4, 1784, on page 7 of the *Bhagvat-Geeta or Dialogues of Kreeshna and Arjoon* (London, 1785).

56. From the same, p. 7.

57. Robert Owen (1771–1858), British social reformer who, after creating a model industrial community at New Lanark, Scotland, tried to create one at New Harmony, Indiana, and failed.

XV. The "Times"

1. John Somers (Sommers) (1651–1716), created Baron Somers of Evesham in 1697, the year he was made Lord Chancellor. I do not know the source of Emerson's quotation.

2. Mansfield was made Lord Chief Justice in 1754. The Duke of Northumberland is presumably Percy Hugh (1742–1817), the second duke. I have not located the quotation.

3. Emerson refers here to Winthrop Mackworth Praed (1802–1839), writer of light verse; Sir John Hookham Frere (1769–1846), verse satirist and translator of Aristophanes; James Anthony Froude (1818–1894), historian; Thomas Hood (1799–1845), poet and humorist; Theodore Edward Hook (1788–1841), novelist and magazine editor; William Maginn (1793–1842), Irish humorist and journalist. By "Mill" he means either James Mill (1773–1836), historian and philosopher of utilitarianism, or his son John Stuart Mill, philosopher and magazine editor.

4. The London *Times* was founded in 1784 by John Walter (1739–1812), known as "Old Walter," and continued under John Walter II (1776–1847) and John Walter III (1818–1894), a friend of Emerson's.

5. That is, supported Queen Caroline in contesting the suit for divorce brought against her by George IV.

6. The so-called poor-law reform of 1834.

7. Up to 1834 the London *Times* had been grossly flattering in its attitude toward Brougham, but in that year it turned on him.

8. The *Times* supported various coercion bills designed to keep Ireland in order, but there was no formal "war" against Ireland.

9. The Anti–Corn Law League, founded in 1836, consistently propagandized for the abolition of protective tariffs on grains. Richard Cobden (1804–1865), with John Bright, was one of the leaders of the Anti–Corn Law movement.

10. The short-lived second French Republic was established by the Revolution of 1848 but was soon succeeded by the Second Empire. Emerson seems to mean that the *Times* used what Tennyson called "the red fool-fury of the Seine" as a device for increasing popular fear of a Chartist Revolution in England.

11. The new French Empire is that of Louis Napoleon (1808–1873), emperor of the French from 1852 to 1870. The English government secretly encouraged the French in their alliance with Sicily, and later openly formed an alliance with France against Russia.

12. Presumably John Walter II, who died in 1847.

13. Emerson lived at the home of John Chapman, No. 142 The Strand, in the spring of 1848. There were two John Chapmans living near each other, and Mrs. Carlyle, desiring to do an errand for her husband at the publishing house of Chapman and Hall, went by mistake to John Chapman the bookseller, where she to her surprise found Emerson. Printing-House Square is near Blackfriars Bridge, London.

14. Mowbray Morris (1818–1874) was appointed manager of the *Times* on August 21, 1847.

15. Old Walter, the founder; Edward Sterling (1773–1847), a great leader (editorial) writer; Francis Bacon (d. 1839), assistant editor of the *Times* in 1835; Thomas M. Alsager, who founded a *Times* City Office about 1820 and committed suicide in 1846; Horace Twiss (1787–1849), biographer and journalist (but a Travers Twiss also worked for the *Times*); Lloyd Jones (1811–1886); John Oxenford (1812–1877), dramatic critic. Both James Bowling Mozley and the Rev. Thomas Mozley wrote for the *Times;* Emerson presumably refers to the second (1806–1893).

16. Joseph Fouché (1759–1820), clever and unscrupulous French minister of police both before and after and during the regime of Napoleon. Josephine was supposed to have given him secret information.

17. Usually Nepal, kingdom on the border of India.

18. Bishops of the Church of England are of right members of the House of Lords.

19. The famous British comic weekly founded in 1841.

20. Douglas Jerrold (1803–1857), British comic writer best known for "Mrs. Caudle's Curtain Lectures."

21. "Officinal" refers to any drug prepared and kept on hand ready for use; thus, sanctioned or authorized.

XVI. Stonehenge

1. In writing this chapter Emerson relied to a remarkable extent upon William Stukeley, *Stonehenge: A Temple Restor'd to the British*

Druids (London, 1740), and to a lesser degree upon the same author's *Abury, A Temple of the British Druids, with some others Described* (London, 1743). These two books were frequently bound together, and reading in them increased Emerson's belief that there was some primitive connection among the Celts, the Druids, the Phoenicians, and the Jews. He seems also to have read a curious pamphlet by Dr. John Smith, *Choir Gaur*, published at Salisbury in 1771, the body (though not the whole) of which is "Abstracts from Various Authors Relating to Stonehenge."

2. A group of huge standing stones and of some that have toppled over, found on Salisbury Plain, the original purposes of which have been long under debate.

3. Hampshire is a county in southern England now comprising the administrative counties of Southampton and the Isle of Wight. Salisbury (originally Sarum) is in Wiltshire on the Avon.

4. A market town in Wiltshire north of Salisbury, the Almesbury (in all probability) of Arthurian legend.

5. The German word for Art, here used as implying a great deal of philosophical and aesthetic idealism.

6. The reference is to a campaign waged against romantic aesthetics by these two German poets.

7. Goethe remained active as poet, dramatist, and polemicist into his eightieth year.

8. Usually, *savants*, men of special learning.

9. Founded in 1547, Somerset House on the Strand in London was occupied, at least in part, by King's College, affiliated with the University of London.

10. Emerson read in *The Works of Confucius* translated by Joshua Marshman, which began publication in 1809; David Collier, *The Chinese Classical Work Commonly Called the Four Books*, 1836; and Sir John Francis Davis, *The Chinese*, 1836. He drew his citations of Confucius (ca. 551–479 B.C.) from these volumes.

11. Traveling salesman, commercial traveler.

12. The association of Stonehenge with the ancient Celts, supposed to be the original inhabitants of Britain, makes the allusion intelligible. The detailed description of Stonehenge which follows is partly from observation, partly from Stukeley, and partly from a guidebook alluded to later.

13. The Turkish Hisslarik.

14. The Dardanelles.

15. Avebury.

16. Fire stones (sarsen stones).

17. Any of the genus of giant ground sloth (megatherium) allied to modern sloths and anteaters, the bones of which are found in geological strata from the Pleistocene.

18. A genus of sloth-like edentates of the Pleistocene period.

19. Made much of in Stukeley, *Stonehenge.* See, for example, p. 5.

20. "The old *Britons* or *Welsh* call *Stonehenge choir gaur,* which some interpret *chorea gigantum,* the giants dance: I judge, more rightly *chorus magnus,* the great choir, round church, or temple." Stukeley, p. 8.

21. The ancient capital of Assyria from which Layard had brought statues of winged bulls. In his struggles with comparative mythology Stukeley makes much of the Near East in relation to the Druids.

22. The authoritative edition of the lives of the saints published by the Bollandist fathers, who take their name from Jean Bolland, a Flemish Jesuit of the seventeenth century.

23. The London Library was founded in 1841 as a lending library for scholars.

24. Iona (Icolmkill), an island west of Scotland (Argyllshire), was a famous center of Celtic Christianity associated with St. Columba, the saint of Iona.

25. Henry Browne of Amesbury, associated with the local museum and described in 1854 as for "twenty-four years attending illustrator at Stonehenge." He published an illustrated guidebook, originally printed at Birmingham, *An Illustration of Stonehenge & Abury,* sold at the museum. Emerson may have used the second edition (1833), though a fourth edition appeared at Salisbury in 1854 with a preface by the son, Joseph Browne.

26. In Stukeley and Browne. But debate still continues over the purpose of Stonehenge.

27. This is in Geoffrey of Monmouth, *Histories of the Kings of Britain,* Book VIII, cols. x etc., but Emerson seems to have picked up this information either from Stukeley or from the Browne guidebook. For example, Browne reads (fourth ed., p. 4): "called, in the publication to which I now refer, the Giant's Dance, by the magical art of Merlin, at the command of Aurelius Ambrosius, as represented by Jeffrey of Monmouth in the year 1130." Killaurus is Mount Killaurus. See also Stukeley, *Stonehenge,* p. 48.

28. See Stukeley, *Stonehenge,* pp. 2–3, and Browne, p. 4.

29. Edward Davies (1756–1831), author of *Celtic Researches; or, The Origin, Traditions, and Languages of the Ancient Britons* (London, 1804).

30. The Rev. William Stukeley (1687–1785) was rector of the church of St. George the Martyr, London; hence Emerson's reference a few lines later to "the courage of his tribe," meaning clergymen. Stukeley's preface, which Emerson partly paraphrases, shows that he wrote his two treatises to counteract free-thinking.

31. "Connected with Stonehenge are an avenue and a *cursus.* The

avenue is a narrow road of raised earth, extending 594 yards in a straight line from the grand entrance, then dividing into two branches, which lead, severally, to a row of barrows, and to the *cursus,* — an artificially formed flat tract of ground. This is half a mile northeast of Stonehenge, bounded by banks and ditches, 3036 yards long, by 110 broad." (Emerson's note.) Since the figures in Stukeley and Browne do not agree with Emerson's, it is possible he and Carlyle measured the distances or that Emerson took them over from some other source. But the passage about the meridian line is from Stukeley, *Stonehenge,* p. 42.

32. Stukeley, p. 57.

33. Stukeley is interested in deriving Amesbury from Ambresbury in order that he may connect Stonehenge with Ambres or Ambrose in Cornwall (p. 9) and apparently led Emerson not to distinguish between Amesbury and Avebury.

34. Stukeley, p. 4.

35. This whole passage is based on Stukeley, pp. 56–61.

36. Secret, mystery.

37. All this is in Stukeley, pp. 59–60.

38. This odd information appears in the *Bibliotheka* of Apollodorus (fl. 140 B.C.), but there the mother of Magnes is Enarete. In Stukeley, however, Emerson read: "So all the writers of the *Argonautics* too will have the ship *Argos* to be loquacious and oracular. Magnes another name of the load-stone is often call'd *Adamas,* which seems to be no other than *Athamas. Apollodorus* makes *Magnes* the son of *Aeolus,* who marrying *Nais,* inhabited the isle *Seriphus*" (p. 60).

39. In Emerson's time a fashionable quarter of Boston.

40. Emerson copies this from Anthony à Wood, *Athenae Oxonienses,* vol. II, col. 432.

41. The twelfth earl.

42. Sidney Herbert (1810–1901), created Baron Lea in 1861, philanthropist and statesman.

43. Sir Anthony Van Dyke (1599–1641), Flemish born, was court painter to Charles I of England.

44. Possibly a humorous reference to Coleridge's "Kubla Khan": "Where Alph the sacred river ran/ Through caverns measureless to man/ Down to a sunless sea."

45. Dates from the thirteenth century.

46. Coventry, Warwickshire. It is scarcely true that in the mid-century the cathedral at Coventry had "no fame."

47. In Wiltshire.

48. The Constitutions of Clarendon (1164) were made up of sixteen articles establishing the supremacy of royal law in England. Thomas à Becket, Archbishop of Canterbury, asserted they were contrary to canon law, quarreled with the king (Henry II), and was murdered.

49. Bishopstoke is in south central Hampshire.

50. Arthur (later Sir Arthur) Helps.

51. Town in Hampshire southeast of Winchester. Once the seat of the bishops of Winchester, the episcopal palace and the castle were reduced to ruins in the English Civil Wars.

52. Charles Maurice de Talleyrand-Périgord (1754–1838), famous French statesman. The remark, however, is Voltaire's and may be found in the *Discours Préliminaire* to *Alzire:* "L'Abbé Guyot Desfontanes: 'Il faut que je vive.' Le Comte d'Argenson: 'Je n'en vois la nécessité.' " It is repeated in chapter iii of Rousseau's *Emile.*

53. Municipal borough for Hampshire.

54. In the southern outskirts of Winchester. Emerson seems to have confused the church with the monastery, in his demand for bread and beer.

55. Henry de Blois (1129–1171), bishop of Winchester, grandson of William the Conqueror and brother of King Stephen.

56. Winchester Cathedral was originally built about the seventh century.

57. The presbytery of the cathedral contains the remains of the Saxon kings, collected and placed there by Henry de Blois.

58. King Alfred is supposed to have founded a minster immediately north of the present site of the cathedral and to have been buried there.

59. William of Wykeham was bishop of Winchester under Edward III.

60. Norman Gothic is to be distinguished from its Saxon predecessor.

61. "*History of the Anglo-Saxons,* I.599." (Emerson's note.) Sharon Turner, *History of the Anglo-Saxons* (4 vols., London, 1799–1905); Emerson quotes the sixth edition in three volumes (London, 1836), from footnote 69 on p. 599 of vol. I. He omits some quotation marks.

62. William of Wykeham did not build Windsor Castle but only supervised the construction of the royal apartments east of the great keep. In 1371 he began a "reconstruction" of Winchester Cathedral, presumably of the nave. He founded Winchester School in 1366, and New College, Oxford, in 1376 if one counts from a gathering of poor scholars, in 1380 if one counts from the laying of the cornerstone.

XVII. Personal

1. *Macbeth,* Act V, scene 3, l. 25.

2. Alexander Ireland.

3. The *Manchester Examiner.*

4. George Bancroft (1800–1891) was United States minister in England from 1846 to 1849.

5. For these clubs and societies and Emerson's admittance to them see Rusk, *The Life of Ralph Waldo Emerson*, chapter 19.

6. Among names not already identified or likely to be unfamiliar are those of Richard Monckton Milnes (1809–1885), Lord Houghton, poet, diplomat, and biographer; Henry Hart Milman (1791–1868), dean of St. Paul's Cathedral and historian; Bryan Waller Proctor ("Barry Cornwall") (1787–1874), minor poet; Benjamin Disraeli (1801–1881), Lord Beaconsfield, novelist and statesman; Sir Arthur Helps (1813–1875), historian, essayist, and antiquarian; John Kenyon (1784–1856), minor poet and friend of Elizabeth Barrett Browning; John Forster (1812–1876), friend and biographer of Dickens; Coventry Patmore (1823–1896), librarian and poet; Robert Brown (1773–1855), librarian and botanist; Richard Owen (1804–1892), paleontologist and opponent of Darwin; Adam Sedgwick (1785–1873), geologist; Michael Faraday (1791–1867), famous pioneer in electricity and magnetism; William Buckland (1784–1856), geologist; Sir Charles Lyell (1797–1875), whose *Principles of Geology* was long standard; Sir Henry de la Beche (1796–1855), president of the Geologic Circle; Sir William Jackson Hooker (1785–1865), botanist; William Benjamin Carpenter (1815–1885), physiologist; Charles Babbage (1792–1871), inventor of a calculating machine; Edward Forbes (1815–1854), zoologist.

7. Joanna Baillie (1762–1851), whose *Plays on the Passions* was once much admired; Sydney Owenson (1783–1859), Lady Morgan, novelist; Anna Brownell Jameson (Murphy) (1794–1860), novelist and writer on art; Mary Fairfax Somerville (1780–1860), mathematician.

8. Kew Gardens. Near London, seat of the Royal Botanic Gardens.

9. Mr. H. is apparently George S. Hillard (1808–1879) of Boston. The Hunterian Museum of the Royal College of Surgeons, in London, is near Lincoln's Inn Fields.

10. Dr. Samuel Brown (1817–1856), physicist and chemist.

11. Mrs. Catherine Stevens Crowe (1800–1876), novelist; Robert and William Chambers, Edinburgh publishers. Robert Chambers in 1844 wrote *Vestiges of Creation*. David Scott (1806–1849), whose portrait of Emerson is in the Concord (Massachusetts) Library.

12. Ambleside, in the Lake District, was the home of Harriet Martineau (1802–1876), reformer. She visited Egypt in 1846.

13. Wordsworth's home in the environs of the village of Rydal, Westmoreland.

14. The revolutionary movement of 1848, which dethroned Louis Philippe.

15. William Robertson wrote among other works a *History of the Discovery and Settlement of America* (1777).

16. What Emerson omitted was: "Carlyle."

17. Frederick Tennyson (1807–1898) and Charles Tennyson (Turner)

(1808–1879) were both older than Alfred Tennyson and both wrote poetry.

18. Properly, Rio de Janeiro, the capital of Brazil. Wordsworth presumably had read Southey's *History of Brazil* (1810–1819).

19. Whose translations of Plato Emerson read.

20. London literati.

21. Wordsworth, "The Happy Warrior," l. 54.

22. "Ode on the Intimations of Immortality Recollected from Early Childhood," composed 1803?–1806, published 1807.

XVIII. Result

1. That is, Anglo-Saxons. Emerson again ignores the other races making up the population of England.

2. After the scheme of making Australia a penal colony was abandoned, joint-stock companies shipped emigrants from England.

3. The Crimean War.

4. England did nothing to interfere with any of the three partitions of Poland, the last of which was "sanctioned" at the Congress of Vienna in 1814–1815. The British did not insist upon the restoration of independence to Genoa in that year, nor oppose the restoration of a Bourbon monarchy to Sicily. Parga, a seaport in southern Albania, occupied by the British in 1814, was promised independence as part of the Ionian Republic (1815–1862), but Britain ceded it to Turkey in 1815. Under Canning the British refused to assist Greece to attain independence and to support it, yet the British acquiesced in the breaking away of various minor principalities from the old Turkish Empire in the first half of the nineteenth century. In 1849 the British government was lukewarm about the creation of a Roman republic, and as early as 1815 had acquiesced in the restoration of the Papal States, including Rome. Finally, the government did nothing to support the Hungarians under Kossuth against Austria.

5. Slavery was finally abolished in the British West Indies in 1833.

6. Emerson condenses passages from chaps. 41 and 42 of the Magna Charta.

7. The *Peerage of England* by Arthur Collins was first published in 1709; there were subsequent editions.

8. By the Act of 1840 uniting Lower and Upper Canada (Quebec and Ontario) Great Britain set Canada on the road to dominion status; by 1856 most of the various states comprising modern Australia had achieved self-government.

9. The British conquest of India, notably in the eighteenth century, was a classical example of *divide et impera.*

10. Vulcan is represented in classical mythology as lame.

11. François Huber (1750–1830) of Geneva, who, though blind, wrote *Nouvelles Observations sur les Abeilles;* and Nicholas Sanderson (or Saunderson) (1682–1739), blind from birth, who was a lecturer at Cambridge University from 1707 to 1711 and who invented a calculating machine for the blind.

12. Temper, genius.

13. Thomas Erskine (1750–1823) was one of the great trial lawyers of his day. Richard Brinsley Sheridan appears here because of his brilliant oratory in the House of Commons, of which Erskine was also a member.

14. This is presumably John Rushworth (1612?–1690), whose *Historical Collections* (the bibliography is somewhat confused) began publication in 1659. But I am unable to find any reference to the Magna Charta in the indexes.

XIX. Speech at Manchester

1. Emerson's address was delivered on November 18, 1847, at the annual banquet of the Manchester Athenaeum. The so-called Manchester school of economists advocated free trade and was opposed to the use of tariff as a protection for British industries.

2. Sir Archibald Alison (1792–1867), principally remembered for his *History of Europe* (10 vols., 1833–1842).

3. Francis Egerton Brackley (1800–1857), Duke of Sutherland (1833) and Viscount Brackley (1847).

4. George Cruikshank (1792–1878), English caricaturist, illustrator of Dickens, remembered for his *Life in London* series of caricatures.

5. The Anti-Corn Law League, an organization devoted to the repeal of the tariff on imported grains.

6. Richard Cobden.

7. Since parietal means that which pertains to the care of or residence within the precincts of an organization (for example, a college), I assume that Emerson has in mind the general truth that *Punch* was primarily edited for the English middle class.

8. "By Sir A. Alison." (Emerson's note.)

9. Dickens' *Dombey and Son* was published in installments in 1847–48.

10. The year 1848 was a gloomy year in business.

11. The equivalent of medals; in athletic and poetical contests in the ancient world the winners were thus distinguished.

12. The Concord River is formed by the junction of the Sudbury and Assabet Rivers, the latter still retaining its Indian name.

Index

THE JOHN HARVARD LIBRARY

The intent of
Waldron Phoenix Belknap, Jr.,
as expressed in an early will, was for
Harvard College to use the income from a
permanent trust fund he set up, for "editing and
publishing rare, inaccessible, or hitherto unpublished
source material of interest in connection with the
history, literature, art (including minor and useful
art), commerce, customs, and manners or way of
life of the Colonial and Federal Periods of the United
States . . . In all cases the emphasis shall be on the
presentation of the basic material." A later testament
broadened this statement, but Mr. Belknap's inter-
ests remained constant until his death.

In linking the name of the first benefactor of
Harvard College with the purpose of this later,
generous-minded believer in American culture the
John Harvard Library seeks to emphasize the impor-
tance of Mr. Belknap's purpose. The John Harvard
Library of the Belknap Press of Harvard University
Press exists to make books and documents
about the American past more readily
available to scholars and the
general reader.